Rob
Christmas 2009

Al Hamilton

Country Lawyer – City Judge

Hon. A.C. Hamilton

Previously published: *A Feather Not a Gavel*

Printed and bound in Canada by Art Bookbindery
www.artbookbindery.com

Published by Rockwood Press
www.rockwoodpress.ca

ISBN 978-0-9784580-0-3

Prologue

Country Lawyer, City Judge begins with some childhood experiences of the writer growing up in Winnipeg. His uncertain academic bent is reflected in his difficulties at school and University, but athletic challenges and an interesting home life seem to have set the stage for the development of determination and independence.

After eighteen months in the army he returned to United College, then Law School which he describes in joyous detail. He was called to the bar in 1951. After completing his tutelage in Dauphin, he moved from one agricultural community to another in search of a challenge. He practiced law in Roblin, Winnipeg and Melita, before moving to Brandon in 1958 where he established his own firm in 1960.

He describes each community where he and his family lived and some of the colourful people he met. When in Melita he struggled to explain to friends how he happened to choose 'the country' as a place to live and practice law when his knowledge of agriculture and farming practices was non-existent.

In Brandon he was finally free to do the sort of work he had been looking for. He was able to go to court for clients who had suffered a loss or injury and seek compensation. In the criminal field, he was able to go before a judge or jury to defend those charged with murder, rape or some other breach of the law.

A sampling of the cases he handled includes many hilarious ones. All are told in the actual dialogue which occurred between him and his clients and sometimes between him and the presiding judge and jury. Unfortunately he feels he has to use some fictitious names to avoid embarrassment to former clients who may still be living. He says the dialogue with his clients is ingrained in his memory and is accurate. He is not as certain about conversations with lawyers, but tries to make the conversations with them as accurate as possible. The facts of the cases he relates are told in precise detail. He admits his distressing losses and takes pleasure in his wins.

His analysis of the judges he appeared before and of the well-known lawyers he watched or had as opponents in court, brings a refreshing insight into the workings of the legal system and the tactics applied in the game of wits. Each lawyer tries to convince the judge of the rightness of his case and the weakness of the case of his adversary.

The extent of the writer's involvement in school boards, chambers of commerce, politics, and other community activities provides examples of the involvement of most lawyers in their communities.

The second half of the book covers the twenty years the writer was a judge of the Court of Queen's Bench until his retirement in 1993. The cases he describes are taken from his original notes. They show how ordinary people can do uncharacteristic things and get into trouble with the law. Some of the stories are funny and pathetic at the same time, but they show the variety of cases judges are called upon to hear.

He spends time explaining, for the non-legally-trained, some of the unusual traditions still followed by Canadian courts. These include the antiquated names that are applied to judges in and out of court, the gowns the judges and the lawyers wear and the rules of evidence which determine what a witness may and may not say.

His appointment as one of the Commissioners of the Aboriginal Justice Inquiry is discussed. His comments on the evidence it heard is more revealing than it was in the 1991 AJI report, or in his later book, *A Feather Not a Gavel*. He comments on the failure of most judicial inquiries to bring about change and gives his opinion as to why they are created.

The author speaks of the mediation he did in family disputes and the high percentage that settled. All the cases he mediated after he retired settled. At his own expense he attended a two week mediation program at Harvard Law School in 1996. Because of these experiences he recommends that parties to every civil dispute be required to go to a qualified mediator and attempt mediation before they can commence a civil action in court.

He recommends changes be made to the Criminal Code to change the manner in which juries are selected. He makes no comment on the length of sentences being handed out today, but indicates the sentences he imposed in the cases he describes where a jury convicted the accused. It is obvious that his sentences were far more severe than those being imposed today.

The book provides an interesting snapshot of the courts of Manitoba and how and why at least one man, a lawyer and a judge, enjoyed his time in them.

Part One

Growing Up

As a child I was small for my age and subject to the usual punishments and dangers of having tougher and stronger friends. I think they were 'friends' as we played hide and seek in the undeveloped lot at the corner of McMillan and Harrow and built a fort in the trees. As we got older we played kick-the-can on the street and canny-can in the back lane. For those too young to have enjoyed that sport, it's similar to cricket, except six empty tin cans, piled in a pyramid, is the wicket. At some point, our activities changed from friendly competition to 'survival of the fittest.' I was beaten up on a regular basis by John Judge who I still considered my best friend. He made one concession, agreeing not to hit me in the face. It was he, I think, who dubbed me 'Hammy'.

My first encounter with 'the law' occurred in those days. For some strange reason the foot and bicycle cops didn't like us playing hockey or baseball on the street. They chased us into back yards for what they must have considered misdemeanours. If there was a complaint of someone swiping crab apples, we were on the most wanted list. Fortunately, I could scale a six foot fence in a flash and avoid being caught. My favourite hiding place was on a garage roof. The cops always looked under bushes and porches but never up.

I went to Grosvenor for grades one to six, often in the company of Jim Daley or Danny Muldoon, two of the biggest boys in the class. In Robert H. Smith for grades seven to nine I got the strap with some regularity. I can't recall what I did but I do recall withdrawing my hand to avoid being strapped by my teacher on one occasion. I was sent to the principal's office for his personal attention.

Until I was ten or so I spent the summers at Sans Souci in my parents' rented cabin and shadowed Monsieur Collede as he worked in his blacksmith shop or on the mower and hay rig. There was dancing and singing in the community hall with hot dogs and soft drinks for all. Madame Collede, also from France, kept the store where the campers could replenish their supplies. The same families came year after year, some for a few weeks and others just on weekends.

My parents then purchased a small cottage on the lakefront across from the station. I used to meet the evening train and haul people's grips in my wagon for twenty five cents. My next enterprise was a Free Press paper route that covered the north half of Matlock. I played tennis on the two courts on the other side of the tracks and biked to friends' cottages in Matlock and Whytewold.

Saturday nights were reserved for a drive to Winnipeg Beach for the rollercoaster and other rides and entertainment. During the war when I worked at Eaton's and the Bay on weekends I would take the 'moonlight' to dance and listen to the music of Jimmy Dorsey, Tommy Dorsey's brother, in the Pavilion. You could dance a set inside the wooden fence for 10 cents or listen all night for free.

After a year of Latin classes at Robert H. Smith, in which I laughed repeatedly at the word 'brazier' I was removed from the class and assigned to shops for my next two years. I learned about wiring, woodworking and drafting, making a metal carrier for my bike and a needle and sewing stand for my mother. In each of grades eight and nine it was recommended I repeat the year. My parents were insulted and refused. In retrospect, the educators were correct. I wasn't as mentally mature or as ready for learning as my pals.

In Kelvin for grades ten and eleven, the athletic program was excellent and I did well in the primary hundred yard dash, hop step and jump and shot-put. I was a member of Clarence Kerr's relay team that had to and therefore always won its inter-high-school races. I was no longer looked down upon by my friends.

At United College we had world class professors like Dr. Stanley in English and later Dr. Arthur Lower. I enjoyed Dr. Victor Leathers' French class and Davey Owens philosophy course. I was however diverted from continuing my formal education when I turned 18 and joined the army. My friends Hugh Dunphy and Frank Pound had both been killed in action and I felt it my duty to join up as soon as I could. When I returned to United for second year in the veteran's course in the spring of 1946 there were only twenty-six of us in the class.

In third year, my independent approach to learning got me into trouble again. I argued with the Sociology professor so much on some of his conclusions that I failed the course. He had the audacity to say that some of my writings sounded like a judgment my father might write. I had trouble with economics as well but passed all my psychology courses with flying colours. On balance, one might say I was not doing well in University.

The summer after third year I got a job as the boatman for the MLA camp in the Lake of the Woods. The Methodist Literary and Athletic Association ran a family camp on an island some distance from Kenora. During my interview I was told that the launch had capsized the previous year and they needed someone who could keep it afloat. I had no special qualifications but when I said I had a motorcycle and could keep it going, Mr. Law, one of the Trustees, was delighted and said I would have no trouble with the launch. The job was to meet the train twice a day to convey the guests to the camp and to purchase the supplies the chef required. I never had any trouble with the launch.

It was a marvellous summer and it gave me time to consider my future. I knew I wasn't academically inclined but I thought of going to UCLA to take a course in industrial psychology. I hadn't reached the point of considering how I would pay for the course. Although I didn't realize it at the time, my father's meagre salary wouldn't enable him to help.

When I was still in Kenora my father took a hand in my future. He had been the only full-time Juvenile Court Judge in Manitoba between 1925 and 1945. His office and courtroom were in the old Vaughan Street jail, near the Law Courts. He spoke to Mr. Russell, the Registrar of the law school run by the Law Society. He determined that I had enough credits to apply for admission so as soon as I returned to Winnipeg he told me of his inquiry and I went to see Mr. Russell. Before I left his office next to the Great Library, I had filled out an application for admission and I started first year law within a couple of weeks.

Looking back, I was lucky to get into Law. There was no LSAT at the time and the policy seemed to be to accept all the veterans who applied. The federal government wanted to get the vets into the work force and assisted both the married and single ones with their education. I don't think the standards of the Law Society were lowered though as some Vets failed courses and had to rewrite. Others decided they didn't want to be lawyers and withdrew, while others were eventually thrown out of the profession.

In retrospect, my introduction to the law began long before I got into law school. Almost every day as I was growing up, my father would talk about the cases he was dealing with. He did that around our dining room table and in our upstairs sitting room with its coal and wood fireplace and heavy drapes over the door openings to keep us warm. While his comments seemed to be directed to my mother, I'm sure he was aware I was interested and was listening.

I particularly remember a phone call that came to our home one evening when I was still quite young. Two juveniles who were in the cells of the Vaughan Street Detention Home had broken out and killed Superintendent Jenner during their escape. He and Mrs. Jenner had a suite on the first floor near the north entrance to the building. My father's office and courtroom were on the second floor but I was never told whether the culprits had been jailed by him. He was nevertheless summoned to see Attorney General Major, later Mr. Justice Major, at the Legislative Buildings in the morning. The only other part of the incident I recall is that the next Superintendent was not to live in the building.

My father always said he would do anything to avoid having to send young offenders to jail. He would meet with their parents and try to get their cooperation. He would have young people monitored by probation officers and he would meet regularly with the operators of the Home of the Good Shepard, the jail for girls in West St. Paul and the Home for Boys in Portage la Prairie.

The Army

My time in the army near the end of the Second World War was a remarkable time in my life. Although, as I will explain, I did not get oversees but ended up in Deer Large for eighteen months, the experience was one I look back on with great respect for those who offered or lost their lives or limbs to save the world from tyranny.

The Air Force wasn't taking recruits for training as a pilot and all the Navy wanted were cooks. Neither appealed to me so I joined the Infantry and signed up at Fort Osborne Barracks. After getting a barrage of inoculations, a bunch of us spent the next day at Minto Barracks marching and shooting 22s on their firing range. The following day we were bussed to the University of Manitoba men's and women's residences the Army had commandeered. We were three to a room.

After two months of basic training we were moved to Shilo for our advanced training. We lived in H huts containing nothing but rows of double bunks. The central toilets, metal wash basins and open showers left no room for embarrassment or privacy. I occupied an upper bunk and Gordon Gillespie had the luxury of the lower bunk. We had to make our own beds and stand to attention beside them every morning so the Sergeant and Lieutenant could see that the bed was properly made, our rifle was being properly held and our boots were shined.

We had to calibrate the .303 rifle we were given so we could hit the centre of the targets.

When we formed up in platoons, our roll call amounted to us shouting out our regimental number and, for a while, the number of our rifle. When we weren't learning how to march, it seemed we were running all the time, sometimes with full pack. Our marches to Waggle Springs on the Assiniboine River were long and tiring but we marched into camp when we returned, with our heads held high and arms swinging, inspired by the bagpiper sent out to lead us into camp in style.

We learned how to dismantle and re-assemble Sten and Tommy guns quickly, how to read maps and know how to use the Fiat anti-tank gun, Bren guns, mortars and hand grenades. Crawling on our stomach during day and night exercises, climbing ropes suspended from the ceiling of the drill hall, along with boxing and unarmed combat, prepared us for action. Discipline and immediate reaction to every command given by a Sergeant or an officer was mandatory.

I did my turn on the garbage truck but was fortunate one day when the temperature dipped to -53 degrees Fahrenheit. We were sent back to our barracks at noon.

We complained to one another about the poor quality of the food but you had to eat it if you wanted to be able to handle the sole-purposed efforts to get us into good physical shape. The cooks all appeared to be recent recruits with no knowledge of how to prepare a meal, but we had no option to take or refuse any part of a meal. Everything was ladled out by the kitchen staff as we walked past them, our tin plates and cup in hand.

I ate what I could get down. Sometimes I could eat the meat, but more often I couldn't. It was the same with the potatoes and vegetables. I ate what I could and threw the rest out. I would then go to the Salvation Army or YMCA service centres for a hot dog to fill me up. I had to be careful as our pay was only a dollar a day.

We didn't dare complain. We knew that would only bring some sort of punishment. It may be that the poor food was to get us used to eating anything, which was probably the situation at the front lines.

As it turned out, I never got overseas with my company. Russ McGillivray and I were slated for officer training at Kingston, so we were held back. That was cancelled before long when it appeared the war in Europe would soon be over. To keep us busy, we became instructors in the infantry at Shilo. For a short time we were loaned to the Air Crew Conditioning Unit at the Brandon airport to help train airmen who had seen action in Europe, in the use of infantry weapons in readiness for service in the Pacific.

That program ended when it became obvious the pilots had no interest in being re-trained. The last straw was one day when we were trying to train some of them how to fall and remain motionless until we gave another order. As we went across the field we hollered

'FALL'. Our students ignored us and kept running. I wasn't sure what they were doing but finally looked beyond them. Two girls were riding bicycles along the road outside the fence. Our charges were only interested in having a visit with the girls or lining them up for a date on Saturday night.

My active duty came to an abrupt halt about three days before V J Day (Victory in Japan day). Our platoon was sent on a shuttle march to Brandon 'to show the flag.' That meant that a third of us would ride in the back of a truck while two-thirds marched. We traded off every few miles. On the way back to Shilo we stopped for lunch at a farm just south of what is now the trans-Canada highway. We were hot and tired so the Lieutenant told us we could take a swim in the little stream.

I waited until my group got into the water. They were standing up and the water came up to their chests. Being satisfied the water was deep enough, I ran towards the creek and did a flat racing dive into the water. Unfortunately, the spot I picked was getting close to a bend in the creek and I went head first into a sandbar just inches under the water. It was apparently obvious I was hurt so I was driven by jeep across the bumpy fields to the Medical Officers' building in Shilo. He didn't know what to do so he told me to walk the quarter of a mile to the Shilo hospital, with what turned out to be a broken neck.

Apparently I got no sympathy from the rest of the guys on the march. According to Gordon Gillespie, the reaction was: "What was that stupid Corporal doing diving into the creek?"

Thanks to a doctor who had spent most of the war in Italy and France, and had seen every kind of injury, he put me in a body cast and shipped me off to Deer Large Hospital in Winnipeg. I spent six months in hospital until the cast was removed just in time for me to get into the second year veterans' class at United College.

The lessons I learned living and working with men from every background stood me in good stead in the decisions I had to make at various times in my life. It is not that I made any connection with the army when a situation arose in court, but the nature of the army training and the development of a single-minded purpose provided me with the self-confidence I may previously have lacked.

A trial, I later decided, is similar to war. To win, a lawyer must have a plan of action. He or she must decide on the approach that should be taken, then try to figure out what the opposition is likely to do. From that point on it will likely be a battle of wits to adapt or adjust your approach to the client's advantage and the enemy's disadvantage.

There is no winning or losing for a judge, but he has a ring-side seat from which to see the lawyers' skills at work and the humour and tragedy the law lays bare. I think enough time has gone by to let me share some of my experiences and inner thoughts.

Law School

Law class of 1947 on the steps of the old law school

The Manitoba Law School of the 1950s was unlike any school or university course I had ever encountered or heard of. While I expected law school would deal with legal matters, I was unprepared for its unusual teachers and their unique styles.

In 1947 when I entered Law School, it was operated by the Law Society of Manitoba and was located on the first floor of the now demolished Art School near the corner of Kennedy and York in Winnipeg. We were given strict orders not to go upstairs. Our assumption was that there were gorgeous nude models posing for the budding artists. A couple of brave souls quickly broke that 'law' but returned to express disappointment.

In later years, the teaching of law moved to the Law Courts building, then to Fort Garry where it became a faculty of the University of Manitoba with its own magnificent building, Robson Hall, its own library, and mostly full-time professors. I was educated under what my confreres call 'the old system.'

Our fifty-two students constituted the largest post-war class. It was so large, it had to be divided in two. Half the students received lectures in the morning and worked in law offices in the afternoon and the process was reversed for the other half.

At that time the law course took four academic years and those with a prior university degree had to article for four years. Those of us who did not have a prior degree had to article for five years, which could be called apprenticeship or slave labour.

Those who had been in the armed forces could deduct one month from their articling time for every month they had served. In addition, there was another option available to veterans, presumably because many were older and the authorities wanted to get them working as quickly as possible. They could take their second, third and fourth years without a break in between.

The result of my taking the 'speed-up course' was that by the time I finished fourth year, with only eighteen months service in the Army, I still had a year left to article before I could be called to the bar and begin practice.

Law School was fun, and for the first time in my questionable quest for knowledge, I enjoyed studying and, to my delight, started to get good marks. Colonel G.P.R. (Pete) Tallin was the Dean and taught contract law. He also gave an optional course in public speaking and, to prove how tough he was, would occasionally lie on the floor and challenge students to jump on his stomach. Colonel Harvey Streight was the Registrar and taught real property, not an exciting but a necessary subject. Both were known for the generous help they gave the numerous married and needy students.

One of our teachers, E. K. Williams, was the Chief Justice of the Court of King's Bench and he taught a less than exciting course in constitutional law. The rest were practicing lawyers although several of them later became judges. Izzy Nitikman fastidiously taught us first year criminal law. Jimmy Wilson and H. G. H. Smith had a witty approach to teaching and seemed to have an off-colour story to fit every legal issue.

Sam Freedman, who later became a Queen's Bench Justice, a Court of Appeal Justice and finally the Chief Justice of Manitoba, was an outstanding teacher. He was also an internationally renowned humorist and after dinner speaker. He regaled us with a wealth of stories he adapted to the principle of law under discussion and had us rolling in the aisles. We had two women in the class. Helen Breen was the wife of lawyer Sam Breen and Helen Arpin was the wife of our classmate, Maurice Arpin. When the ladies were busy with their young families and missed a class, the level of the jokes and ribald examples of law-related stories knew no bounds.

R. B. MacInnes K.C. taught us civil procedure, a difficult topic to make exciting. 'Pop' Sutton taught wills and estates and provided a wealth of case law we would use later in practice.

Every teacher made 'the law' a living reality. We had to memorize important principles of law so we could recite them on our exam papers. We had to memorize the names of cases, the report series and page numbers where they could be found. My marks started to rise as I enjoyed the real-life examples of the law in action.

My favourite course was fourth-year criminal law, taught by Deputy Attorney General John Allen, an outstanding counsel in his own right. He would hold the *Criminal Code* open in his hand and waive it around as he lectured on its contents. Occasionally he would leap into the air, pretending to have discovered a new principle of law. He was making certain we understood the basic principles of guilt and innocence and the basic rights and freedoms of those suspected of having committed a crime. The sanctity of 'Proof beyond a Reasonable Doubt' was drummed into us. He stressed the fact that if the Crown could not present evidence that satisfied that objective, the accused person was entitled to go free. He even told us what the final exam would cover. As strange as that approach seemed, it made us study the matters he wanted us to understand and to remember. I got a 98 on his final exam and couldn't understand why it wasn't 100.

The only non-lawyer who taught us was Fred or Frank Johnson, a chartered accountant who tried to explain his specialty to us. All

I can remember him saying was, "if you have a problem, consult an accountant." Unfortunately, he didn't teach us, or me anyway, how to keep a good set of books. That might or might not have had anything to do with the five or six of our classmates who ended up being disbarred and spending a few years in Stony Mountain Penitentiary. I just mention that in passing to show that the practice of law was and is serious business.

I did all my studying in the Great Library of the Court House five or six nights a week, along with many of my classmates. The collegiality seemed to make the learning easier. In any event that was where all the cases and statutes could be found.

Murray Coughlin, later of the Pitblado firm, and I walked home together most nights. After a coffee at Westminster and Sherbrook, he would carry on to his home in the Wolseley area and I to McMillan Avenue. We also sat beside one another in class. If the lecture was dull we played hangman.

Roy Gallagher was the star of our class. He became an outstanding Crown Attorney, then an equally effective defence counsel and civil litigator. He was much in demand by police and other unions during their contract negotiations. Roy was also a regular in the Great Library, as it was called. He wouldn't let anyone talk to him as he studied. He was so engrossed in his research that he often had two cigarettes burning at the same time.

Friday afternoon at five seemed to be reserved for at least a dozen of our male classmates to gather in the basement pub of the Abbey (the Aberdeen Hotel) on Edmonton Street. The liquor laws had not yet been modernized so our lady members couldn't attend. We may have made up for their absence by commenting on the "prettiest girls in Canada" who marched to work and filled Portage Avenue sidewalks at noon and after work.

Law Office Student

The other part of our training began with an agreement signed with a practicing lawyer who agreed to involve the student in the day-to-day practice of law and to provide experience in the type of law he practiced. The system was apparently based on the medieval apprenticeship approach to trades training in England.

Frank Allen and I started articling with Parker, Parker, Hunter and Hamlin at the same time. Our offices were on the fifth floor of the Bank of Commerce Building on Main Street, a block north of Portage Avenue. We worked in the office every school day afternoon and on Saturday mornings. In addition to the training we received, we were paid $25.00 a month and given a bus pass.

The work of the firm was mainly commercial so we spent many hours at the Land Titles Office searching titles for the names of owners, mortgagors or lien holders. The L.T.O. staff was helpful as they put a new batch of students through their paces every year. It was a pleasure later on to find many of them in the County Court and Queen's Bench offices. I seemed to spend the rest of my days delivering documents or packages to other law offices or drawing separation agreements. The most exciting part was running the open cage elevator by myself.

By the end of the first year I thought I knew everything there was to know about titles, liens and other encumbrances. I could prepare a transfer of land, read a mortgage and search the records in the County Court office.

I prepared my first separation agreement under the watchful eye of my father. As I took each succeeding draft home, we would examine every word and my Dad insisted I keep making changes until I was satisfied the document was perfectly clear. Thirty five years later I was revising and revising some forms for a Metis election. One of my assistants, Laurie Messer, asked why I was doing so many drafts. I told her the story and she said: "So, it's your father's fault."

As I did not seem to be learning much law and never went to

court, I transferred my articles to C. T. Wyrzykowski after a year. He had a small law practice on the second floor at 663 Main Street. He was a dapper and smooth court room lawyer. Mr. Morrisey did his legal research and Mr. Borowski did solicitor work. Mr. Rigby, an English remittance man, lived in the Salvation Army Hostel around the corner on Logan. He ran errands and was a delightful conversationalist. He apparently had a bit of a drinking problem and was pleased to have Mr. Wyrzykowski make certain he didn't receive all his pay at the same time.

There were two drawbacks to being with that firm. The first was that almost all the clients were Polish and I couldn't participate in the conversations with them. The second problem was that I hardly ever went to court with the boss and spent a lot of time searching the neighbourhood for family members whose overseas relatives had lost track of them during or after the war.

I did learn about the 'Police Court' as it was called. It was in the Rupert Avenue Police Station, the one where Jack Krafchenko was held after being arrested for the murder of the bank manager during a robbery in Plum Coulee. He escaped from the third floor of the jail after his lawyer, Percy Hegel, persuaded a guard to give him a gun and a rope. He was arrested, convicted by a jury on the ninth of April, 1914 and hanged on the ninth of July, 1914 at the Vaughan Street jail. The guard went to the penitentiary for seven years and Hegel got three years. The legal system moved quickly in those days.

When I started to appear in that court, Charlie Tupper was the Crown Attorney and Maris Garton was the Judge. Each day a parade of nuisance offenders was brought into the courtroom from the adjacent cells. Some were vagrants and others had been apprehended by the Railway Police for riding the rails or hitching a ride in empty boxcars. Both types usually ended up getting a 'Floater.' That meant that the charge against them would be dropped as long as they left the city within twenty-four hours.

Generally, I just went to court to obtain an adjournment until a case could be settled. Very few went to trial. I had to go to the County Court office on the main floor of the Law Courts building to deal with small claims I was working on or to file documents dealing with the administration of an estate. It was usually on those occasions that I would steal some time to sit in court and watch the judges and the lawyers at work.

The most interesting display of the interaction between the judge and lawyers I can recall was a case where Louis Morosnic was defending a client in a trial before a judge and jury. He got very worked up and yelled at witnesses. Chief Justice Williams interrupted him on several occasions and told him to calm down. Louis would bow deeply and thank the judge for his assistance but within minutes he would be yelling again. When he was making his final argument to the jury he broke his eye glasses on the railing of the jury box, presumably to show how certain he was of his client's innocence. The Chief Justice tried to calm him down but finally gave up and saved his breath for his own instructions to the jury, when he would instruct them on their duties and straighten everything out. He left no doubt about the verdict he expected.

The story was that Morosnic kept several pairs of glasses in his brief case so he could repeat his performance for the next jury he appeared before. Harry Walsh was a star performer at that time as well. He was ferociously serious but equally entertaining as he tore prosecution witnesses to shreds.

A benefit of having the law school down town was that we had easy access to the courts and the court offices. Even when delivering documents to lawyers' offices we came to know how interesting they were. Mr. Lamont Sr. (the father of John and Frank who later joined the profession) upset me when I visited his office in the Avenue Building by abruptly asking some question about the package I knew nothing about.

There were many sole practitioners in the Paris Building, the McIntyre Building and the Confederation Building as well. Phillips and Tallin had an office in the Canadian Pacific building at the corner of Portage and Main. Taking a document there was a trip back in time. After I got through the ferns I was confronted by the sort of teller's cage I had only seen in banks in western movies. Leon Mercury, who articled there, made it clear that the office was designated "Law Chambers."

B.B. Dubienski, of large stature and a booming voice, was in the Confederation building. His son, Ian, became one of the two judges who presided in the Rupert Avenue court. His humanity and, some would say, leniency, brought a new approach to the work of the provincial bench. That continued when he became an Associate Chief Judge in the new quarters attached to the old Law Courts. Unlike most judges, he was active in the various associations that helped former offenders to reform.

If I hadn't been working downtown I would never have met the many lawyers I did and seen them at work in their modest quarters. I met many of them again in later years in court or when I attended the annual meetings of the Manitoba Bar Association at Clear Lake, Minaki, Brandon, Flin Flon or Winnipeg. Those meetings and articling in downtown Winnipeg were a real introduction to the workings of the profession.

There was no direct connection between what I learned in class and what I learned as an articling student in Winnipeg. I now think it was like having two separate but related educations. One was of the book-learning type and the other involved live people and the legal system in operation. In Dauphin, I saw the two interacting with one another.

Articling in Dauphin

As the time for graduation neared, I started to look around for an articling position that would cover my remaining apprenticeship and provide me with more experience in court. I heard that Ernie McGirr of Dauphin did a lot of court work and was looking for a student. I contacted him and we met in Winnipeg. He was the Dauphin member of the coalition provincial government and the Town Solicitor as well. His partner, Stewart McLean, who shortly thereafter succeeded him as the local M.L.A., did mostly real estate and other solicitor matters. The result was that Mr. McGirr was interested to hear that I wanted to do court work.

I moved to Dauphin in April or May 1950. I cannot remember the exact date but I was out of Winnipeg at the time of the devastating 1950 flood. I heard tales of our classmate Gordon Barkman from Steinbach, (and later a Queen's Bench judge,) operating a bulldozer on the dikes.

I boarded with Charlie Shaw, his wife and their son. Charlie worked for the local dairy and liked to golf. He had a magnificent Golden Retriever which he was allowed to take on the nine-hole course at Lake Dauphin. The dog would follow our balls into the bush and bring them back to Charlie. When he wasn't retrieving our balls he returned to the bush to bring others out as well.

Dauphin was a friendly town. I learned to curl there. One of Charlie's friends, Ab Gowanlock, asked me to play lead on his club rink. That was quite an honour as Ab and his competitive rink had won the Canadian championship. There was a Little Theatre group lead by Wilf Booth, the Superintendent of Schools. Apart from a little acting, I directed Eugene O'Neil's The *Long Voyage Home* in which I had acted at United College.

Another activity I was engaged in was helping the local young liberals who were enlarging their group and preparing to host the annual provincial meeting later that year. The local people I met became good friends and at the convention I renewed my association with the young people from Winnipeg who ended up running the organization ten years later. Bill Ward, the local Member of Parliament, supported the group and the convention.

After being introduced to court personnel and the law library in the Court House by Ernie McGirr I was pretty well on my own to arrange adjournments and hearing dates. Before long I was doing guilty pleas on my own and I negotiated sentences with the Crown Attorney, C. S. A. Rodgers. I would have our client plead guilty and Mr. Rodgers would recommend the agreed upon sentence to Magistrate Tommy Little. I don't recall doing a contested trial of any significance.

Going to the Court of Queen's Bench, when McGirr was making an application or putting in evidence for an uncontested divorce, was another matter. He was meticulous in his wording of supporting documents, brief and to the point when examining witnesses and making submissions to the presiding judge. The Q. B. judges, all of whom had to live in Winnipeg, took turns coming to Dauphin but one of them presided in Dauphin each month with the exception of July and August.

McGirr dealt with contested civil trials in a different way. He was positive, careful and caring when examining his own clients and their witnesses, but rough and demanding when he put on his bulldog persona to cross examine an opposing witness. In most civil cases his opponent was Jack McFadyen of the firm of Bowman and Company. Each used every trick in the book, and ones that weren't in the book, to defeat one another. They would interrupt the examination of a witness if things weren't going to their liking and would laugh out loud if they thought a statement by the other side was damaging to their case. They always kept one eye on the judge to make sure he understood the point they were making.

The adversaries goaded one another as they presented their cases and tore one another to shreds as they presented closing arguments to the judge. It was always a rough and tumble, no holds barred, demonstration of verbal and mental agility. It was exciting to watch. If McGirr won, as he most often seemed to do, he would be on cloud nine for days. I wouldn't be surprised if the judges liked to come to Dauphin to enjoy the spectacle.

In spite of their legal battles in court, the Dauphin lawyers got along well. Every time a visiting judge came to town, the bar would invite the judge to drinks and dinner in the Dauphin Hotel. Someone from the bar would bring greetings and the judge was invited to speak. Some like Chief Justice Williams and Justice Arnold Campbell would exhort members of the bar to hone their skills and to participate in the functions of the province-wide bar association.

After dinner, most would leave and those remaining would play poker. Isaac Johnston, a busy solicitor who lost his legs in the First World War, along with Ernie McGirr, were reputed to be regular winners. I knew better than to tangle at the table with either of them.

There were some rough spots in my relationship with Ernie McGirr but they were part of my education. On one occasion I was directed to draft a by-law amendment to go before the Town Council. When I looked over some of the material I noticed that a by-law dealt with the extension of roads and I noticed the term "kerb and gutter". I checked the dictionary, found that the correct spelling was "curb" and changed the proposed amendment. When I left the amendment in his office you could hear McGirr hollering out on the street, "Hamilton, get in here."

I rushed in to be greeted by "the spelling of kerb is with a K. That's the way it is in the by-law and it's gonna stay that way. It's not up to you to change it. Do you understand?"

Ernie (although I wouldn't have dared call him that) had a cigar in his mouth most of the time. It didn't seem to matter to him whether it was lit or not. He chewed on it incessantly and swirled it from one side of his mouth to the other, and his volume of speech or yelling was not decreased by its presence. Another outburst was caused when I was asked to draft a chattel mortgage to secure a loan on some farm machinery. He had given me a brief description of the items to include and I made my own notes of his requirements. When I finished the document I took it into his office.

It wasn't three minutes before he hollered my name. "Get in here" was much more than an invitation.

"What's this?" he said, glaring at me with disdain.

"The Chattel Mortgage Sir," was my reply, not knowing what

was wrong.

"What in hell is a sprung-tooth harrow and don't you know how to spell John Deere?"

Of course, I didn't know there was an 'e' on the end of 'deer'. I was quaking in my boots and had to admit, not that it wasn't obvious, that I had no familiarity with agricultural terms. You would think the experience would have been enough to divert me from my growing attraction to the rural way of life and the pleasant people who made me feel welcome. On the other hand, maybe the reaming-out was worth it as I was never asked to draw another farm related document.

My beautiful yellow Triumph motorcycle had to be left in Winnipeg, not that it was very practical. I couldn't drive it after dark as the lights would drain the battery and the bike would stop. I couldn't afford to get it fixed. I needed some transportation in Dauphin, so I sold the bike and bought my first car. It was a 1932 Chevy Roadster with a soft top, even if it wouldn't fold down, and it had a rumble seat. Spare tires were mounted in the front fenders. It would start no matter how cold it was in the winter. All I had to do was put it in neutral with the choke out, go to the front and crank.

I had to be careful driving though because as soon as I went over 30 miles an hour it would start heading for the ditch. Another shortcoming was that it couldn't climb the hills between Dauphin and Clear Lake. Before I left Dauphin, I had to trade it in on a slightly newer Pontiac sedan that was no fun at all.

For several months before I left Dauphin, I spent a lot of time at the Dauphin Land Titles Office. Mr. McGirr had obtained a contract with an oil company that was doing some seismic work in the area. Before deciding on whether it wanted to lease the mineral rights, the company had to know whether the farmer owned them, or who did. Many mineral rights had been reserved by the federal Crown when the land was first settled, or held back by the railroad or the Hudson's Bay Company when they sold the sections that had been given to them. The rights might also have been sold or leased by the original owner later on.

I went to the Land Titles Office and did hundreds of 'historical searches.' I had to examine the original grant from the Crown on each property and every sale, mortgage, lease or other encumbrance that had ever been filed. I did so many searches, the Registrar of the office, Mr. Marsden, let me go into the vaults to locate the lists and documents I wanted to examine. I paid for the number of documents I examined before I left for the day.

Some were Torrens Titles, with a new title issued by the Land Titles Office each time a parcel of land changed hands. Others were still Old System Deeds. In either event I had to certify who owned the mines and minerals, so Mr. McGirr could send a certificate to the oil company.

In the spring of 1951 another event occurred that brought about a change in my life. When I was in third year Arts at United College, the English class was so large the professor had us sit in alphabetical order so he could keep track of us, to see if seats were empty because someone was skipping class. Lorna Hasselfield of Deloraine, who lived in residence, and I sat next to one another. We never socialized and probably didn't say much to one another.

It was a surprise then to run into her when we both ended up in the same café on Main Street in Dauphin one Sunday evening. We had a nice conversation and saw one another regularly from then on. We married in October 1951.

Lorna, I discovered, in addition to Arts had just completed her degree in education. A teacher at Smith Jackson junior high school was going to have a baby and Lorna came to Dauphin to teach literature to her grade 7, 8 and 9 classes until school was out at the end of June. She was slated to join the staff at the new St. James Collegiate in the fall but had to resign before she started because we would not be living in Winnipeg.

I received my call to the bar in the spring of 1951 and was finally free to practice law on my own or with a firm of lawyers. Mr. McGirr asked me to stay on as a member of his firm but he imposed a condition. I would have to give up my involvement with liberals and the liberal party. He said something like – "you'll have to give up this foolishness with the liberals." I thanked him for the offer but declined. I felt badly about having to leave Dauphin, but as a matter of principle, I felt that my choice of political affiliation was my own business. Mr. McGirr renewed the offer some years later, without the condition, but by that time I was getting settled in Brandon.

I had many regrets about leaving Dauphin. The main one was that my tutelage was far from complete. Mr. McGirr would have taught me a lot about how to defend alleged offenders and how to put in or defend a civil case. My stubbornness and principles dictated a less expert and precise method of learning the trade. I still didn't feel qualified to practice law.

Signing the Rolls of the Law Society in the Great Library

Roblin

I didn't know what I was going to do after leaving Dauphin, but within two weeks I found employment searching titles for W. L. Griffith Lease Brokers, an American company with a temporary office in Brandon. Because of my experience searching for mineral rights, they hired me to do that in the Brandon, Neepawa and Boissevain Land Titles Offices.

While I was happy to have a steady job and a fair income, I had no idea how long the oil activity would last. In addition, I was not happy with the misleading stories some of the land men were telling farmers. In any event, I was still anxious to practice law.

On one of my weekend visits to Deloraine, I met the local lawyers, Mart and Mac Colquhoun and Glynn North. I must have expressed an interest in practicing law because one of them said Doug Watson, who was born or raised in Deloraine, wanted to sell his law practice in Roblin.

I phoned him and confirmed that he did want to sell his practice and the insurance business that went with it. Lorna and I drove the 200 or more miles to Roblin the next Saturday. We drove around the town of about 1000 and liked the look of the houses, its small lake, the row of six or more grain elevators and the farm machinery agencies displaying new farm equipment. We both thought it would be a pleasant place to live.

We then went to the small law office above Harvey's general store and spoke to Doug Watson. When I expressed some concern about the size of his office, he said larger offices and living space were available in the building across the street. He phoned Mr. Hawryluk, the owner, who showed us the space he had for rent above a hardware store. Part of it was used by Spigelman and Lichter to store the furs they had purchased from trap line operators until they could be shipped to Winnipeg. The rest was vacant.

There were six unoccupied rooms on the second floor and we decided they would do for my law office, a waiting room and for our living quarters until we could find a better place to live. There were no doors between most of our private rooms so, apart from the kitchen and bedroom, we had to go into the public hall to get from one to another.

We discovered that the Village, as it then was, had no sewer and water. There was, however, a sink and a hand pump in the kitchen to bring water from the cistern in the basement. For drinking water, I would have to cross Main Street and walk another half block to the well and hand pump. There was an indoor biffy on the second floor but, I quickly found, I would have to empty the pail myself.

Doug Watson introduced us to a lady on west Main Street who would take me in as a boarder until we married and moved into the apartment or into a house if we could find one to rent. We learned that Roblin was named for an early Premier of the province, Sir Rodmond Roblin. His grandson, Duff Roblin, would shortly succeed to that office.

It was hard to tell how busy the law practice had been but the insurance business included agency connections with a dozen or more companies. It seemed that part of the practice would produce enough income to get by on. A desk, typewriter, a few chairs and an old wooden filing cabinet were included in the purchase price. The greatest asset seemed to be the fact that there were no other law offices within 30 miles. There were lawyers north of the Duck Mountains, a classmate, Bob Smellie, in Russell, 30 or so miles to the south, and one at Gilbert Plains, 35 miles to the east. Dauphin was 50 miles to the east and the border with Saskatchewan was about 10 miles to the west of Roblin, where the east-west highway crosses the Assiniboine River.

We talked to Lorne Stevenson who managed the hardware store. He liked the town and was enthusiastic about its future. He thought there should be work for a lawyer. He told us there were two relatively young doctors in town, a dentist, a theatre and a number of people our age. Lorna ran into Arnold Purdy in the café we went to for coffee. He had been a classmate of hers at United College and in the Faculty of Education. He was teaching in the high school and spoke highly of the school, its Principal Sam Wright, and the friendliness of the Village.

I couldn't tell from Doug Watson's records how much legal work there might be but I thought that if Deloraine, also with a population of 1000, could support three lawyers, Roblin should be able to support one. After a week's contemplation, we decided to take the plunge and finalised the deal.

Lorna and I were not yet married so in the interim I boarded with Mrs. Coughlin in a little house near the edge of town. She was a lovely mother-hen of a lady who insisted I eat well and didn't work too late. She introduced me to her neighbours, including Mayor McBride, who lived across the street.

By the time Lorna and I moved into the Hawryluk building, I had met and was able to introduce her to the dentist, Mike Kobewka and his wife Ruby, to Ed Somers, the Ag. Rep, and his wife Dee and to Dr. Art Large. I had been to meetings of the Chamber of Commerce and the Legion and we had been invited to attend the United Church when Lorna arrived.

After we married in October, we moved in. We spent many an evening driving the country lanes and byways. The rolling country and winding roads were picturesque. Being at the western end of the Riding Mountain chain, the land was rolling. Deep valleys led to small lakes where we later learned to catch jackfish and how to cook them. The Shell River valley took water from the west end of the Duck Mountain watershed to the Assiniboine River. The bush covered banks gave shelter to ruffed grouse, deer and other animal life city dwellers would never see.

Mixed farms still showed signs of the recent clearing of trees, and the boulders along fence lines gave testament to the back-breaking task of clearing the land to produce a crop. Stone boats were still in use, as were homemade log splitters. For city folk, a stone boat is a sturdy log or lumber sled, built close to the ground so farmers could roll boulders onto it and move them from the productive fields to an unproductive area. This seemed to be a never-ending task. Most farms grew a variety of grain crops, raised cattle, some sheep, and had Clydesdales and Percherons for heavy work and to show at country fairs.

Many of the farmers were first and second generation Ukrainian. When I prepared papers to transfer a parcel of land from one farmer to another, it was not unusual for the buyer to arrive at my office with a tin can filled with bills. Possibly because of a bad experience during the depression, a lot of farmers didn't trust the banks. The bank tellers weren't surprised though when I deposited a wad of bills to my trust account.

Two rural Municipalities had their offices in Roblin. One was the large Shell River Municipality with Mr. Filewich Senior as its long-term Reeve and Manager. The other was Hillsboro Municipality where his son, Charlie Filewich, was the Secretary Treasurer. He and I became close friends and, as couples, we visited back and forth. He had recently returned from an auctioneer course in Nebraska and put on quite a show in town or at a farm sale. We still have a massive family bible we bought at one of his sales.

As it turned out, I was not deluged with legal work. Things were so slow that Charlie and I had time for several games of pool every afternoon. That came to an end when the Hillsboro counsellors told Charlie to cut it out and stay in his office. Otherwise, they said, he would be out of a job.

One of the reason things were slow for me, I finally discovered, was that a long-time resident and land speculator who loaned money to farmers who wanted to expand their holdings, did legal work. Whether he charged for doing it, I don't know, but he was quite aggressive in seeking business. Worst of all, he blatantly placed a 'Law Office' sign in his second storey office window.

I complained at one of the meetings of the Dauphin Bar and the matter was referred to the Law Society. As a result, the Law Office sign was removed. It was impossible to tell whether he continued to practice.

Lorna and I divided our out-of-town travel between Yorkton and Dauphin. The former had the best restaurant at the time and Dauphin had the best theatre. It was not that Roblin didn't have a theatre but we liked to have an excuse for a little trip now and then. We bought Dusty, a cocker spaniel, at Saltcoats, Saskatchewan during a meandering Sunday drive. I would tie trips to Dauphin in with what I had to do at the Court House or Land Titles Office, so we were there every couple of weeks. When I attended the monthly Bar meetings, Lorna would visit Milton Barr and his wife, the people she had boarded with when she taught in Dauphin.

At one of the bar meetings, Sam Freedman, who was presiding in court, came to the monthly bar dinner. He had been appointed to the Court of Queen's Bench on the 8th of April, 1952. I felt honoured when, without any warning, Ernie McGirr, who was chairing the proceedings, called on me to express the bar's welcome to the new judge. I described the pleasure it had been to have Sam as one of our professors in law school and said what a great judge he would be. I was equally pleased with Ernie McGirr's gesture. I was happy to know that he wasn't mad at me for declining to join his firm.

Roblin nestled in the rolling forest and farmland between the western slopes of the Riding and Duck Mountains. When we lived there, the interior of the Duck Mountains was accessible only by horse, jeep or truck. Childs Lake with its crystal clear water, tall reeds and shale bottom, wouldn't be opened to cottagers for another decade. Sleepy hamlets like Deepdale and Makaroff, with their one or two-sheet curling rinks, were hidden in the hills. Today if you drive through them, the rinks are gone and residents stop and stare, wondering who the stranger in their midst may be. A wave will be tenuously returned, but your presence is an unusual event.

Roblin's hospital, schools, a Catholic Seminary, Manitoba Pool Elevator No. 1 and a variety of churches, made it the social, agricultural and commercial centre of the region. Church feasts and weddings, with traditional cooking, were a regular part of the social scene. Dancing to the fiddle and accordion was sometimes slow and smooth, but hectic when the strains of a polka brought everyone to their feet. Drinks at wedding dances, after a presentation parade, were on the house. The choice was beer or homemade 'hooch.' My first attempt at the latter persuaded me to stick to the gentler libation.

The next year, Lorna was invited to teach at the Roblin high school. She enjoyed the work immensely and her income helped us to survive. Because of my lack of attention in law school, I was never sure whether I was making any money or not, but we were having a good time.

We played bridge with Sammy Lebedowicz and his wife. Sam was a character and when he took a trick he liked to say he had been ‘hiding in the bullrushes’. He was the owner of an appliance store. When we bought a fridge from him and I was writing out a cheque he said, “You didn’t ask for a discount. Everyone asks for a discount. I’ll give you one anyway.”

The Mighty Moose

One afternoon, when I had been in Roblin for a few months, there was a pounding on our kitchen door. When Lorna answered, three bearded men in overalls were standing there.

"We want to see the lawyer," one of them announced.

"His office is at the end of the hall," Lorna replied as if their appearance at our suite was a common occurrence.

When they walked straight into my office, one of the fiercest men I had ever seen said, "Are you the lawyer?"

"Yes," I said, trying to stay calm.

"We got a ticket," another of the giants said. That didn't sound too serious but then he added, "over a moose."

Thinking they must have hit one with their car or truck, I said, "Well you better tell me about it."

Lorna lurked in the background although she was undaunted by tough looking mountain-men. She had dealt with many of them when she worked in her father's drug store in Deloraine below the Turtle Mountains. She nevertheless followed them down the hall and listened as I started to talk to them, until she was satisfied she didn't have to run to the police for help.

In case an uninformed reader thinks these stories are set in the Rocky Mountains or the Alps, I should explain that Manitoba contains a number of 'mountain' ranges. None of them have a vertical rise of 1000 feet above the surrounding plain, but early settlers or map-makers must have decided the pleasant rolling hills deserved a lofty designation.

It turned out the mountain men were just that. They lived at Boggy Creek on the southwest slope of the Duck Mountains south of Childs Lake. They had gone ploughing through the bush looking for 'their Moose' as soon as the season opened. Moose, I learned, was not only a source of meat for hungry families during winter months, but its mighty antlers were lasting proof of the skill and vigour of the intrepid hunter. Bagging a moose was no small accomplishment, my clients informed me.

In a slow step by step process, I continued to question the men as they told me their story, using as few words as possible. They said that, in accordance with the law governing hunting parties, they had only one licence between them. All were entitled to join in the chase, but when one shot a moose, the others had to stop hunting. If another member of the party shot another moose that would be an offence. I also learned that when a moose is bagged, the tag that is attached to the license is supposed to be removed from the licence and wired to the animal's ear.

One of the threesome shot a moose and was dragging it through the bush behind his horse when he was stopped by a Conservation Officer. He had the license in his pocket but the tag was still attached to it and not to the ear of the moose. When he saw that, the officer said an infraction of the law had been committed, wrote out a summons on the spot, and confiscated the hunter's rifle and the moose as well.

The hunter who had received the summons told me he was innocent and all three went on at length condemning the unfairness of his arrest. They expressed their displeasure with the law and with the Conservation Officer in particular. Their bravado, supported I assume by their usual ability to intimidate all comers, led to their joint decision to refuse to pay the fine and lose the rifle and the moose. They instructed me to fight the case and to give no quarter (my word, not theirs).

After they left, I prepared two letters on my ancient Underwood. One was to the court office in Dauphin, letting the Court and the Crown Prosecutor know that I was representing the hunter who had been charged and that he would plead Not Guilty when the case came to trial. The second letter went to the Conservation Department of the Provincial government in Winnipeg saying the same thing and demanding the return of my client's rifle and the moose.

After they had engaged me to fight the case, it seemed that my clients told everyone they met what had happened and that 'the lawyer' was going to fight the charge. The impending case attracted the interest of all gun owners within thirty miles. That included all the farmers and a good percentage of the townsfolk who owned shotguns, rifles, or both. Long before it came to trial, the public interest was even greater than for my most important civil rights case of later years.

To fully appreciate what follows and put it into a broader context, it may help to consider the intended purpose of our laws. Laws are enacted and put in place by members of Parliament, Provincial and Territorial Legislatures, City and Municipal governments. Licensing powers, through delegated authority, add untold numbers of rules and regulations that limit and restrict our basic rights and freedoms. These too have the force of law. 'The Law,' if it succeeds, is the glue that holds a civilized country together. In its pristine form it provides a set of rules, privileges and limitations to enable citizens to live and work in harmony with one another. It is intended to strike a balance between individual freedom and responsibility. If it works, it provides peace and harmony. If it fails, it can breed charges of privilege, corruption, contempt and disrespect for the law.

On the other hand, some things are not totally black or white. Sometimes the public is left asking: 'Was the result correct? Was justice done? Did someone get away with something they should not have?' This, my first case since becoming a full-fledged lawyer, showed the interaction of these choices and principles. I leave it to others to decide whether justice was done.

When my client, his burly bearded friends and I appeared at the Shell River Municipal Office on the date set for the trial, I was surprised to see the Mayor of the Village presiding. The Crown Attorney, who had driven in from Dauphin on the loosely gravelled road, explained that the Mayor was a Justice of the Peace and the appropriate person to hear the case. The prosecutor wanted to talk to me about the case so I agreed to an adjournment for a month. The heavy bags in the corner of the room, containing the rifle and the remains of the moose that I expected would be entered as Exhibits, were returned to storage.

I knew the Crown Attorney was going to follow his usual procedure of trying to persuade defence counsel to have their client plead guilty. Needless to say, the pressure from the Crown had no effect on my stubborn clients and their growing number of supporters. My clients appeared to have had some previous experience with the law and they were not going to be dissuaded from this fight. This was a *cause celebre* for them and most of the hunters in the district. It was obvious the game wardens were not popular.

When the appointed day arrived the next month, every space in the 'courtroom' was filled with spectators and the exhibits were once again waiting to be recognized. The room was sufficient for municipal business, but had none of the space or decorum of a courtroom. The building only had two rooms. The back room contained a long table and six or eight chairs where the Municipal Council had most of its records and where it met to conduct business. It was closed during the trial. The front room was where the Secretary Treasurer sat when collecting taxes or dealing with ratepayers' concerns. There was normally a counter across half the room and one desk.

Converted to serve as a courtroom, the counter was pushed against a wall and there was a single collapsible table across the room. The judge sat on one side of the table and the Crown Attorney, an Enforcement Officer, my client and I, squeezed together on the other side. There was no Court Reporter and barely room on the table for a pad of notepaper. The spectators stood and occupied every other inch of space in the room.

Excitement ran through the crowd as the prosecutor rose, presumably to begin his case. We were disappointed again. He was having trouble getting his witnesses together and he requested a further adjournment. The spectators groaned their disapproval but back the carcass went to cold storage. I didn't see the rifle. On the third try, the case finally got under way. This time the desk had been moved to the back of the room so the Judge wouldn't have to squeeze through the crowd to get to his seat. He was able to come in and leave through the Council Chambers.

The Crown called its first witness, an official from the Department of Natural Resources in Winnipeg. He explained the law that was contained in the Provincial Regulation. The first indication of a problem arose as this rather pompous law-and-order public servant turned towards and started to lecture the crowd. More than a murmur of discontent was audible as the independent farmers displayed their dissatisfaction with the authority they were being told they had to respect. Farmers as a whole are an independent lot and this was a situation that touched the freedom of them all.

When it was my turn to cross-examine the witness, I asked about the need for a moose season. He explained it was meant to control the numbers of animals that would likely not survive the harsh winters if there is insufficient food for them. He agreed that some population control was needed and agreed the hunters were performing a public service as they garnered food for their families. He made it clear he was not anti-hunter at all. The murmuring of the crowd seemed to suggest they weren't so sure.

I then asked about his experience as a hunter as, from what he said in direct examination, it was apparent he didn't have much. A common rule of courtroom advocacy is that a lawyer should never ask a question unless sure of the answer. A bad answer can ruin a case. In this case I was sure enough of what the answer would be. When asked if he had ever pulled a carcass through the bush with a horse, he said he had not. The next few questions dealt with the likelihood of a tag being torn loose and lost while dragging an animal through the bush. By then I was absolutely certain he would have no experience with that happening, so I suggested problems that might arise. By that time the spectators were voicing their own experiences. One shouted "that's right" when I suggested the tag could easily have been pulled off while dragging the animal through the bush. When I suggested that my client was a responsible hunter, the congregation murmured its agreement.

The next prosecution witness was the Conservation Officer who followed the tracks in the snow and came upon my client in the process of hauling the moose through the bush by a rope attached to his saddle and to the animal's legs. In direct examination he told the Prosecutor of asking my client for his license and his surprise at seeing the infamous tag still attached to it instead of to the moose. He spoke of how a tag is supposed to be attached to the ear of an animal and the importance of doing that. He said he gave my client a summons and took charge of the dormant beast. His strict application of the law did not impress the hunters in the audience and his comments were met with a chorus of not very silent boos.

It was then my turn to cross-examine the less than popular policeman of the woods.

"Is it not true that my client was towing the animal through very dense and tangled bush?" I asked.

"Yes, it was quite thick," he started in a positive tone.

"Isn't it possible that if the tag had been attached to the animal, it could have been torn off during the dragging operation?"

"I don't see why," he replied.

"Oh, have you ever dragged a moose through the bush with a tag attached?" I reasonably and quietly asked.

"No and I don't shoot animals either," was his surly reply.

"Well then, you don't know if the tag could be lost or not."

"Well --- no," was his reluctant reply.

I didn't realize I was in the Clarence Darrow club but the crowd enjoyed the questions and the exchange so much they clapped when I sat down. The Crown closed its case and it was time for our defence. My client was sworn "to tell the truth, the whole truth and nothing but the truth," and then I asked him questions that coincided with the questions I had asked the arresting officer in cross-examination. He maintained his belief that he was in the right and should not have been charged. He said he followed the law as far as he could under the circumstances. He made a more effective witness than I thought he would, buoyed no doubt, by the enthusiasm displayed by his supporters.

He said, "I knew the law and would have attached the tag to the moose as soon as I got it out of the bush. I didn't attach it earlier as it could have been torn off in the dense and tangled bush."

He was impressive as a poor hard-done-by citizen. His statements were met with even louder comments of agreement and support from the audience.

The judge called for quiet and said the prosecutor was entitled to some respect. He was booed. The chorus caused the judge to keep quiet until the case was over. This was a very unusual scene for a court of law. The judge, known by all as "Bill" or "Mr. Mayor," tried to retain control, but couldn't. He didn't intervene again, probably because he was also an insurance agent and couldn't go too far in chastising those in the courtroom, some of whom were surely his customers; and besides, he was up for re-election in the fall.

The Crown Prosecutor threatened the spectators with expulsion if they didn't behave themselves. I didn't want to antagonize either the judge or the prosecutor. We were certain to meet in other cases and the Mayor was a pleasant person who had welcomed me to town when I first arrived. I had known the Crown Attorney, C. S. A. Rogers, when I was in Dauphin and we always had a good relationship. He was reasonable when negotiating a penalty on a plea of guilty and in refraining from over-charging (laying a more serious charge than the facts warranted) so I wanted to keep on his good side. I therefore joined in the effort to allow each witness to have their say without interruption or reaction. I urged the crowd to keep silent and to permit the Crown Prosecutor and me to complete our questions. It seemed for a few minutes that our requests had been observed.

Little did I know that the worst was still to come. As the Crown Attorney cross-examined my client, the fury of the crowd was fanned. When he asked my client why he hadn't obeyed the law he knew existed, a number of boos were heard. When he suggested that his excuse of being concerned about the tag being torn off was false, the lid came off. Not only boos, but calls of persecution and not knowing what he was talking about were clearly and loudly expressed by faceless people buried in the crowd. Now, whatever question he asked, it was greeted with disdain. He gave up without even introducing the remains of the moose or the rifle into evidence.

Closing arguments were listened to without too much interruption. I went first as I had to because I had called my client as a witness. The spectators listened to the Crown Attorney with some degree of decorum, probably because their anger had been spent. We each only spoke for about three minutes, the Crown Prosecutor asking for a conviction and I for an acquittal.

The case came to a speedy conclusion when, without any formality or reference to the evidence, the Mayor said "Not Guilty," closed his note book, gathered up his papers, and left by the back door. He was undoubtedly relieved that the ordeal was over. I can't remember appearing before him in another case, presumably because he and the Crown Attorney agreed that all contested cases would be heard by the Dauphin Magistrate or by the County Court Judge.

The crowd poured onto the dusty street to congratulate the offender and one another on the victory they hardly expected to achieve. I cannot pretend it was my legal prowess that secured the acquittal, but I was content to wallow in the congratulatory comments none the less. My greatest reward was being recognized as a lawyer who fought for his clients.

Business started to pick up after this initiation into the community and an issue that touched its very soul, but the story was not over. A month after the trial, my wife had another visit from the three stalwarts, looking for 'the lawyer.' My name was either incidental or unknown. They again arrived and pounded on our kitchen door, and when my wife opened it, they said "here." The men of few words presented her with a sizeable package of moose meat, turned and left.

I thought that was a wonderful gesture on their part. My wife wasn't persuaded. She refused to keep or cook the roast, concerned that it's travels to and from court and in and out of some unidentified sort of cold storage would have caused it to spoil. As the roast was thrown unceremoniously into the garbage she proclaimed, "and besides, I've never cooked moose, and I'm not interested in learning how to do it now." The sweet taste of victory was still not a bad start in Roblin.

With Lorna teaching at the school and bringing in needed income, she and I decided to move out of our quarters over the hardware store and try to find a house of our own. Our kitchen and bedroom next to my two-room office were wearing thin for both of us. There was no potable water and the biffy across the hall was a mess and we were tired of having to take a bath in our metal washtub.

We finally found a small asbestos-covered log house looking down on Goose Lake. In our snug little nest we had the luxury of a coal and wood kitchen stove with a hot water closet at one end. It was a little hard to get into the dug-out basement, but the briquettes I shovelled into the little furnace each morning and night kept us toasty warm. It was there Lorna began to display her love for and interest in building, renovations and interior design. She got me involved in laying a hardwood floor. Little did I know that interest would continue to this very day.

In any event, I was happy to have my wife removed from the invasion of her privacy by unusual clients and from my sometimes-different practice of law. In spite of the disruption to our lives, and the comic aspects of the case, I thanked the Mighty Moose for propelling me on my way. The case was only the first of many where serious issues were involved but where the human element was the part I remember.

An unusual aspect of our move was that the house we bought turned out to be an investment holding of Bill McBride, the reluctant Judge and Mayor of Roblin. Our courtroom encounter had fortunately not damaged our friendly beginning.

Thinking back on the case years later, it was not surprising that the Federal Government's plan to introduce a compulsory gun registry system ran into the emotional resistance it did. It must have rekindled the same emotions the farmers and hunters of Roblin felt in the case of the Mighty Moose.

The Roblin Riot

The riot in Roblin occurred on a warm summer's night. 'Riot' may seem an extreme word to apply to what happened in a usually sleepy, law-abiding Village of a thousand peaceful souls, but a riot it was. My dictionary describes a riot as a tumult, disorder, disturbance of the peace by a crowd and its refusal to disperse when an officer of the law demands it.

The evening in question started as all Saturday nights had for years. Country folk were in town to visit their neighbours on the street and the townsfolk parked on the main drag early in the afternoon so they would have a ring-side seat from which to view the passing parade as the evening wore on. It was a time to catch up on all the news and gossip, and some always could be found. It was an exciting day. During the week, the winds whirled the dust or snow through the funnel created by the one and two storey buildings that supported one another on each side of the two-block business sector.

On Saturday night the clothing merchants, grocery stores (there were two), drug store, butcher and the barber, enjoyed their busiest day of the week. The street was packed with visiting town and country folk catching up on one another's family and activities. Men would lean against a wall discussing municipal affairs or politics and women talked of upcoming community events. It was the place to get the latest news on the condition of the crops and the prices being offered by elevator agents.

As might be expected, many of the men were tough and hard living. Saturday night was their time to visit their friends and let off steam in the only drinking hole in town – the men-only beer parlour in the town's only hotel. There was still no government-operated Liquor Commission and it would be another six years before the Bracken Commission recommended women be admitted to these male sanctuaries.

The hotel was a peaceful retreat for some, but a raucous freewheeling attraction for others. Saturday nights were the worst. Long held and usually controlled antagonisms became unleashed and challenges and fights erupted regularly. There was a fair amount of competition and animosity among farmers, though I never understood where it came from. As far as I could tell, it began a generation earlier when land was being purchased from the government or allotted to the first settlers. Some farms certainly had better land than others and that may have had a bearing on the smoldering antagonisms.

Not all the patrons were farmers. Rough and ready woodsmen from San Clara and Boggy Creek were in a class by themselves. They were tough and enjoyed the excitement of a Saturday night in town. They were happy to tangle with anyone who looked at them sideways.

The hefty hotel owner was sure to be on duty Saturday night. It took someone as tough as the customers to keep things under control. He was usually able to calm things down by ejecting those who had too much to drink. His ultimate weapon was to have a troublemaker interdicted and barred from the hotel indefinitely. That was a fate worse than death to the party crowd.

One warm and humid autumn night, tempers were running high before closing time as threats and challenges were hurled across the room. When 'Last Call' was hollered by the barman, the tradition was that each patron could order two more glasses of beer no matter how many they still had in front of them at the time. The boys had to down their final beers in a hurry as the closing time was eleven, or if the owner was in a good mood, eleven fifteen.

It was therefore a well-oiled crowd that flowed onto Main Street and across to Jimmy Foo's Chinese restaurant. The booths and stools quickly filled and the insults and arguments started up again. A couple of bearded bushmen started to shove one another and before long a full-scale fight broke out. Others were on their feet, ready to join in, but the diminutive Mr. Foo, used to calming things down, jumped on a table, screamed at the crowd, and threatened to call the police if they didn't go outside.

The crowd didn't want to get Jimmy upset enough to close the only late-night eatery in town, so they headed for the street en masse. Soon a dozen fights were in progress. While some of the fighters limited themselves to haymaker punches and the occasional kick or bite, others wrestled on the gravelled street, trying to get up. Within minutes, the late night shoppers, waiting to drive the drinkers home, surrounded the fighters and egged their favourites on. They made as much noise as those in battle and added to the bedlam. Before long, the non-combatants stood three to five deep and kept moving to watch the best fight.

The ferocity of the fights made some of the spectators believe someone might be killed and a call for help went out. It was into an unruly crowd that the guardian of peace and order strode. Dick Bogle was a civilian cop employed by the Village. He was a small man but his war experience had made him as tough as nails. His bravado and commanding voice usually controlled any situation, but the problem he faced that night was that his strict approach to law enforcement hadn't made him many friends. His calls to the brawlers to stop had no effect; nor did his order to the crowd to go home. His every shout was met with taunts and boos.

Not to be deterred, he called out the volunteer fire department. One of the farm implement dealers was the Fire Chief and one of his employees was his Deputy. A pig farmer close to town, a mechanic, plumber and a few spare volunteers made up the fire brigade. When a call came in, the Chief would determine the number of fire-fighters needed and phone them. In this case, three men appeared to be all that would be required.

It took ten or fifteen minutes to assemble the crew and to get the fire truck out of the garage next to the Village office. With no water or sewage system in town, there were no hydrants. The firemen, directed by Dick Bogle, drove the fire engine with its full load of water, to Main Street a hundred yards away. They had to stop outside the ring of spectators to unwind the hose and get it closer to the combatants.

They dragged the heavy hose into the centre of the crowd. While two attached and adjusted the nozzle, the other was sent back to the truck to turn the water on. The crowd was told to stand back but few moved from their vantage point. Water gushed out of the hose and the firemen took aim at the wildest fight.

This attempt to quiet things down might have worked, but as

soon as the firemen got the hose working, the flow of water stopped. A fireman rushed back to the truck only to find that someone had turned off the tap. He turned the tap back on and returned to help direct the flow to where it might do some good. After breaking up one fight, the water died again. Someone had turned the water off again.

The sequence was repeated once again but by that time Dick Bogle was beside himself and the crowd was enjoying his frustration. Each time the water started, the crowd booed and each time the water stopped, the crowd cheered its approval. In their anonymity, they had a great time badgering and defying Mr. Law and Order. The minion of the law finally gave up and announced he was calling in the Mounties.

The well-liked resident RCMP Corporal, Dunc Young, was away on a course, so he couldn't help. If he'd been in town he could probably have settled things down. As it was, Bogle could only carry out his threat by phoning the Mounted Police detachments in Dauphin and Yorkton, each an hour away. He called both detachments and an hour and a half later, uniformed officers finally arrived from east and west. By the time the Mounties arrived, the energies of the frolickers had been spent and most had gone home. There wasn't much the Mounties could do. After questioning a few stragglers, and giving Dick Bogle a hard time, they went home as well.

Cpl. Young and Dick Bogle later got the names of many of the fighters, and some who may have egged them on, but they could never find anyone who would identify the mischief-maker who kept turning the water off. If any had seen who it was, they weren't telling. Although the star of the evening kept silent, he became a folk hero.

Fourteen men were charged with "disturbing the peace and interfering with a police officer in the exercise of his duty." They appeared in court a month later. The Crown Prosecutor from Dauphin, C. S. A. Rogers, remembering his unfortunate experience in the crowded Municipal Office in the case of the Mighty Moose, rented the movie theatre to serve as the courtroom. Tommy Little, the Magistrate in Dauphin sat behind a table on the stage.

When court started, the theatre was full and a spectator entertained the crowd by announcing, "It's the best show in town."

The charges were read and the judge asked each accused: "How do you plead, Guilty or Not Guilty?"

"Not guilty Your Honour," they replied in the manner I had suggested. I advised the judge we were ready to proceed to trial, but the Prosecutor said the police were still investigating. He asked the judge to adjourn the case until the next sitting of the court. The judge agreed and the disappointed crowd left the theatre.

The Prosecutor called me aside: "You know Al, if your clients will plead guilty to disturbing the peace I'll ask the judge to be lenient and give them a suspended sentence."

There was no need to consult my determined clients so I said, "Sorry, my instructions are to fight the charges all the way."

When we returned to the theatre a month later, Mr. Rogers "stayed" a number of charges, meaning they were adjourned indefinitely. In layman's language, and in reality, that meant the charges were dropped. The Crown was obviously having trouble finding witnesses to come to court. The remaining cases were adjourned for yet another month.

The anonymous spectators at the riot played a large part in the final result. They had no desire to see anyone punished for providing the best entertainment the Village had ever seen, nor did they mind being part of a good joke on the sometimes officious town cop. They appeared to have a common case of amnesia as they were unable to identify any of the entertainers.

When the third hearing began, the remaining and all the original accused and a smaller crowd, were present. There were only four accused left. The red-faced Prosecutor rose slowly to his feet and quietly advised the judge he was withdrawing all the charges. Apparently none of the Crown's hoped-for witnesses could or would say who started a particular fight. More to the point, they couldn't say that some if not all the accused weren't merely defending themselves from an attack by someone else.

It was unlikely any of the accused would have been convicted even if a trial had taken place. The spectators had only a vague recollection of what happened and had no idea how the fights started in the first place. My clients actually wanted to give evidence. They weren't about to have Dick Bogle spoil their fun and there was no way they were going to accuse one another of assault. Each of them enjoyed the brawl and the whole scenario immensely. Sitting together in court, they looked the best of friends. I didn't think it necessary to tell them, but I wouldn't have called any of them to take the witness stand in any event. I didn't want them cross-examined by the wily Prosecutor.

I was also saved from playing my ace in the hole. If the trial had gone ahead, I would have argued that all the participants consented to the fighting, like boxers in a boxing ring; that all the fighting was for their common enjoyment, and that none were guilty of an assault.

The community came out of the incident quite well. One of the municipal councillors made no secret of his feelings. He thought the incident allowed people to get rid of old animosities that needed to be put to rest, and helped to establish a stronger and closer-knit community. The locals enjoyed telling, re-telling and embellishing the story. They relished the spirit of the "old west," still alive and well in their frontier community. No guns were used, but the story was repeated as an epic on a par with the Shooting at the OK Corral.

Although I represented all the accused, my main contribution was to have them plead "not guilty." Without doing so openly, I was telling the prosecutor: "If you say my clients are guilty, you prove it." That is the job of the Crown and Rogers knew it. He also knew my job was to do the best I could for my clients.

Lorna and I didn't see the riotous scene as, like Corporal Young, we were away that weekend. While at first I was sorry to have missed the fun, my absence was fortuitous. As unbiased as I would have tried to be, it might have been difficult to act for the accused if I had witnessed what happened.

Insurance Salesman

When I bought the practice, it included a general insurance business. That was fortunate because the income from it kept me afloat until the practice of law could. It provided good contacts, but also presented problems I had no idea might occur. I also inherited a real estate practice or, to be more precise, the right to sell houses and farms if the owners gave me the authority to find buyers. The law at the time permitted a lawyer to act as a realtor and I must have let it be known this was another service I could provide. The law governing real estate agents was later amended to remove that automatic authority and to require training.

Realtors will be pleased to know that, in spite of two listings over a period of three years, I never made a single sale. I don't think I even had a formal listing – merely permission to show some land if I had an inquiry. It must have been evident to buyers and sellers alike that I couldn't even speak sensibly about farm land and didn't know one piece of machinery from the next.

Property and car insurance were in a slightly different category. I was left with a large number of current automobile policies and farm insurance. The latter described the home that was covered and the number and use of various out-buildings. It wasn't too difficult to phone or write the policy-holders to remind them their policy was due for renewal. They would come to my office and see me or the part-time secretary I finally acquired.

I must have been an agent for more than a dozen companies. There was Saskatchewan Mutual, Halifax, Lloyd's of London and other Canadian and overseas companies, but the largest was the Wawanesa Mutual Insurance Company. Charlie Lawrence was my contact person and he visited my office two or three times a year.

Charlie was born and raised in Wawanesa, a pretty town atop the high banks of the Souris River a few miles before it joins the Assiniboine. The major office of the company has long since moved to Winnipeg, but its Board of Directors still holds an annual meeting in its red-brick building at the corner of Fourth and Cliff in Wawanesa to maintain a connection with its place of birth in 1896.

By the way, Wawanesa is still a 'Village' and is happy with the designation. It has a magnificent museum in the original Wawanesa Mutual building across the street and an old church that has been attached to it. The museum displays clothing, pictures, period clothing, and a map showing the names and location of early Indian Tribes. The Kriddle family history and a section on Nellie McClung make it unique.

During one of his early visits Charlie suggested that, when I was renewing a farm policy, I should discuss the possibility of increasing the coverage on the buildings and see if the insured had other assets that weren't covered. He impressed on me that I should always visit large farms to make sure the buildings were still in place.

Determined to do my duty and be seen as a productive representative, I looked for opportunities to increase coverage. I was writing very few new policies, although the odd friend and acquaintance took pity on the young and starving lawyer. When a middle aged couple came to my office to discuss the renewal of their soon to expire farm policy, my questioning about sufficient coverage was pleasantly received and when they agreed to consider expanding the policy, and I said I would have to inspect their farm before that could be done, they encouraged me to come to their farm the next week and to bring my wife.

When we arrived, the farmer showed me around and I made note of the buildings and what they were used for. He explained the rising cost of operations and the current value of each building. We looked at the existing policy and agreed that some of the buildings now had a greater value. The increases he suggested sounded reasonable to me. When we returned to the farm house our hostess had tea and sandwiches prepared. The concluding *piece de resistance* was a wonderful German fruit cake. We thanked our hosts for their hospitality, the increase in business and headed back to Roblin taking scenic side roads all the way. The next day I submitted a renewal application with increased coverage to Wawanesa Mutual. Their bill and the new policy arrived in due course. The farmer came to my office, received the policy and paid the premium.

Some months later I received a call from Charlie Lawrence. That was not unusual but this time he spoke of this particular farm and asked me to have my file available on the day he wanted to come to my office. I saw no problem with that and we agreed to meet on a certain date. Charlie was punctual as always but his entry and opening comments were more brusque than during earlier meetings.

Instead of "How are ya" and "how are you doing," he exploded: "The whole bloody farm burned to the ground."

No one had told me there had been a fire and none had been reported in the local paper. "You mean the Gelder farm?" I asked.

"You're darn right," he said. "How come you put on all that extra coverage?"

I was taken aback by this attack on my performance. "What do you mean? You told me to see if I could increase the coverage on farm buildings."

Ignoring my comment, he continued to question my performance. "Why didn't you go to the farm and inspect the buildings?" he roared.

"I did!" was my shocked reply, and I explained that Lorna and I visited the farm and I looked at all the buildings with the farmer.

"But his wife has claimed she lost forty dresses, three mink coats and a raft of expensive furnishings."

"Well I didn't look in her clothes closet," I explained.

"We think they started the fire themselves," seemed to be his parting shot as he was running out of steam.

"Well then, they should be charged with arson," I said, relying on an area about which I had a little knowledge.

"The problem is we can't prove it. We've had our investigators going over the place with a fine tooth comb and they can't tell what started the fire." He looked at me, hoping I could help the company confirm its suspicions.

"Have you spoken to the owners?" I inquired.

"Of course we have, but they have no receipts and no proof they bought what they say they had in the house. They say they might have had some receipts, but any they did have were destroyed in the fire."

Wawanesa never took the agency away from me but I felt our

relationship had been strained so it wasn't long before I sold the insurance part of my business to Les Spear who had helped me with insurance during the preceding year. In any event, the much easier practice of law seemed to be increasing and I was glad to dispose of the uncertain requirements of fire and automobile insurance companies. I never heard of the fire again. I would see Charlie from time to time when he came to town and our relationship returned to a friendly one as we were no longer in business together. He and Les got along well, probably because Charlie now had an agent who knew the insurance business and had a good farm background as well.

Years later, after I retired from the bench, I was having my hair cut at a barber shop in Charleswood. As I got up to leave, I noticed what I thought was a familiar but long unseen face on an older gentleman waiting his turn for a cut. I went over and asked, "Charlie Lawrence?"

In his usual pleasant way he replied, "Yes."

"Al Hamilton" I said, but he still had a blank look on his kindly face. "I was a lawyer and your agent in Roblin."

He immediately brightened and replied, "Oh yeah, the fire. How are you Al?"

We had a good chat about earlier days and about the infamous fire. I reminded him of the wonderful welcome my wife and I had received during our visit to the farm. Wondering what Charlie would say, I added, "They were such a nice couple."

Charlie rose to the challenge immediately and gave me a shot in return: "I've followed your work over the years Al. I think you made a good career change."

"Touché," I happily replied.

An Important Loss

My first appearance in the Court of Queen's Bench in a contested civil case was in the old but still majestic Dauphin Court House, positioned at the very end of and seemingly in the middle of Main Street. It contained a sizeable Law Library next to the Judge's private office, a Registry office, a Sheriff's office and a court room for the Magistrate and his busy dockets. The second floor contained a large court room with a jury box, formal witness stand, and a wooden fence to separate those involved in cases from the theatre-style seats for the public.

Behind the courtroom was an office for the visiting Queen's Bench Judge, with a pull-down bed and a separate bathroom. Also behind the courtroom, off an adjacent corridor was a barred jail cell where persons on trial before a jury were held when the court was not in session. Across the hall was the barristers' robing room where local lawyers kept their gowns and changed to go into court. There were also witness interview rooms, a room for the Court Reporter and public washrooms.

The basement contained the Dauphin Jail where those sentenced for up to two years less a day served their sentence. It had traditional iron-barred cells, although most were replaced in later years when inmates were encouraged to seek employment in the community. The prisoners plowed the snow around the Court House, cut the grass and looked after the large flower and vegetable gardens.

Although I had processed a few uncontested divorces in Dauphin, I had never appeared for a client of my own on a contested civil case. I was about to receive my initiation under fire. I had been in the Q. B. with Ernie McGirr when I articled to him, and had witnessed him and Jack McFadyen tearing strips off one another, even though it was just good-natured bantering. I never dreamt it could happen to me.

My opportunity to go to the Q. B. arose one wintry day when Dorothy, a woman for whom I had obtained a divorce, came to my

Roblin office and introduced Molly, a young country girl. She had had 'a child out of wedlock.' Dorothy sat through the initial and all subsequent interviews, encouraging Molly to speak, and adding her own evidence and opinions from time to time. She seemed more concerned than Molly that "justice be done."

Molly told me the child's father was Gordon Brewster.

"Of course it's Gordon," Dorothy confirmed.

"Gordon visited me in the hospital and drove me and the baby home," Molly added.

"And he gave Molly $25 a month to help with the baby's care," Dorothy added with authority.

I was a little shy and reticent in the presence of these prim and proper females. I asked when Molly had sex with Gordon but didn't go into a great deal of detail.

"We only had sex once and that was nine months before the baby was born. I told Gordon I was pregnant about two months afterwards," Molly told me.

"Did you put his name on the birth certificate?" I asked, believing that was standard procedure.

"No, I didn't want to embarrass him," was her immediate reply.

"Did you discuss what you would call the baby?" I asked.

"No, I was trying to keep him out of it, and anyway, I was looking into an abortion."

"Did you discuss abortion with him?" I asked, assuming the answer would be 'Yes'.

"No, I didn't want to."

Dorothy came to her rescue. "She came to me and I said we should keep Gordon out of it. After all, it was her baby! I also told her it was her duty to keep the baby."

"Tell me how Gordon came to give you money." I asked.

"Well, we had been friends in high school and when he came to visit me in the hospital I was crying. He asked what was wrong and I told him my parents were mad at me and I couldn't afford to support the baby on my own. He said he would help me out."

"How much did he give you?"

"He gave me $25 a month for three months, then he stopped and I haven't seen him since."

"I phoned Gordon's mother," Dorothy chimed in. "I had a real battle with her. She had the nerve to say it wasn't Gordon's baby and he wasn't going to give Molly another cent."

By that time Molly was sobbing and I didn't think I should make matters worse by asking about her sexual experience with Gordon, let alone with anyone else. These women would think it insulting, so I accepted what Molly and Dorothy told me as the whole story and all I needed to know.

After the women left, I wrote Gordon saying I had been retained by Molly to seek regular payments to help support their baby. Reference was made to the $25 a month he had paid for several months and I said that amount would be acceptable in the future. I asked him to send me the first payment along with his agreement to pay that amount each month and said I would prepare an agreement for them to sign if he wished.

No reply came, so I sent another letter renewing my request and threatening court proceedings if he didn't agree to pay. When it became clear he wasn't going to contact me, I researched the law in the Dauphin Court House library. The cases I read on situations where the identity of the father was in issue, indicated that a blood sample may be demanded from a "putative" (alleged) father. They also said that, if the man refused to provide a sample, his refusal might be taken as an admission that he was the father. The cases cautioned that it was still up to the trial judge to decide whether to draw that inference or not.

Following the authorities, I sent a formal notice to Gordon demanding that he go to Dr. Ed Otke or to another doctor of his choice, and have his blood type confirmed. I explained that Dr. Otke had delivered the baby and would have a record of the baby's blood type. Again, my letter was ignored. I tried again, suggesting that a blood comparison could show he was not the father, but that didn't bring a response either.

It was obvious I was in an uphill fight when I received a reply, not from Gordon, but from my former principal, Ernie McGirr. He said he was acting for Gordon Brewster and had my letters. He said his client would not provide a blood sample, as there was no evidence he could possibly be the father. That position was unheard of in the cases I had read. I decided the refusal to provide a sample, which I now had in writing from his lawyer, would provide all the evidence we needed to win the case.

My attempts to reach a negotiated settlement failed. McGirr wouldn't negotiate. I knew he was a tough bargainer, so without further delay I prepared a Statement of Claim, filed it in the court office in Dauphin and delivered a copy to the office of McGirr & McLean. Their Statement of Defence was filed within a week and the case was placed on the docket for hearing in two months time.

When the trial date arrived, my client and her ever-present supporter arrived well before the 2 o'clock starting time. I had them wait in the corridor while I went into the lawyers' robing room to change into my court attire. Ernie McGirr arrived shortly after I did, threw his Q. C. gown on over the rest of his attire he must have put on at his office. "Ready for battle are ya, Al?" he chortled.

As if that wasn't unsettling enough, his partner Stewart McLean showed up and put on his gown. He was also a Q. C. and I assumed he had another matter to speak to in court, but that was not the case. When the Court Clerk called the case, I advised the judge I was acting for the Plaintiff. Ernie McGirr rose and announced that he and his partner, Stewart McLean Q. C. acted for the Defendant. That surprised me, as I had never seen the two of them in court together. The precarious nature of my position started to sink in.

My unease increased when it became obvious that Ernie McGirr would be the only one to question the witnesses. McLean's presence was only to impress the judge with how seriously the firm considered the attack on their client. If the tactic was intended to intimidate me, it worked. I was as nervous as could be when I rose and called my client to the witness stand. I asked Molly her age and where she lived.

"I understand you are the mother of a baby," I began.

"Yes I am."

"And when was the baby born?" She gave the date of birth.

"Do you know Gordon Brewster?"

"Yes I do," she replied in a strong forthright way.

She was doing well. After asking how long she had known him, I asked, "Does he have any connection with your baby?"

"He's the baby's father," she said in a calm controlled voice.

"Did you have intercourse with Gordon?" I began, being careful not to lead the witness.

"Just once," she said.

"When was that?"

"About nine months before the baby was born," she replied.

"And did you see Gordon after the baby was born?"

"He came to the hospital every day and drove me and the baby home when I was discharged."

"Did he ever give you any money?" I enquired as if I didn't know the answer.

"He gave me $25 three times, and then he stopped."

"Did he say why he stopped?"

"No." At that point Molly looked at Gordon who was sitting between McGirr and McLean at the counsel table, and sobbed, "I didn't see him again till today."

Changing the topic, I asked if she had instructed me to ask him for a sample of his blood. I had warned her that was the way I would ask the question and she correctly answered, "Yes." I show you a copy of a letter addressed to Gordon Brewster. "Is that the letter you directed me to send?" "Yes" she said, calming down.

"My Lord, I ask that the letter be entered as Exhibit One." Turning back to Molly, I asked, "Do you know if Gordon provided a blood sample?"

"I don't think so," she faintly replied.

"Those are all the questions I have My Lord." I sat down.

With brutal precision my cigar-chewing mentor, without the cigar to slow him down, ridiculed every statement my client had made in the witness stand. He went over her friendship with Gordon and had her confirm he was a kind person and a good friend. She agreed he had helped her out when she was in need of money after the child was born. When Molly started to cry, he turned into a soft-spoken father figure, sympathizing with her situation. He brought out the fact that she had lost her job and was almost penniless.

He went back on the attack and asked her in his gruffest voice, "How many times did you have sex with Gordon?"

"Just once I think," she said weakly.

"You think? If you can't remember, you must have had sex many times, or is it because you had sex with so many boys you can't keep them straight in your mind?"

"No. I never had sex with anyone else."

"How many men have you asked to give a blood sample?" he switched topic.

"Only him," she whimpered.

"I suggest to you that you had sex with several boys from your school," McGirr was back on the attack.

"No, I didn't," she cried.

"Why should we believe that?" he roared.

"Because I'm telling the truth," she sobbed.

"You are not," McGirr grumbled as he sat down.

Molly had stubbornly held to her position but she was not an impressive witness. Although he hadn't been able to get her to admit to any other relationships, McGirr had raised a number of questions the judge might consider. When Molly returned to her seat beside me she said, "I just want to go home."

I closed our case, having no further evidence to offer. Mr. McGirr then called his client as the next witness. After the clerk swore Gordon to tell the truth, Mr. McGirr, with a sneer on his face, asked: "Gordon, what do you say about Molly's evidence?"

"It's true I went out with her a bit but we only had sex once."

"When was that?"

"It was on my birthday in her uncle's barn," Gordon said, as if he was sorry he had to tell.

"And when is your birthday?"

"March 22nd and here's my birth certificate." He hadn't waited for anyone to ask to see it.

"And I see from Exhibit 1 the baby was born on August 17th. Do you know if the baby was premature?" McGirr asked.

"How would he know?" I commented, without making a formal objection.

"All right, if my young friend wishes, we will call the doctor as a witness."

I really couldn't be angry at my former mentor for his demeaning use of "young," although "my learned friend" was the usual way to speak of opposing counsel in court. It would have been evident to the judge that he had a young lawyer before him who was having trouble with his case. At that point I felt a tug on my gown, so I leaned over to hear my client whisper so the whole courtroom could hear.

"I don't want Dr. Otke brought here. It was a full term birth."

Trying to make the most of my embarrassment, I said: "My Lord, my client admits that the baby was born approximately nine months after she became pregnant."

"Thank you Mr. Hamilton," the judge said with a twinkle in his eye.

Ernie McGirr returned to his witness. "Are you the father of the baby born to Molly on August 17th?"

"No, I couldn't be" he said in a straightforward manner.

"Why is that?" he asked.

"Well that was only five months after we had sex. I finally figured out she must have already been pregnant when we had intercourse."

He got the answer out before I could decide if it was admissible or not.

"Did you help Molly financially after the baby was born?" McGirr continued.

"Yes I did. I guess at that time I probably thought I was the father."

His obviously honest answer was not an admission of liability but sounded reasonable, the way it was said by this polite and generous young man. McGirr sat down with a flourish and a nod of satisfaction to his partner. The judge saw the gesture as well and may or may not have decided by that time that McGirr had won the day.

During my cross-examination, I couldn't shake Gordon from what he had said in direct examination. He politely answered my questions but he stuck to his story and repeated it again and again. I couldn't challenge his clear recollection of the day and place of the sexual encounter. "Why wouldn't you give a sample of your blood?" I asked, having decided to take another approach.

McGirr was on his feet in a flash. "That decision was made on my advice as his counsel. There was nothing to support the allegation my client was the father and I told him to refuse."

"I object My Lord." I blurted out. "My learned friend is giving evidence."

McGirr got around my objection by asking the judge's permission to ask his client a few more questions. He quietly asked, "Very well, Gordon, why did you stop giving Molly money?"

"Because you told me to stop," Gordon replied to my chagrin.

"And why did you refuse to give a blood sample?" McGirr asked.

"Because you told me not to," Gordon quietly replied.

I had made things even worse by opening the door to Mr. McGirr's agile reaction. He had his client make his closing argument for him and he managed to get his client off the hook at the same time. His aggressive approach was reminiscent of the court battles with Jack McFadyen I had watched with amusement as a student. It wasn't so funny when you are on the receiving end.

I tried to persuade the Judge the girl had proved he started out supporting the baby and that his refusal to give a blood sample should be taken as an admission he was the father. I quoted from the cases I had with me where a refusal to give a sample was enough to find the person responsible. There wasn't much more I could say as Mr. McGirr had demolished both positions with his carefully crafted questions to his own client. I had no way to prove that Gordon's clear recollection of the one and only time they had sex, was a lie.

McGirr argued that the cases I relied on didn't apply in this case where it had been conclusively proven that Gordon couldn't possibly be the father. He stressed the fact that Molly had admitted the child was born after a full term pregnancy. He argued that her evidence was weak and unsure. His final point was that she, as the plaintiff, had the obligation to prove that Gordon was the father. The law did not require a man to prove he was not the father. In any event, McGirr said, Gordon had proved he was not the father and could not have been. He quoted no cases to support his argument but he made it with conviction and the judge obviously accepted it.

Although we may have had the right man in our sights, Mr. McGirr's refusal to have his client give a blood sample, as risky as that was, won the day. He obviously knew his client would make a good impression and he knew how impossible it would be to contradict him. He was sure enough of his own cross-examination skills that he could make Molly's case appear weak, if not untruthful. I had to accept the fact I still had a long way to go before I could go up against a professional like Ernie McGirr again. Although I'm not sure what else I could have done, I felt I must have been, at least in part, responsible for our loss. I felt inadequate and downhearted.

It is unfortunate that clients suffer as lawyers learn their trade, but I learned more from cases I lost than from those I won. This case taught me three important lessons: Never interview a client with someone else in the room. Never assume your client is telling you the whole story. Cross-examine your client in your office to see how he or she will stand up in court.

I was sorry to leave Roblin and the friends we made. While there I learned to curl under the watchful eye of Art Large and Doug Young. My wife and I learned that the best mushrooms grew on old farm manure piles. We learned to enjoy the monster fish caught in Jackfish Lake and how to operate Reeve Filewich's homemade log splitter. We learned how to square dance and the protocol of community gatherings for newlyweds. We made good friends with other young people who were entering their parent's businesses or were trying to establish their own medical practice or position as an Agricultural Representative.

I was, unfortunately, not satisfied with the amount of court work I was doing and it was the prospect of an almost totally criminal law practice that drew me from Roblin to Winnipeg.

The Winnipeg Experiment

Whether our move from Roblin to Winnipeg was inspired by my occasional success and enjoyment of the courtroom drama was hard to determine, but for some reason I had a nagging desire to do more civil and criminal litigation. The converse was probably the more compelling reason. I found little interest in processing land deals, drawing wills or providing advice in matters I knew little about.

Somehow or other I learned that a lawyer had returned to Winnipeg after spending the war years in the Merchant Marine. As I later discovered, he had sailed the seven seas and dealt with rough and ready sailors and tough characters in every port. He was doing criminal work in Winnipeg and developing a reputation as a strong advocate for the underdog. I heard he was looking for a young lawyer to join him in that work and to do some civil litigation as well.

My time with him was exciting and close to dangerous at times. It introduced me to a level of criminal society and facets of the law I never knew existed and most lawyers would never encounter. Some years later, a friend even questioned whether some of the things I did were legal. I still don't know whether they were or not, nor have I felt compelled to do any research on the subject.

He was a good judge of humanity and understood the problems of the less fortunate. As I was to discover, he could bring tears to the eyes of the most hardened judge when he made a plea for leniency on behalf of a derelict or someone who ended up on the wrong side of the law. He was at his best when speaking to sentence after a plea of guilty or before the Court of Appeal.

It was undoubtedly his own experiences that enabled him to lend a sympathetic ear to those in trouble with the law. His name and successes were well known in the penitentiary and in the tanks where new offenders were held in the city. The Law Society had reinstated his lapsed practicing certificate. I don't recall his age but it must have been at least fifteen years since he had practiced law.

By the time I joined him he had been named the Swedish Consul.

He once invited my father and me to have dinner with a visiting dignitary, Count Raoul Hamilton, Sweden's Minister of Agriculture. It was interesting to hear the Minister say there were many Hamiltons in Sweden, some of whom resembled my father. I had never heard that our family might have Swedish roots but it was possible that our branch of the clan came from Sweden to England en route to their eventual homeland in Scotland and Ireland.

He was developing a substantial criminal practice but was in need of an associate who had some experience in commercial law and civil litigation. My experience in those areas was skimpy at best but sufficient to get me the job. Most importantly, from my perspective, it enabled me to observe his unusual abilities in the field of criminal law. With his worldly experience he was able to communicate well with the down-and-outers who make up the largest percentage of people who continuously get into trouble with the law.

The experience I gained proved useful in later years. It let me see another side of the law and some of the shady characters who acted as intermediaries with the criminal element. One of the middlemen I had to deal with was Billy Bain who had a stable of bondsmen who would help offenders get out of jail on bail. Another in the same business was a woman known to me only as Mary. I had her phone number, saw her occasionally at the police station, but knew nothing about her. When my boss received a late night call from someone who had been arrested, he would contact one of them. When the terms of their employment were arranged he would phone me and dispatch me to the jail to attend to the paper work and get the client released on bail.

Billy or Mary would apparently get in touch with someone in their select group of bondsmen who was prepared to go bail for a price. I had no idea how many people they had in their stables, or how many properties each of their bondsmen had, but to go bail a person had to have a clear title to a house or other property and pledge it as security, guaranteeing that the offender would show up in court as and when required.

A "clear title" in this context, meant they could not have pledged their title as security for any other person at the same time. The length of time their property was under pledge would depend on how long it took to have the accused dealt with by a plea of guilty or a trial. When that happened their title was cleared and could then be used as security for another person needing bail.

It became obvious that Bill and Mary had contacts in the jail and at Stony Mountain Penitentiary as well. Their contacts could find out and tell them whether a certain accused was a safe risk and would show up in court when required. If a person was known to run after getting bail he would never get bail through these crafty money-makers. I never did hear what efforts were made to recover bail money from a runner and that was probably just as well. Those who couldn't get bail just had to stay in jail until their case was disposed of by an acquittal or by their being sent to jail. When Billy or Mary got hold of someone to go bail for a client, I would meet them and the bondsman at the Police Station.

Occasionally a bondsman would be leery about going bail without talking to my boss first. On one occasion he sent me to the Bell Hotel on Main Street to talk to a Fred Smith. The name sounded a bit fishy to me but when I arrived at the hotel about 10 o'clock at night, and I approached the night clerk with "I'm looking for Fred Smith. He's expecting me."

"Never heard of him. Anyway, who the hell are you?" the leery clerk said, eyeing me with suspicion. "I've never seen you here before."

"I'm a lawyer and my boss wants me to talk to Fred." I gave him my business card.

"There ain't no Fred Smith here."

As I started for the door, the clerk said, "Sit down."

I settled into a filthy armchair and watched as a variety of characters who, for no apparent reason, wandered into the lobby, looked at me and left by the door they came in, presumably back to the beer parlour. Fifteen minutes passed before a rough looking character wandered in and looked me over. "You want to see me?" he said without any preliminaries.

"My boss told me to speak to Fred Smith. Is that you?"

Without answering, he said, "How do I know he sent you?" I handed him our business card. After looking around to make sure no one was listening he said, "What d'ya wanna see me about?"

"We want to get Keith Carlton out on bail and Billy Bain says you have a clear title."

"What's he charged with?"

"B and E" I said in the most knowledgeable voice I could muster, using language I knew he would understand.

"What did he knock over?"

"A corner grocery on Elgin."

"What sort of record does he have?"

"Billy says, 'a few of the same,' but always Provincial time." I knew that meant he had never been sentenced to more than two years for any offence and had never done time in the Federal Penitentiary at Stony Mountain.

"What are you paying?'

"A hundred to cover you and Billy. I don't know your deal with him."

"Sit down. I'll phone him," he said before disappearing again.

After what seemed like an hour, he came back and said: "A hundred and fifty, a C note for me and fifty for Bill."

I had been told to expect some dickering and had been given some leeway so I said, "It's a deal."

"OK, let's go," Fred said as he headed for the door.

As we walked down Main Street to the Police Station on Rupert, Fred kept looking to left and right. I wondered what kind of character he was and why everything had to be so secretive, but I knew better than to ask. My guess was he was in some trouble with the law and didn't want to be seen but thought it safe to take a short walk at that time of the night, with some easy money to be made.

Billy Bain was at the Police Station, Carlton was brought in from the cells, and with little discussion, the Magistrate completed the $5,000 bail documents, had them signed and took Fred's title. I gave Bill $150 and left Keith in their tender care and took the bus home. I never heard of the case again but assume Keith pleaded guilty and got some negotiated sentence.

After I had been in the bail bondsmen business for awhile, I got to know some of those who regularly put up bail. For some reason, I phoned one of the regulars directly. That was a mistake. I received a call from Mary who tore a strip off me and told me never to do that again. If I wanted a bondsman I was to phone her. She obviously had a loyal stable of bondsmen who she kept on a short leash.

Billy Bain was more accommodating. I was having trouble finding someone to go bail for a slimy little fellow called Roger who was being held on a charge of assaulting a police officer. He must have failed to show up in the past because none of Bain's people would touch him. A bondsman had to be careful about guaranteeing the appearance of the accused. If an accused absconded, the Crown would ask the Court to give it title to the property or to have the property sold so the Crown could recover the amount of the bail from the sale.

Having been turned down by his regulars, Billy suggested I go to the beer parlour in the Mount Royal Hotel and ask for Louie. Billy said, "He used to be a runner for Percy Hegel in the 30s."

I wasn't sure what a "runner" was but I'd heard of the lawyer and some of his nefarious cases. I assumed a runner did odd jobs, including finding people and getting clients out on bail.

"He'll ask you for seventy-five bucks to cover expenses. Don't give him a cent or you'll never see it or him again."

The bartender said he knew how to get in touch with Louie and told me to come back the next Friday. When I arrived, the barman pointed to an older man slouched over a corner table. "Louie?" I asked.

"Take a seat," the stranger almost crooned. He stared right at me as he talked and I was nervous knowing he must have had a colourful past. When I told him I was looking for a bondsman and gave him all the information I had, he said, "I'll see what I can do but I'll need an advance of fifty dollars. There will be phone calls and I'll need a taxi."

Forewarned by Bill I said, "I'm not authorized to pay you a cent 'til I meet you with the bondsman. Here's my card. Phone me when you have someone lined up." I got him another beer and left a disgruntled Louie in the bar. Billy Bain knew people. I never heard back from Louie.

Another of my tasks was to go from room to room in some of the seedier parts of town looking for an accused client or a witness who had failed to come into the office. That seemed more like police than lawyer work but it was good training.

Often a persuasive witness wins a case in court and we needed to interview them ahead of time. It was unwise to call an accused to testify if they had a criminal record and I was supposed to check on that as well. The Crown Attorney would be able to check his and the court's records. If the accused or his witness had a record, he would make mincemeat out of them on the witness stand. It was part of my job to find out what a witness could and couldn't say and to find out if they had a record.

One of the first clients who came to see me directly, rather than going to see my boss first, was scared out of his wits. He had been arrested and spent a night in jail and was now summoned to appear in what was then the "Rupert Avenue Police Court." He had been swimming in the popular Sherbrook Baths. It had a large pool, with an upper diving platform and a lower springboard. I knew the place as my pals and I used go there from time to time. On Saturday mornings it is filled with boys and girls. There were separate change rooms and lockers for men, women, boys and girls.

After Jimmy finished his swim, he was heading down the tiled stairs to change and go home. On passing the entrance to the girls' quarters, his imagination and curiosity got the better of him and he decided to peek in to see what he could see. There was no one in sight so he moved toward the sounds of giggling and laughter. Within seconds, he was grabbed by a husky woman attendant and hauled up to the administration office.

His feeble excuses carried no weight. The police were called and he was whisked away in the back of a police car. He was charged with trespassing and was threatened with a charge of sexual assault, even though he hadn't touched anyone. He was placed in a cell with "a dozen dirty old men", to use his description. He stayed there overnight before he was released, crying to his father. He was given a summons to appear at a later date.

The Crown Prosecutor was Andy Moffat and the judge was Magistrate Maris Garton. I decided to follow the pattern I had seen some of the better lawyers apply. I asked a Secretary if I could speak to Mr. Moffat. I told him the circumstances and said Jimmy would plead guilty. I also explained the tremendous impact the arrest and detention had on my young client. I said I was convinced that if Jimmy could be given a suspended sentence he would never appear in a court of law for the rest of his life. I likely used some of the terminology I'd seen others or my boss use so effectively.

I was convinced Jimmy had not been lying to me and I sincerely believed the treatment he had received in jail had so impressed him that no better or other punishment was needed. I suggested that, if he was sent to jail, he might get in with bad company or the punishment might harden him. I suggested he had learned his lesson.

The rumour was that the Crown Attorney went over the docket with the judge before court opened. Whether that was the case or what they might have discussed I didn't know. I did know it was a busy court that had a long docket to complete every day. I was careful to be on time when court opened. I had seen some lawyers who arrived after their case had been called, having to wait until the rest of the docket was dealt with before they got a chance to speak. When Jimmy's case was called, I made a few short remarks, then sat down with my fingers crossed. The Crown Attorney said he would be satisfied with a suspended sentence and Judge Garton imposed it without comment.

In later years when I was sentencing people convicted by juries, I often thought of Jimmy's case and tried to find a punishment that best served the interests of the accused, the victim and the public interest. Much of course turned on the attitude of the offender.

My time with the criminal lawyer came to an unfortunate end as a result of a disagreement. He was supposed to appear at an Examination for Discovery in a civil action and it seemed to me he wasn't prepared. He hadn't gone over the material or decided on the approach to take. He directed me to phone the lawyer on the other side of the case and say he was in the hospital. I refused. We carried on for a while but our personal relationship had been damaged beyond repair. I left Sten Goerwell six months after I started with him.

Disaster struck. I couldn't find another job in Winnipeg. The law firms were taking as many law students and recent graduates as they could handle. Another problem was that the experience I had gained since being called to the bar wasn't great and there weren't criminal lawyers who were interested in my recent brush with the seamier side of the law.

An attempt to get a job with a commercial firm looking for an assistant to work with the manager came to naught. I was politely shown the door. I wasn't very robust looking and the impression I got was that the manager thought I was still wet behind the ears. There seemed to be nothing to do but open my own law office. I did that but after exhausting the few family members and friends who needed a new will, I really had nothing to do.

We were quickly exhausting the meagre savings left over from Roblin. I had no commercial clients, no criminal law connections and insufficient income to support my wife and newborn daughter, Irene. My father was retired from the Juvenile Court and he couldn't help us anymore. We knew we couldn't afford to keep living in Winnipeg but didn't know what to do.

Melita

Lorna's home town of Deloraine again played a part in our next move. Her father Charlie knew the area and had gone through the process of getting established as a pharmacist in rural Manitoba. He had apprenticed with Wesley McClung, the father of Nellie McClung and the pharmacist in Manitou. Lorna's father then established his own drug store in the small community of Waskada, fifteen or so miles west of Deloraine, early in the century. In 1903 he moved to Deloraine and established his own business in a building next to the bank. A few years later he went to San Francisco and got certified in optometry, which he also practiced in the same building in Deloraine.

Lorna clearly recalls growing up in the "dirty thirties." She recalls looking out her second-storey window and being unable to see the houses on the other side of the street for the blowing dust. Those days seemed to be ancient history as now the cattle and grain farms were flourishing once again.

Her brother Don studied pharmacy at the University of Manitoba after he was discharged from the Navy, and his son John now runs the drug store which has been in the same family, in the same building for 104 years. When visiting, I would join Don and his pals on their 6 a.m. duck and goose hunts, dogs and all, in the nearby Whitewater marsh. I also met many of the local residents in town or at Lake Metigosh on the American border. The farmers and town dwellers curled and played hockey together, and had a common interest in their community.

We had been wondering what to do after my disastrous experience in Winnipeg and wondered if we should consider another move to rural Manitoba. I took a look at a junior position in Virden where the search for oil was just beginning. The senior partner was on the verge of retiring and Jimmy Doak had recently or was about to join him. For some reason, I decided to keep looking.

We had heard that George and Nellie Bureyko, who had been

friends of ours in Roblin, had recently gone into business in Melita, so during one of our weekend visits to Deloraine we decided to see what Melita looked like and how our friends were doing. Someone in the Melita drug store directed us to their business on Main Street, a few doors up the hill.

George phoned Nellie and we went to their home for afternoon tea. They had been in Melita for six months and were excited about the town and its future. Business was good and they liked the people they had met. When I indicated we were thinking of moving out of Winnipeg they encouraged us to come to Melita.

Looking out their living room window, Nellie pointed across the street and said: “You should be able to rent that house cheap. It’s the Manse for the Presbyterian Church and it’s been empty since the full-time Minister left last year.”

It was a big, unpainted, two-storey weather beaten hulk. Lorna, obviously not impressed, said: “It looks awfully big.”

Nellie countered with, “Well it would do while you look around, and besides I can keep an eye on you.”

George gave us the name and phone number of the church warden, then added: “I’ll see if he’s home.”

He was, so I talked to him, told him what I did and asked what the rent would be on a month to month lease. “$25.00 a month” he said without hesitation. “We would be happy to have someone living there while we decide what to do with it.” When I explained we hadn’t decided whether we were coming to Melita or not, he countered with “I hope you come. It’s a nice place to live.”

I asked George, who I’d come to know as an astute business man, what he thought about the business aspect of opening a law practice and where I could find an office. He said, “You should see Bill Powne. He knows all about that sort of thing and can tell you whether there’s room for another lawyer in town as well.”

I took Bill Powne’s address and phone number but Lorna and I thought we had gone far enough for the moment. We hadn’t even talked seriously about whether we wanted to live in Melita.

While looking over the town to see if we would like to move there, we peeked into the United Church. A woman was playing the organ and looked up as we entered. Without a moment’s hesitation she charged up the aisle, introduced herself as Laura Furtney and asked if she could help us. Lorna took the lead, introduced us and mentioned she was a daughter of Charlie and Babe Hasselfield and had grown up in Deloraine.

"My dear," she said. "I know your mother and father well and Don and Verna too. If I'm down that way I get my prescriptions filled at their drugstore. What brings you to Melita?"

She was one, as we would find out, who always came directly to the point.

"We're thinking of moving here and opening a law office." was my reply.

"Boy, do we ever need another lawyer," she said. "Winnifred Yuill is OK but there should be lots of work to go around."

Jumping ahead, Laura asked, "Where are you going to live?'

"We don't know, we haven't got to that point yet, but we have just come from talking to the Bureykos who we knew in Roblin. They're right across from the Presbyterian Manse and it's available."

"I know," Laura said, "I play the organ there too."

Without further discussion she bundled us into her car and gave us a tour of the town. We saw the residential areas, including some new veterans' houses, the schools, the modern hospital, the hockey rink and the agricultural park next to the Souris River. She drove through a bit of the countryside and said she and her husband Ken had two children and that, although their farm was six or so miles south, they lived in town.

She told us what a great minister they had. Her daughter Shirley, she said, was just the right age to baby sit our daughter.

Over the next week we talked about Melita, the trouble of another move and getting settled in a new community but finally decided to make some more inquiries. We knew we had to move out of Winnipeg and we had no other place in mind. Finally we decided to go the next step and see what Bill Powne had to say. I phoned him and agreed to be at his office in Melita at two o'clock on Saturday.

When I arrived, it was obvious George Bureyko had been talking to him about our interest in Melita. Bill Powne and I discussed the boom in business the town was experiencing. Then we picked Lorna up at the Bureykos and Bill drove us around town in the largest pink

Cadillac I'd ever seen, pointing out the homes of business people and explaining what each one did. He painted a rosy picture of town activities and the need for legal services. I didn't know at the time that he had a reputation as a high-pressure salesman with a penchant for exaggeration.

When I got back to his office he picked up the phone, dialled a number and said: "He's here. C'mon over Tom."

Tom Gould was a short, older man wearing overalls. I guessed he was or had been a farmer. Mr. Powne told me he had been the Reeve of the surrounding Municipality. "This is the lawyer George Bureyko was telling us about."

Here was another character who got right down to business. "Know anything about the oil business?" he asked.

"Well yes," I was able to reply. "I worked for W. L. Griffith Lease Brokers for a while in Brandon and did historical searches in the Dauphin, Neepawa, Boissevain and Brandon Land Title offices."

"You're kidding." he replied. "We've got oil companies swarming all over the place doing seismic work. I'm more or less in charge of getting leases on the farms they want to test. The title of every parcel of land has to be searched in Boissevain to make sure who owns the mines and minerals."

I knew exactly what he was talking about. "Who's doing the searches now?" I asked.

"We're using a lawyer in Boissevain, but it's awkward as all I get are written reports and they're slow in coming. There's lots of work for you here if you're interested."

Tom Gould left as quickly as he came. Bill Powne, who I was still calling 'Mr. Powne' took me across the street to meet the Barker brothers who ran a nice looking men's clothing store, and Mr. Morrow, the druggist next door, who had been a long-time Mayor of the town. They all thought there was room for another lawyer in town and enough business to keep me busy.

Back in his office, Bill showed me a back room I could use until I found a larger space. "You can have it rent free for two months," he said when I explained that my finances were not in great shape. "And I may be able to steer some business your way. I work closely with Tommy Gould and there's no doubt he'll do the same."

I was a little concerned these fast-talkers might think I was going to be in their pockets and do things the way they wanted them done. On the other hand, I had dealt with fast-talking salesmen in the oil business before and was able to do things in the way I knew they had to be done.

I thanked Bill for his time and encouragement and said Lorna and I would make up our minds and be in touch before long. Lorna and I headed back to her parents' home in Deloraine and started to consider Melita in earnest. It didn't hurt to know that her family was 100% behind the move. We bundled up our daughter the next day and made our decision by the time we got back to Winnipeg.

We broke the news to my parents and they were supportive of the move, as they knew the prospects in Winnipeg weren't good. Our home on Claremont Avenue in Norwood went on the market the next day and we had an offer by the end of the week. I called the caretaker of the manse and Bill Powne to say we would move in on the first of August.

Yuill & Yuill had a long established law office in a small stone building on Main Street. Almost as soon as we moved, I dropped in to pay my respects. Mr. Yuill, the father, was in his 80s and liked to visit the office every day and chat with his friends. We had a nice talk and he welcomed me to town. His daughter Winnifred ran the office and prepared the documents needed to transfer farm lands and town properties. She also prepared wills for everyone in the district and had a substantial estate practice. She had no interest in the oil business.

As it turned out, Winnifred was tough competition because she was still transferring farm land for the fees she had charged during the depression and her clients resisted any change. She would set her fee and divide it equally between the buyer and seller. In Winnipeg, lawyers charged the seller a fee and the buyer another fee for the services provided to each. I tried to follow that example in a sale I processed but the farmers abruptly told me I couldn't charge two fees if I wanted any farm business.

On entering the Yuill building you were met by Winnifred's large golden retriever curled up in an upholstered chair. The dog never budged unless it was to follow his mistress home or down the hill to the bank or grocery store. Winnifred's office contained a large desk and two chairs. Files were piled everywhere, testifying to a busy practice. Mr. Yuill had a small room with a desk and a couple of chairs.

Winnifred had no secretary, nor did I. She preferred to do all the typing herself. I later learned that she had a special agreement with the Registrar of the Land Titles Office in Boissevain where all south-western titles were kept. An announcement had been sent to all the lawyers in the area that, after a certain date, all transfers of land and other documents had to be typed or the Land Titles Office would reject them. That meant that when I prepared a mortgage I would have to prepare five copies on my ancient typewriter and not make any mistakes. If I made a mistake, I had to re-do the whole page. That meant inserting four or five legal sized pieces of paper and four pieces of carbon paper as well.

Winnifred received separate instructions. She was to write all her documents with pen and ink. She was a notoriously bad typist and documents prepared in that manner had misspellings and gaps that made the document almost illegible.

I had my own problem with typing, although of a different sort. When I started in Melita I smoked cigarettes and I often blamed them for my mistakes in typing, as the smoke would get in my eyes as I typed. I discussed the problem with the gang that gathered for coffee at the Chinese café near my office. Chick Jones, my dentist, smoked like a chimney and his fingers were yellow. In spite of that he was an expert on smoking and many other subjects. I was told to quit cold turkey when I still had half a pack of cigarettes left. It was then important to give them away.

Someone else told me to take the 'dark test' and they explained how to do it. One evening when I had something to do at my office, I turned out all the lights and, with some difficulty, lit a cigarette. I had been told to see what my reaction was to smoking at that point. When I inhaled, I could see a red glow at the end of the cigarette, but that was it. I couldn't feel any smoke going into my lungs and when I exhaled I couldn't see any smoke. It was a nothing experience. To complete the cycle, I put the rest of my cigarettes on the restaurant table the next morning and asked my pals to help themselves.

I stopped smoking and never smoked cigarettes again. My typing, or the need to re-type a document, improved. At times after that I would occasionally have a cigar at the end of the day but I never inhaled. It took a few years before I realized that all my clients didn't think the practice added the nice ambiance to a law office I thought it did, so I stopped smoking them as well.

The Presbyterian manse was even worse than it looked from the outside. Mice were everywhere. Lorna would sometimes chase them with a broom and I had traps set in the kitchen. When we turned the lights out at night, it was like living in a tomb. It was even unpleasant to approach the place from the street. I can't remember how we slept or how long we stayed there but it wasn't long.

We found a small red brick storey and a half house within a couple of blocks of the Furtney's. It was on a pie-shaped lot with gravel streets on its three sides. The second floor or attic was unfinished and the house had a low dug-out basement which contained a furnace and a cistern. It wasn't free of vermin but we got rid of the rats with warfarin. That just left the mice we could hear running up and down between the walls. Fortunately, they kept out of our living space. We put in a vegetable garden and on the other side of the house there was a magnificent birch tree. I could reach up and put our daughter Irene on one of the lower branches.

Farough was a kindly woman who lived across the street from the back of our house. She had no hair but had a cloth head cover and a heart of gold. Her husband and son were forever getting into trouble with the authorities over their truck licences or the materials they were hauling. They were not well educated but determined to fight the 'big boys' and to run their business in their own way. They were small operators and rather than take them to court the department seemed satisfied to let them off with warnings.

Several trucks were always parked on their lot. The men had never finished the inside of the house. The floors still had diagonal planking and the kitchen walls were bare. In spite of that, Farough was happy. She didn't want to be called 'Mrs Farough'. She was Farough and that was it. She was the kindest person in town and gave Lorna emotional support as she struggled with our daughter and later with our first son.

One day, our daughter Irene disappeared and Lorna and Farough searched the neighbourhood after phoning me. As it turned out, Irene had decided to walk to my office pulling her little red wagon. She was very upset that her adventure had been interrupted. Eventually she was found and Lorna and Farough came downtown and took her home.

Dr. Hank Kay was an outstanding general practitioner but he had a number of likes and dislikes and strong opinions on how people in authority should conduct themselves. He was not on good terms with the other doctors in town or with the Mounties, whose offices were next to his home. My first recollection of him was when he rushed to our home when Irene was scalded by a cup of boiling water she pulled off the counter. He took off her shirt and plastered her with gelanet and bandaged her up. Hardly a hint of the damage remained after a couple of weeks.

He had a run in with the other local doctors and the hospital Board. At one point they barred him from using the hospital because of the controversies he stirred up. Fortunately, our son Jeff was born in the hospital before that happened. Hank, who was quite progressive, allowed me to stay in Lorna's room while Jeff was being born. Although I thought I was fine, he said to a nurse, "I think you'd better get Mr. Hamilton a chair."

Hank and his wife quarrelled a lot. Once she had another doctor certify her husband and she got the Mounties to take him to the Brandon Mental Hospital. I had to read up on the procedure in a hurry, but was able to get a court order for his release. The couple, and we liked both of them, were like fire and oil together and they finally agreed to separate. Laura Furtney, another individualist, was another of the doctor's staunch supporters.

In spite of the entertainment provided by Chick Jones at Wong's Café, I spent half my coffee breaks enjoying the light-hearted banter at Lefty's, a café on the other side of the main drag. While Lefty regaled the morning coffee drinkers with his comments on the issues of the day, and kept the refills flowing, his wife Mary served the toast, doughnuts or pie some would order. These morning sessions built loyalty but it was the noon and evening meals that allowed Lefty to display his culinary skills. Town and country folk enjoyed his full course meals. His specials, as I recall, were his succulent steaks and his well done liver and onions. He still kept up the chatter and kidding that made his meals an entertaining experience.

As with Roblin, we became immersed in the activities of the community. The Legion was like a service club and it sponsored dances and raised money for local causes. The Chamber of Commerce was equally active and it participated in local and provincial issues. The Commission on reforming Manitoba's liquor laws, chaired by former Lieutenant Governor McWilliams, was holding meetings throughout the province and I was the spokesman for the Melita contingent when we went to Souris to present our suggestions.

The under-forty Kinsman Club met at Dave Snitka's hotel on Railway Street. It had its own projects to improve the park and work on other local issues. All the groups sponsored dances in the community hall. When I was still new in town, I decided to go to his beer parlour in the same hotel for a drink, presuming that might put me in touch with more people. That was a mistake. Sure enough, a man came over, sat down and told me of his domestic troubles. When I asked what he wanted me to do he said, "Oh Nothing, I just thought you could tell lawyers these things."

When he left, another came over and told me of a dispute he was having with a neighbouring farmer over drainage. When I said I would need more details and asked him to come to my office so we could discuss a court action, he backed off. He wanted some advice but he wasn't going to pay for it; or he may have known what he could do but didn't want to cause trouble.

The people who came to my office had legitimate concerns. I had to write a letter to a Winnipeg lawyer when a woman who was trying to settle a divorce matter told me the lawyer was making sexual suggestions and she was afraid to go back. I warned him that any more inappropriate remarks or conduct would be reported to the Law Society. It worked. She had no further trouble.

I did the occasional divorce but most people seeking that service preferred to go to Brandon or Winnipeg. They didn't want their friends or neighbours to find out their marriage was in trouble. It was the same with criminal matters, whether it was a driving infraction or something worse. People would arrange to deal with those matters in Souris or Virden.

For a break, if we were not going to Winnipeg or Deloraine we would occasionally drive to Minot in North Dakota. It had a few outstanding restaurants but it was the chance to get away on our own that appealed to us.

I used to see Winnifred at political meetings. We both supported the liberal party and hard workers like John McCrea kept us involved. The area was mostly conservative and it was at that time that John Diefenbaker became the Prime Minister. He was extremely popular and I thought the best thing he did was abolish the death penalty.

My election to the School Board was of course non-political. That was my introduction to the management of schools by local residents. Lorna and I became good friends of two of the teachers, Keith Wilson and Keith Cooper. The latter went on to become a Principal, School Division Superintendent, the Director of the Children's Home in Winnipeg and the Director of Child and Family Services in the Provincial Government.

His future wife Diane White was a Melita girl whose father was a farmer who lived in town. She served as Director of the Manitoba and North Western Ontario Conference of the United Church of Canada for years. Her father Larry White, was active in the life of Melita and was looked up to as a wise and solid citizen.

When we arrived in Melita in 1955, stories were still being told of the 'dustbowl' and the 'dirty thirties' when the topsoil was blown off the land and many farmers went broke. Depression thinking still dominated local commerce. My work as a lawyer involved the drawing of wills, the administration of the odd estate, preparing share-crop leases and notarizing documents. In the spring I did a brisk business preparing farmers' income tax returns from the boxes of disorganized receipts and grain slips they dumped on my desk. After deducting the cost of machinery, operations, and depreciation, I don't think I ever did a tax return where money was owing to the government.

I did have one difficult estate to administer. I had been discussing the preparation of a will with a gentleman for some time but he could never make up his mind on what he should do with his properties. I had prepared several drafts but I could never get him to come in to sign any of them. He died quite suddenly.

There were substantial business assets and a number of under-age children. A nephew agreed to act as administrator and he had a difficult time over a period of years. He had to decide who would purchase or manage which asset. He also had to keep a set of books for the estate so he could keep track of income and expenditures. When disputes arose within the family he initially discussed them with me but eventually he had to settle them. Some member of the family always disagreed with his decisions.

Ian McMillan was the minister of the United Church. We became good friends of Ian and his wife and we attended church when we were in town. One of the most unusual experiences I had in Melita, occurred one Sunday morning about 8 a.m. Ian phoned to say he was unwell and asked if I would deliver the sermon in his place. He was phoning others, including Laura Furtney, to do some readings. He made no suggestion about what I should say.

When church started, Laura announced that Ian was sick but he wanted us to carry on as usual. Some read pieces of scripture, the choir sang the pieces they had prepared during the week and then it was my turn. I hadn't decided what to say although I had finally started to develop a theme that would have a biblical base.

I tried to equate the call from Ian to one from a higher authority. I asked the congregation what they would do if God called on them to do something and discussed what a challenge that would be. "How would you respond?" I asked, assuming they would do their best to do what was asked of them. I have no notes of what I said and can't recall what else I said. The only thing I remember is Ian calling me an 'evangelist' the next Sunday.

That was probably the closest I came to pleading a case when we lived in Melita. It was nevertheless a marvellous experience to be so deeply immersed in the life of a close knit rural community.

My work was pretty well tied to the local oil activity. In those days the Land Titles Office for the district was in Boissevain, 50 miles to the east. It was in the process of modernizing its procedures but there were exceptions. Lawyers weren't usually permitted to go behind the long counter that separated the public from the staff and the rooms with safe-like doors where the records of land transactions were securely kept.

Due to the quantity of searches I was doing, I was allowed to go into the back and pull down the Registry books that contained the original grants from the Crown and the documents that had been filed with respect to each parcel of land since that time. I dug out old documents myself until I had a complete history of the parcel of land I was examining. I made notes on the chain of ownership so I could type out a report when I got back to my office. Finally I had to certify who owned the mineral rights or a shared interest in them if some had been sold.

When Irene was four, I occasionally took her with me on my trips to Boissevain. I propped her up on the counter as I went about my work. Fortunately the office was not that busy and some of the staff were always willing to talk to her. When Jeff was born, he and Lorna would visit in Deloraine until Irene and I returned. It's possible, I like to think, that this early introduction of Irene to legal matters may have sown the seeds of her later interest in the law. I could never persuade any of our three sons to consider law as an avocation.

I also took Irene duck hunting when she was four. At dusk, we crouched in the weeds as we heard the birds coming in to land. I fired my single-shot shotgun and, of course, I didn't hit anything. The result was that I had scared Irene, and she and Lorna ganged up on me and made me promise that I would never go hunting or try to kill those pretty birds ever again.

If the Legion or another organization had organized a dance, we would usually go with a group of the young people we had come to know. Wes Feader the jeweller, and Doug Minnis, the shop foreman of a car dealership, kept us busy in the community.

When it came to fowl suppers in the country, Laura and Ken Furtney were our hosts and our guides. We visited their farm regularly. Through them we met the Downey clan and eventually sold our little home to a Downey. They were the kindest farming family we met. We didn't know Jim Downey who went on to become the local MLA and a Minister of the Crown because he was away at university when we lived in Melita.

Why the Country

Some of my Melita friends had been after me to tell them why I had moved to an agricultural community when I had grown up in Winnipeg and knew little about farming. I was reluctant to tell them the embarrassing truth, but I finally caved in and said something to the following effect.

"The only answer I can think of is, it just happened. One thing led to another and that is where I ended up. In retrospect, I think there were more basic causes. One is that, although I didn't think of it at the time, I was stubborn and independent. My father was a well known Juvenile Court judge in Winnipeg and was involved with a number of community initiatives. I didn't want to impose on him or have to rely on his connections to get ahead.

Another reason may be that I seemed to have a death wish where agriculture was concerned. My first taste of farming was one Saturday when I was in grade ten. A call had come for volunteers to help with the sugar beet harvest. A busload of Kelvin students was bussed into the country. We were each handed a sizeable knife and put to work. All I did, all day long, was cut the tops off and toss the remaining beets into a wicker basket a muscular type emptied into a truck. I didn't learn anything of value, but I was doing my bit for the "war effort."

The next year a call came to all Winnipeg high schools for students to help with the harvest. A hundred or more students jammed the rotunda of the CNR Station in Winnipeg as we waited for our names to be called. I didn't see anyone I knew. When my name was called, I was directed to a certain rail car. I had no idea where we were going. Unknown to us, the organizers had a list of our names, the name of the person we were paired with, our destination, and the name of our employer.

As we pulled out of the station and headed west across the rusted plains, my mind turned to the thought of riding horses, milking cows, driving tractors and operating threshing machines. The August sun shone on the waving wheat, or whatever kind of grain it was, and we were off on a romantic adventure.

After we got past Carman, the trip was ponderously slow. It seemed that as soon as the train got up some speed, the brakes would squeal and we would start slowing for the next stop. As the morning wore on, beautiful billowy clouds began to turn to cumulous black-bottomed ones. By the time we got into the hills it had begun to rain. By Ninette it was pouring cats and dogs. It never crossed my mind that the weather might affect our adventure.

Finally my name and nine or so others were called. Tom Haddad, who I had never met, and I were told we were to go to the same farm and we were given the name of the farmer, who I'll call Mr. Flynn. When we got off the train it was pouring and there were no trucks or wagons or any other sort of transport to be seen. There was no railway station at Margaret, so we stood in the rain wondering what to do. Finally, as the train pulled away, an old man in a shiny slicker and rain hat sauntered over.

He asked if we were the kids from the city. A tough kid, who immediately assumed the role of spokesman, asked where the farmers were that were supposed to meet us. The man said: "Can't get in, it's been raining all afternoon and the roads are a mess."

Our leader asked how we were supposed to get to the farms and whether we were supposed to stand out in the rain all day. His belligerent attack didn't seem to carry any weight, nor did his demand for food. Our greeter calmly said the farmers would probably come in the morning as the clouds were starting to break. He said we could sleep in the loft of the livery stable.

I don't think I wanted to go to sleep, but after tucking my few dollars into the money belt I'd bought for the trip, I fell asleep and the sun was shining when I woke. We all got up about the same time and made our way down the ladder and into the mud and gravel street. Slowly, farmers began to appear, most with a horse and wagon and one in an old green truck. Haddad and I waited and waited. About ten o'clock a gruff Irishman, Mr. Flynn himself, appeared. He didn't look too excited about the scrawny kids he saw but he called our names, told us to get into his wagon, and away we went.

No "pleasantries" were exchanged. He was mad at the delay the rain had caused to his harvest and mad at having to come to town when he had other things to do. He cracked the reins and away we went, sloshing along the muddy road, along a stretch of gravel and then up the grassy road to his farmhouse. The narrow two-storey house stood on a rise a quarter of a mile in from the main road. There was a good-sized hip-roof barn and a dugout. He told us to head up to the house as he had chores in the barn to do. Mrs. Flynn was a delightful woman and she welcomed us as if we were family. She introduced us to their children, a girl about 10 and a boy of 8. We had a massive breakfast and were promised a bath and supper after work.

After breakfast we went down to the barn where we were told we would find Mr. Flynn and sure enough he was hard at work cleaning stalls. He told us we could start stooking the nearest field and asked if we used a pitchfork or our hands. Not knowing exactly what he meant, we said what sounded the most professional to us – a fork. He gave us each a pitchfork and told us to go the corner of the field and get started, saying he would join us in a few minutes.

We started, but couldn't seem to make the pitchfork lift and place a bale. We changed tactics and began standing one bale straight up and piling others on each side. That didn't work either and the whole mess was spread out on the ground. We then decided to work together so while one of us held a couple of bales together the other would pile more on each side. That seemed to work and by the time the farmer joined us we had a few stooks built. We met our employer with smiles as he walked toward us with a fork in his hand. We expected he would thank us for the good work we had done.

As Mr. Flynn got closer he was red in the face and yelling like a stuck boar, not that I had ever seen or heard one. I don't think he swore but he looked and sounded furious. "What do you guys think you're doing?"

"Stooking" we said, not knowing what he expected us to say.

"You've got the bloody stooks upside down." he said in a sense of raging disbelief. "You put the heads of the grain up, so they don't rot in the mud," he explained.

I should have kept my mouth shut but I said, "I thought if we put the heads down they wouldn't get wet if it rains."

"Have either of you ever been on a farm before?" Without waiting for a reply he ended his tirade with, "Where did they ever find you guys?"

"Come on," he said, "we've got to finish stooking in two weeks as the threshing gang will be starting then. If you have to work till its black out, you're going to get the job done. Grab two sheaves like this, lean them together and put four more around them. They've got to stand up in a wind so make sure they won't fall down. Now you do it."

He stayed with us until he thought we could carry on alone, then wandered back to the barn shaking his head in disbelief. We finally completed three fields within the two weeks, sometimes on our own and sometimes with him along to speed us up.

When we finished, without any discussion, Mr. Flynn paid us and sent us on our way. There were no thanks and there was no ride to town. We walked to where no. 10 highway crosses the Souris River then hitched a ride to Brandon. We stayed in the YMCA for the night then walked up the north hill to No. 1 highway and finally got a ride to Winnipeg.

Working at Purity Flour in St. Boniface on weekends and over the Christmas break completed my agricultural education. I swept warehouse floors, filled 98 pound bags of flour and moved 140 pound bags of alfalfa around on carts. One of the nastier jobs was to dig the fermented grain from under the conveyor belts that bounced each time they passed over one of the 100 rollers in the underground tunnel leading to the chop house. My mother made me take my work clothes off in the basement entrance when I had been doing that job. They reeked of fermented grain.

The best part of the job was when I was assigned to the full-time painter. When I was painting the outside of the corrugated metal buildings from a scaffold or bosun's chair I felt as free as a bird. If my boss wanted me to do something else, he had to holler from below over the sound of shunting boxcars. It's strange how my hearing would fail as I kept on painting and enjoying a break from nastier work.

Over the Christmas holidays, I and two other university students had a good time loading 24 pound bags of rolled oats into box cars for shipment overseas. The bags weren't heavy so we set up our own version of a chain gang. One of us would take a bag from a cart, throw it to another in the box car and he, without losing momentum, would throw it to the third guy who started piling at the front of the box car.

As it was winter, we ate our sandwiches in the employee lunchroom rather than outside on the lawn. After we had been applying our newfound organizational skills for a couple of days, we were approached at lunch by three of the largest and toughest looking warehouse workers. Without any opening, one of them said, "You guys think its fun to load a box car quickly, but we don't."

Another joined in, "You kids are just here for a few weeks. We work here all year long and you're setting a bad example."

The third giant, not wanting to be left out, added: "The bosses have started timing you and they'll expect us to be as quick. Cut it out."

They stood there, waiting for our reply. We got the message and agreed. We were as good as our word. Some might call their comments 'a word from the wise.' We took it as a threat and a lesson in reality."

My friends got a kick out of my background and said they could understand why I never pretended to know anything about farming.

Brandon

It was a chance meeting with Ken Stevenson of Clement & Stevenson in the law library of the courthouse in Brandon that got me interested in another move. Bob Clement's father and uncle had established the firm of Clement and Clement in earlier days. Ken grew up in Belmont where his father was a doctor so he knew rural living. He asked me how I was enjoying Melita. I said we enjoyed Melita but I missed going to court.

A week or two later he phoned and said he and his partner had been talking about getting another lawyer to join their firm to do court work. "Would you like to come in and discuss the matter with us?" he asked.

I said I'd get back to him. Lorna and I decided it wouldn't do any harm to listen, so I set up an appointment. I found the partners to be very pleasant and I knew from my earlier days with W. L. Griffith that there were other firms in the city as well. They were Kerr Meighen Haddad and Kerr, Stordy Alder and Buckingham, Coleman and O'Sullivan and Kempston & Pearson. The first two were well established second-generation firms.

When I met with the partners, they said they had decided to look for someone to do their court work so Ken could concentrate on the substantial real estate practice he had built and Bob could devote his time to the administration of estates and the corporate work he enjoyed.

They said if I joined them they would pay me a salary of $300 a month and after two years I would have my name added to the firm and I would receive a share of the profits. Lorna and I decided that, unless I would be content with continuing to do the sort of work there was in Melita, I should accept the offer. I signed the agreement they prepared.

We moved to Brandon in the summer of 1958 and rented a small house on Eleventh Street near the tracks. The heat was so unbearable the kids couldn't sleep so Lorna took them to Deloraine. We started looking for better accommodation as soon as the weather cooled and ended up buying 544-16th Street, a large two and a half storey home that had previously been owned by the Wankling family. A bank manager again made the purchase possible. Our younger sons, Bill and John, were born while we lived there and before we built a house on Cedar Bay a few years later.

As strange as it seemed, my most vivid recollection of the Clement Office was the accounting and billing procedure. In the general office, with its hardwood floor, there was a high sloping accountant's desk where all expenditures had to be recorded. To make an entry, I had to sit on an elevated stool, insert the name of the client, the date and the amount of the expense that had been incurred. It was obvious from the records that the most common expense was postage. If I used a three or five cent stamp to send a letter, I had to enter it immediately. It was the task of the part-time bookkeeper to gather up the records from time to time and post them into each client's account. This was an indication of how western Manitoba was still recovering from the years of drought and depression. The fees charged for a lawyer's time were low and much lower than in Winnipeg.

The office was stark and business-like but the ancient furniture, dictating machines and typewriters, added to a sense of stability. The other law offices were similar and they all frowned on any show of opulence, such as a rug on the floor. These practices, along with the pinch-penny accounting procedure, although I didn't realize it at the time, were a pretty good indicator of the penurious approach of the partners and the reason for rejecting my suggestion of loosening the purse strings.

The work given to me and my relationship with the partners was enjoyable. Bob Clement had me assist him in one civil trial, then let me handle others on my own. Lorna and I made new friends and enjoyed Brandon. By the end of the second year I had become involved in community activities. The Rotary Club, Artillery Mess, Chamber of Commerce and the Liberal Association put me in touch with many people. I continued my involvement with the Manitoba and Canadian Bar Associations.

The Chief of Police, who I saw regularly as my criminal work expanded, and I established a branch of the John Howard and Elizabeth Fry Society to help reforming convicts get a job, clothing and a place to stay until they got settled. A little later I was appointed to the Brandon Branch of the Alcoholism Foundation of Manitoba which Jimmy Toal from Winnipeg and Terry Penton of Brandon had established.

The pay I received from the Clement firm was barely enough to enable our growing family to meet its needs. I was hoping for a substantial increase in pay as the end of the two-year probationary period approached. The partners seemed satisfied with my work and we got along well. It was therefore a shock to be offered only a miniscule improvement in my financial situation when the senior partner and I discussed my future.

Several attempts were made to get a better deal but Bob Clement was firm and I was shattered. We just could not live on the amount he proposed. It appeared we would have to leave Brandon and start all over again somewhere else. The reason the choice seemed that stark was because, when I had joined the firm two years before, the partners and I had signed an agreement which included a clause to the effect that if I left them I couldn't practice law in Brandon, or within 50 miles of it, for 10 years.

The more I thought about my position and nine years experience, the more I convinced myself that not only was the offer unfair but we couldn't live on it. Our daughter Irene was now six, Jeff was three and Bill was a few months old. It was also clear to me that I could produce a good level of income for the firm. I even suggested basing my pay on a percentage of the fees I was able to earn for the firm but my employers wouldn't budge.

My greatest concern was the thought of subjecting my family to another move. They had made friends and were settled into Brandon. Provoked by these thoughts, I decided I should examine the law on 'restrictive covenants' to see if the courts had dealt with a situation similar to mine. As in Law School days, I headed for the law libraries in Brandon and Winnipeg. It took some hunting but 'restraint of trade' led me to a number of cases dealing with Restrictive Covenants.

The most persuasive case I could find was a 1935 decision of the Supreme Court of Canada. The presiding judges were Duff, the Chief Justice of Canada, Justices Lamont, Cannon and Davis of the Supreme Court, and in addition, Mr. Justice Dysart as an ad hoc judge. I'd never heard of a member of a Manitoba Court sitting ad hoc in the Supreme Court, but even more unusual was the fact that Mr. Justice Dysart (if indeed it was the same Dysart) was a Judge of the Manitoba Court of King's Bench where the case originated. The trial decision had been rendered by Justice Adamson of the same court.

The Manitoba Court of Appeal, made up of Chief Justice Prendergast and Justices Dennistoun, Trueman, Robson and Richards, had overturned Justice Adamson's decision. The Supreme Court of Canada overturned the Court of Appeal and restored the decision of Justice Adamson. The most amazing thing about the case was that Justice Dysart, of the Manitoba trial court, wrote the Supreme Court of Canada decision. In effect, a judge of a lower Manitoba court overruled the decision of Manitoba's highest court.

The case was *Maguire v. Northland Drug Co.* (1935) S.C.R. 412 and it involved an agreement signed by a druggist in Flin Flon who had signed a restrictive covenant when he was first employed. He was discharged by his first employer and then hired by a new drug store that opened up next door. The Supreme Court of Canada held that an agreement in restraint of trade was illegal and unenforceable unless the person relying on it could prove it was necessary to protect the proprietary rights of the first employer. The agreement must not unduly restrain an employee from making use of his skills and talents. If the limitations in the agreement were too wide, either as to time, place or scope, the agreement would not be enforced. The employee was protected even if a customer followed the employee to his new place of employment, as long as the employee had not solicited or encouraged the customer to move his business from the original employer. I thought the case would carry a lot of weight in Manitoba.

As a result of this research I concluded that the restrictive covenant I had signed must have been intended to protect Clement and Stevenson. Even without the research, I knew it would be improper for me to take any of their clients or business with me if I left. I concluded that the restrictive covenant I had signed was valid in protecting the business of my employers but too broad to stop me from starting my own practice as long as I didn't interfere with their clients or business. The research resulted in my decision to sever my relationship with the Clement firm and to start my own Law Office.

My decision to go on my own was supported by Lorna and by friends who had lived in Brandon for years. They encouraged me to go out on my own. They thought there was a need for an aggressive lawyer who would go to court for people with a problem. I also sought the advice of Mayor Steve Magnacca. He not only encouraged me to start my own business, but offered me the use of two rooms in a building he owned on 8th Street. He said I could pay him rent when I could afford it. He also gave me the name of a stenographer whose husband had just been posted to the army base at Shilo.

With only $300 in the bank, we decided to take the plunge. A steno was out of the question but I took the Mayor up on his offer and moved into his building. With my old Underwood typewriter, a crank-type adding machine and some supplies, I started my own practice on the first of June in 1960. I put my old Melita 'Law Office' sign in the window.

Within two weeks I was so swamped with good wishes and requests to draw Wills and do other minor matters, I couldn't keep up and had to take the next step. I phoned Sylvia Cockman, the stenographer the Mayor had mentioned. She agreed to start on a part-time basis until I needed her full time. She was a fun person to work with. She had lots of office experience in eastern Canada. Not only was she a crackerjack stenographer, she got along well with clients and was an outstanding office manager. She was delighted to have an interesting and challenging position and stayed with me as long as I practiced in Brandon.

Criminal defence work, while not paying a great deal, enabled me to make a living. Few other lawyers in Brandon elected to deal with the 'seamy' side of the law and most couldn't. Frank Meighen was a vigorous part time Crown Attorney so he and his partners couldn't do any defence work. Bill Stordy and his partner Ed Alder were part-time Judges so they were eliminated. Joe O'Sullivan had moved to Winnipeg to work with Walsh, McKay, and Bernard Coleman was only interested in defending cases in Magistrate's Court and stayed away from the County Court and the Court of Queen's Bench. My former associates, Clement and Stevenson, and Bill Pearson, then on his own, did no criminal work. Harry Walsh came to town for the occasional jury trial, but otherwise the field was wide open.

My former associates never said a word to me about starting my own business or about the restrictive covenant. They apparently agreed with my right to go out on my own and had no concerns about my interfering with their clientele.

It soon became obvious there wasn't enough room in the Mayor's building. Cam Donaldson, who had just stepped down as the owner and Manager of Brandon Packers, owned a small building across 8th Street. He had recently sold his business interests to Paton and Cox from Toronto. They were delightful individuals but their corporate manoeuvring and alleged mismanagement caused trouble with the Securities Commission and local shareholders. Mr. Donaldson retired and sold me his building, directly across the Street from my temporary quarters.

The little building had a large bank-style walk-in vault, one private office, and a reception area large enough to accommodate Sylvia's needs and waiting space for a few clients. A small parlour clock made in Berlin, Ontario, and a desk were included. Before I left practice and sold the building to my partners, it had to be enlarged twice. The first expansion was to provide space for a full-time accountant-receptionist, Sylvia, two more stenographers, two new offices with carpet to the wall and a library. I departed from the stark appearance of the other offices in town. We had wall to wall carpeting in the offices and hallways and the offices were soundproofed.

The next extension came a few years later when the shoemaker next door agreed to sell his little building and narrow property. This time we built a two-storey addition with more offices, a large library in the basement that doubled as a conference room, and a sauna.

I believe our firm was the first in Manitoba to have its own sauna. While the idea of a sauna was probably inspired by my enjoyment of them during our annual ski trips to Banff, it provided a valuable addition. Each Friday at five, the towel-clad male members of the staff would gather in the sauna for a review of the week's work and an informal get-together. The tradition was that the youngest lawyer or student, armed with the necessary funds, would go to the Brandon Hotel on 9th Street and come back with a dozen beer. The session let us keep abreast of what each of us were doing and provided an opportunity to discuss issues anyone wanted to raise.

The move to my own practice and my own building was a success from the start. During the first month I had a greater net income than when I had worked for Clement. The income improved from then on. Being independent, I didn't have the same connections other lawyers had with realtors and people in the business community, but it left me free to take on interesting and challenging cases. I was fortunate to have Al Hunt join me as a law student and then as a partner. He had been a farmer in Saskatchewan who left active farming due to an allergic reaction to grain dust. He knew farming and communicated well with the farmer clientele he developed. He preferred to process real estate transactions, administer estates and do commercial law, none of which I enjoyed, so we made a good team.

Ron Myers, the Director of the fledgling Legal Aid system in Winnipeg, appointed me as the Brandon representative so I got a start by representing indigent offenders. I didn't get paid for the work but it helped me become known to the rotating residents of the Provincial Jail. I also started to appear in court in Souris, Killarney, Virden, Minnedosa, Russell and occasionally in Portage la Prairie and Winnipeg. For a while I had branch offices in Glenboro and Hamiota, but I sold them for next to nothing when it became obvious I was losing more business when I was away from my office in Brandon than I gained in those locations.

The Town of Souris was and still is famous for its suspension bridge over the Souris River and the agate deposits nearby. The business section, on intersecting streets, was high above its delightful park in the Souris River valley. Harry Forrest was the Magistrate in the tranquil town and I occasionally appeared before him to speak to sentence where a client wanted to plead guilty to a traffic or other minor offence.

Most of my trips to Killarney were for similar reasons, although

County Court Judge Milton George from Morden sat on a couple of contested cases I had there. One was a criminal case and the other dealt with a dispute between brothers and sisters over the distribution of farm lands in an estate. Judge George, formerly a lawyer in Deloraine, was a good judge and he told me he enjoyed a case involving disputed facts and an interesting point of law. Bill Scurfield of Manitou was the part-time Crown Attorney for the Southern Judicial District and he prosecuted criminal cases in Killarney.

Killarney was later the site of a two-day School Board and Teachers Society arbitration hearing where Mel Myers of Winnipeg was the Arbitrator appointed by the Teachers and I was the Arbitrator appointed by the School Board. Mel and I couldn't agree on the appointment of an independent chairperson. Mel wanted someone from Winnipeg and I wanted someone from rural Manitoba. We had to leave the choice to Chief Justice Freedman. He appointed Cy Buckingham of Virden. That was an excellent choice as far as I was concerned as he knew the rural situation and rural schools as well.

Minnedosa was an active court in the Western Judicial District as well. Judge Lindal was the resident County Court Judge and Bill Ferguson was the Crown Attorney. George Lauman of Shoal Lake, a part-time Magistrate, sat there quite often when he wasn't in Florida watching baseball. He would also sit behind a card table in Russell from time to time, but contested cases were heard in Minnedosa where there was a large courtroom and jury box.

Judge Fred Coward from Brandon sat in Minnedosa to handle Preliminary Inquiries where the case was headed for a jury trial in the Queen's Bench. All the jury trials were held in the Brandon courthouse after Judge Lindal retired and Justice Ferguson was appointed to the Queen's Bench.

Virden was a busy Magistrates' Court and Cy Buckingham, after he moved there from Brandon, heard cases from a large part of south west Manitoba. Virden was booming as Manitoba's oil patch had a fair number of criminal cases.

Brandon was a good place to do business. The business people I got to know were positive about their businesses. The city of course had a massive trading area which extended to the American and

Saskatchewan borders, up to Dauphin and half way to Winnipeg. The story was that if you were an average business person you could do well in Brandon. If you were above average, the sky was the limit.

In spite of that, a lot of Brandon people were jealous of the much larger City of Winnipeg. At one time I was caught up in that sentiment as well. I used to think, 'If only those Winnipeg lawyers would just stay in Winnipeg, I would have more work to do.' It took some time for me to realize I was wrong. Being 120 miles away, not many outside lawyers were asked to take criminal cases in Brandon. In civil cases, on the other hand, it was almost always a Winnipeg lawyer who represented the insurance company or party I was opposing. It gradually became apparent to me that most Winnipeg lawyers didn't want to go 'all the way to Brandon' for an examination for discovery or a trial. That made it easier for me to negotiate some good settlements. Of course, I kept that little secret to myself.

The object of this explanation, with the occasional diversion as to how I settled into my practice in Brandon, is merely to record that I was at last free to devote my time to my beloved civil cases and the criminal law.

The Royal Bank

Although I started with criminal cases, it wasn't long before I got challenging civil cases as well. Within a year of starting my own practice, I received a phone call from Dr. Fridrik (Fred) Fjeldsted, who was known for going beyond mere treatment to help his patients. He asked if I would see a lady who had suffered a severe and debilitating hip injury in a fall in the Royal Bank. He thought she might have a claim for compensation.

She arrived at my office, a lovely lady on crutches. She said she had consulted two civil litigation lawyers in Winnipeg, both of whom told her she had no claim and no chance of successfully suing the bank. I was surprised, as one of the lawyers was the most litigious I had ever encountered and seemed to fight every case with vigour, whether it was clear cut or not. His practice was devoted almost entirely to civil litigation.

My youthful bravado and belief in justice must have spurred me on, as I decided she might very well have a valid claim. This was tort law at its finest. One principle that remained in my mind from law school was that "for every wrong there is a remedy." If I was to live up to another maxim of the legal profession, I owed the client a duty to represent her "without fear or favour," an ideal or standard more often defined by judges when informing jurors of the nature of their task, but equally apt when discussing the profession to which I was happy to belong.

Mrs. Campbell made it clear she was not "out for blood" but felt the bank should accept some responsibility for her injuries. The bank had never apologized, nor had it told her it was sorry she was injured in their premises. An insurance adjuster had come to see her in the hospital but told her the bank was not responsible for her injury. He made it clear that in his opinion she had not been paying attention and was totally responsible for the fall and the injuries which resulted.

The bank in question was a branch of the Royal Bank and it

was located on Rosser Avenue at the end of the block my office was in. Mrs. Campbell and I visited it the next day and she pointed out where the puddle of water in which she had slipped and fallen had been – a short distance from the tellers' cages. Strange looks from the tellers and other staff greeted us as she pointed and I took measurements and made notes. If the Manager was watching, he stayed out of sight and I was just as glad of that. This was, after all, the bank where I had my business and personal accounts and if the staff didn't know my name, I imagined they knew I was the young lawyer from farther up 8th Street.

After some further discussions with Mrs. Campbell I prepared and forwarded a letter to the manager of the bank in Brandon and to its head office in eastern Canada, demanding compensation for my client. I wasn't surprised when I received a reply from a firm of insurance adjusters denying liability. I sent another letter, presenting arguments for why they should make a payment to my client, but again their denial of responsibility was absolute.

There was no time to waste as a claim in tort, a civil wrong, had to be filed in court within two years of when the alleged negligent act or injury occurred. She had fallen on the 25th of November, 1959 and our Statement of Claim was filed in the Brandon office of the Court of Queen's Bench on June 12, 1961. It was only two pages long and our position was basically explained in one rather poorly constructed paragraph:

"The plaintiff was walking towards a counter in the said premises in a normal, careful and prudent manner, when due to the slippery and dangerous condition of the floor, she slipped in an accumulation of water on the floor resulting from melted snow the Defendant had negligently and carelessly allowed to be and to remain upon the floor and she fell and suffered severe and permanent injuries."

The bank's insurer engaged lawyers in Winnipeg. Jim McLaughlan, a classmate of mine who was with the firm of Fillmore, Riley, McLaughlan, Norton and Yarnell, filed a Statement of Defence. It said the bank was not in a dangerous condition, that it had taken proper care of its premises and that it was the carelessness of my client that caused her to slip and fall. Among other things, the defence alleged that my client wasn't wearing proper footwear at the time. In fact, Mrs. Campbell had already left with me one of the rubber soled boots she had been wearing at the time. I made another attempt at reaching an out-of-court settlement but Jim stood by his position and completely rejected the possibility of a negotiated settlement.

In view of the outright denial of responsibility, there was nothing left but to proceed with Examinations for Discovery and they were held in the Law Library of the Brandon Court House. Discoveries are part of the procedure available in civil litigation that are intended to give each side an opportunity to question someone from the other side, to see what they have to say and to cross examine them on the various matters in dispute. Where a corporation is involved, it can select the person to be questioned. The bank chose to have its local manager appear for questioning by me, probably because he would be the main witness for the bank at the trial. Mrs. Campbell, as the plaintiff, was questioned by Mr. McLaughlan. All the questions and answers were recorded by Stan Smith, a popular Court Reporter, on his stenotype machine, transcribed and distributed so they could be read into evidence at trial or used to cross examine the party at that time.

During her examination, my client told of the snowy day on which she entered the bank to cash a cheque that had been drawn on that branch. She was questioned as to the care she had taken for her own safety, about the puddle of water she described and the boots she was wearing. She told of the work she had been doing as a realtor and how the injury to her hip and her continuing disability prevented her from earning a living.

Our case was inadvertently helped during my Examination of the Bank Manager. He was incensed that we had dared to sue "his" bank. He was aggressive in his statements and swore there never was any accumulation of water on the floor of the bank and said it was regularly mopped by staff in any event. The more he spoke, the more excited he became and the more offended he was at the unscrupulous attack he thought I was making on his integrity and the safety of the bank. I had no wish to stop him in his defensive tirade. On the contrary, I encouraged him as he defended himself and exaggerated the safety precautions he had established in the bank. He was, fortunately for our side, a little inconsistent. He insisted there was no puddle or accumulation of water on the floor in which anyone could possibly slip and fall and in the next breath said a member of his staff cleaned the floor of the moisture that had accumulated on it that very day.

I found the atmosphere at the bank cool and uncomfortable after that, as did Sylvia Cockman. We actually felt we weren't wanted in the bank so we transferred my personal, business and trust accounts from the Royal Bank to the newly opened branch of Canada Trust. I intentionally stayed away from the other banks in the city as I was unsure how they felt about me suing a local bank.

A few days after the transcripts of the examinations were received, I again wrote Jim McLaughlan and suggested we discuss settlement. I can't recall the amount I suggested but I thought it was quite reasonable in view of the difficult case we had to prove. The request for payment was rejected again so I set the case down for trial. I re-interviewed the witnesses I wanted to call and prepared an outline of the matters I would have to prove during the trial.

The trial began in the Court of Queen's Bench before Mr. Justice Ralph Maybank on the second of June, 1962. The amount of the special damages was agreed to by Jim McLachlan, but liability was still denied, meaning we would only receive the special damages, made up of doctor and hospital charges and lost income, if the bank was found liable in law. Otherwise no payment would be received.

My arrangement with Mrs. Campbell was that I would receive 15% of the court's award if we won, and nothing if we lost. Although we ended up going to the Court of Appeal and the Supreme Court of Canada, I never changed the arrangement. I could have charged more but was satisfied with that amount in view of the extensive experience I was gaining.

The trial lasted four days, three for the evidence of the eleven witnesses who were called to testify and half a day for the oral submissions of counsel. The judge reserved his decision but delivered his reasons for judgment in writing on the 15th of June, 1962. He found in favour of Mrs. Campbell and awarded her general damages of $28,800, special damages of $7,089 and costs.

The judge accepted Mrs. Campbell's evidence and her

explanation of how she came to fall. He found she had been taking care for her own safety and was walking in a careful and prudent manner. He found as a fact that she fell in an accumulation of water on the slippery floor. In spite of a different version given by a bank employee, the judge found that she had been wearing low-heeled curling boots and a fur coat. He accepted the evidence given by our weather expert that there had been one and a quarter inches of snow on the previous night and 2.8 inches more on the day of the accident and a daytime temperature of between 23 and 27 degrees Fahrenheit.

Mrs. Campbell was a lovely lady and the judge, also a good judge of character, knew she was telling the truth. Her evidence of water on the floor was supported and reinforced by another credible witness, Mr. Edworthy, who also slipped in the water and almost fell when he was helping Mrs. Campbell to get off the floor and into a chair.

Justice Maybank made positive findings of fact. He said, "I think there can be no doubt that water on the floor of the bank lobby caused this woman to fall and I find this as a fact. The place was too slippery for safety. The bank did not take care to have its premises safe for its customers. The plaintiff did walk in a careful and prudent manner."

Mr. McLaughlan and his clients were understandably disappointed with the result and they appealed Justice Maybank's decision to the Manitoba Court of Appeal, but it wasn't until we were in the Court House in Winnipeg that I received an offer of settlement from Jim McLaughlan. Mrs. Campbell was pleased we had done so well up to that point and she directed me to reject the offer. We had a good hearing before a five member court but unfortunately we lost. Mr. Justice Guy wrote the majority decision and he was supported by Chief Justice Miller and Justice Schultz. The minority opinion was written by Justice Freedman, Justice Fred Monnin concurring. The result was that the decision of Justice Maybank was overturned. The majority and minority judgments were delivered on the third of January, 1963.

There was no doubt what had to be done. We had to appeal to the Supreme Court of Canada. I knew absolutely nothing about how that should be done, what sort of forms were required, or how they should be worded. None of the lawyers I spoke to in Winnipeg had ever been to the Supreme Court and I was told this would be the first civil appeal to that court by a Brandon lawyer.

I decided to fly to Ottawa to find an agent and get some help from him. I did find a firm who would act as my agent but the young member of the firm I saw had no personal experience in launching an appeal. He did say the people in the Supreme Court office were easy to talk to and suggested I go there and speak to them.

I went there the next morning. The building itself was (and is) an intimidating structure with its divided outdoor staircases. I expected I would be stopped and questioned by a security guard as I looked around trying to figure out where to go. That didn't happen, but as I could only see signs of direction to the Exchequer Court I had to ask a guard where the Supreme Court of Canada's registry was located. He directed me.

When I got off the elevator I saw the sign "Registrar" and as its doors were open I went in and approached the counter. When a man asked if he could help me I explained I was a lawyer in Brandon, Manitoba, and wanted to file an appeal from a decision of the Manitoba Court of Appeal. Although I'm sure it was obvious to him, I explained that I had never been to the Court and wondered if someone could provide me with the Court rules. He couldn't have been more helpful. He sat me at a table and brought me a number of documents. The first was a copy of the rules dealing with an appeal. They outlined the various documents the court required and gave detailed instructions on how they were to be prepared. He then produced several Cases on Appeal from earlier cases containing copies of the Statement of Claim, Statement of Defence, the evidence given at the Examinations for Discovery, the evidence at the trial, the judgment of the trial judge and the judges of the Court of Appeal. There had to be a short and succinct statement of the grounds of appeal, indicating the matters I wished to rely on and where the evidence on each point could be found in the various documents.

The Clerk or Assistant Registrar told me the cost of filing the various documents and pointed out the strict time lines that had to be followed. It turned out that all documents had to be printed by a recognized printer, and only on the left side of each page. Covers had to be of cardboard strength. The right hand pages had to be left blank so the judges could make their notes there as the hearing progressed. I spent the better part of a day in the court building, including an hour in court watching an actual case being argued before the full panel of nine judges.

On the way back to Brandon I drafted various cover sheets and indexes for each document. Once back, I rushed to see my friend Bud Leech of Leech Printing to see how soon they could print the substantial number of copies I would need. As the father of the two sons who ran Leech Printing had once been the Provincial Printer at the Legislative Building in Winnipeg, I knew the firm would be acceptable to the Court. In fact I had run the name by my Supreme Court helper.

I spent countless evenings revising and completing the documents. When all was done I had to be present at the printers when the printing was done to make certain everything was completed in accordance with the Supreme Court requirements and exactly as I had prepared them. My recollection is that I ordered about 50 copies of each document because I had to send thirty or so to the Supreme Court and copies to opposing counsel, the Queen's Bench and the Court of Appeal. By April 25th I had served a Notice of Appeal on Fillmore Riley and had a certificate from the Registrar of the Manitoba Court of Appeal certifying the correctness of the various Judgments and Orders of the Court of Queen's Bench and Court of Appeal in Manitoba that were included in my printed material.

As I still had to do a lot of work on my oral argument for the Supreme Court, I decided to take the train from Brandon to Ottawa and holed up in a duplex roomette. That turned out to be the best decision I made as I virtually re-wrote my argument during the three-day trip. The problem I had was to get my message across to the Justices in the twenty or so minutes I was allotted.

I was so nervous in front of five of the top nine judges in Canada that I can't recall what I said. One of the judges apparently said at one point, "there's no need to deal with that matter Mr. Hamilton," telling me to move on. In my nervous condition I didn't even hear him, but plodded on with what I had planned to say.

The case was argued in the fall of 1963 and the decision was reported in the 1964 Supreme Court Reports at p. 85. The five judge court was divided on the result. The majority, Justices Ritchie, Hall and Spence allowed the appeal and restored the decision of Justice Maybank. The minority of Justices Martland and Judson would have dismissed it.

Much of Canadian law is based on English common law and English court decisions. It was a case from England I had cited in the Campbell case that was used by the Supreme Court to confirm the law in Canada. The Case of *Indermaur v Dames,* 1866, L.R. 1 C.P. 274 (1866 Law Reports, Volume 1, Common Pleas at page 274) set out the responsibility of occupiers of property, like the Royal Bank, for the safety of people coming onto their property. Two of the quotes used in the majority decision were:

> *"And with respect to such a visitor at least, we consider it settled law, that he, using reasonable care on his part for his own safety, is entitled to expect that the occupier shall on his part use reasonable care to prevent damage from unusual danger which he knew or ought to know (existed)."*

> *"If the danger could have been prevented by these economical and easy precautions then surely a member of the public frequenting such a busy place would have been entitled to expect such precautions or others equally effective, and their absence would tend to make the danger an "unusual" one."*

As soon as I received the written decision from the Supreme Court I phoned Mrs. Campbell and told her the majority of the Supreme Court judges agreed with the decision of Justice Freedman, and the findings of Justice Maybank. She was elated, as was Dr. Fjeldsted when I called him.

I was personally pleased as the Supreme Court of Canada had departed from some earlier Canadian cases on 'slip and fall.' The decision represented a significant change in tort law and is still studied by Canadian law schools. The case also resulted in a substantial increase in my civil work to the point that, along with my still growing criminal defence work, my work now involved cases that were either in or were going to court.

A few years later I was pleased to have Don Fjeldsted, a son of the doctor, join me as a law student, then as a member of our firm.

When I was being considered for appointment to the Queen's Bench in 1971, apparently two of the considerations were the Campbell case and my experience in civil and criminal trials.

Still Learning by Losing

Lest it be thought I won all my cases, let me set the record straight. I won more cases than I lost but my first civil case in Brandon was a loss in a case I clearly should have won. It involved a collision near Virden; and Cy Buckingham, before he became a Provincial Judge, was on the other side. My client had his truck damaged when another farm truck went through a stop sign and hit it.

My demand letters were ignored so I filed a Statement of Claim in the County Court seeking the $800 it cost to repair the damage. The first inkling I had that the defendant disputed the claim was when I received a Statement of Defence from Cy Buckingham of Virden. He had left Brandon shortly after I arrived and was practicing in the Virden "Oil Patch" with Jimmy Doak, Q. C., a tough litigator.

After some fruitless negotiating, I set the case down for trial before County Court Judge Jack Kerr, recently of the Brandon firm of Kerr, Meighen, Haddad and Kerr. He had succeeded Cy's father, County Court Judge Buckingham. The only witnesses were the owners of the two vehicles.

As the Plaintiff, we had to go first so I called my client to the stand. "I understand you were driving your truck near Virden on August 13th of last year when you were involved in a collision."

"Yes, that's right," he said.

"Please tell the Court what happened."

"Well, I was driving south on this gravel road, going about 40 miles an hour, when I noticed a truck coming from the east. I'd say he was going about the same speed. I didn't pay too much attention as I was on the through road and the other truck had a stop sign facing it at the corner. I thought he was slowing down to stop, but when he got to the intersection he drove right into the left side of my truck."

"Did you say anything to the other driver at the time?"

"Yeah, I asked him why he hadn't stopped at the stop sign. He said, 'I didn't see you.' We exchanged names and that sort of thing and I went home."

"I show you a bill from Virden Motors. What is that?"

"That shows what it cost to get my truck fixed."

"I file the bill as Exhibit 1, Your Honour."

Cy Buckingham cross-examined my client but he stood his ground and refused to admit any responsibility for the accident. Cy then called his client to the stand and asked for his version of the accident. He confirmed that he hadn't seen my client and suggested he must have been going very fast. In cross-examination I asked if he had stopped at the stop sign.

"Of course I did. I always stop at stop signs."

He was quite aggressive on the stand and I thought my client had been much more believable. I argued that the bill was ample proof of the accident and the considerable damage that had been caused to the left door and box of my client's truck.

In his closing argument, Cy Buckingham repeated what his client had said. He then paused and said to Judge Kerr, "and besides, your Honour, my learned friend has failed to prove that the accident happened in the Province of Manitoba."

He was right. In asking where the accident occurred, after my client had talked about the intersection, I should have asked: 'and that was in the Province of Manitoba?' I didn't ask that vital question, although I should have known I had to establish the jurisdiction of the court.

The judge dismissed my client's case. I had been 'non-suited' by Cy Buckingham. The only thing I could say, which of course was no consolation to my client, was that I was never non-suited again. I subsequently used the same defence in a couple of trials myself. I had learned an important lesson. Needless to say, I didn't send my client a bill for my services.

I can't recall anyone moving to non-suit a case when I was a judge. I wonder if the rather antique requirement to prove the territorial jurisdiction of the court has been removed by legislation or by the decision of a higher court.

Judge Buckingham

Not long after this encounter, Cy Buckingham was appointed a Magistrate and later a Provincial Court Judge. He was certainly the best part-time Provincial Judge I ever appeared before. He sat mostly in Virden and occasionally in Brandon. His factual and legal findings were sound and he demanded a high degree of propriety from the police in the performance of their duties.

I had a case before him where my client had been stopped by the RCMP for speeding and driving erratically. When the police officer was giving his evidence, I questioned him in some detail about what he did when he went up to the driver's side of my client's car after he stopped it.

"Did you have a conversation with Mr. Curtis?" I asked.

"Yes, I asked him for his driver's licence and for the car registration."

"Did he comply?"

"Well he was a bit slow and didn't seem to want to show them to me."

"What gave you that impression?" I continued.

"Well he was fumbling around and I was in a hurry."

"So what did you do?"

"I waited," he said.

"Was there any physical contact between the two of you?" I asked.

"Of course not," he replied.

"I suggest to you, you hit him with your revolver. Isn't that true?"

"Certainly not."

I didn't press the matter any further, but by the time he left the witness stand, the officer was obviously mad. I then called my client to give his side of the story. He said he hadn't been speeding but confirmed that the officer had pulled him over and had walked up to his window. My client said he was nervous and upset about being stopped and admitted he had trouble finding his licence and ownership papers.

"What was the police officer doing while you were fumbling for your papers?" I asked.

"He was getting very impatient and he was badgering me," the older gentleman said.

"Anything else?" I asked.

"Well," he said in a hesitant way, "when I found my driver's licence and had my left hand on the window sill, he hit it with the butt of his gun."

"Did that do any damage?" I inquired.

"I thought my hand was broken, but the doctor x-rayed it and said it was just bruised. I had it in a sling for a while."

The Crown Prosecutor spoke to the policeman but never called him back to the witness stand to refute what my client had said. Judge Buckingham threw out the case. I assume he wasn't prepared to believe anything the officer said after he decided my client was telling the truth.

I usually got along well with RCMP officers, both in and out of court. In this case there was a sad sequel to the trial. During the trial the officer had said he used to be stationed in Virden but was now in The Pas. When I was getting into my car to return to Brandon, the officer approached me and said, "You better watch out. I'll get even with you if you ever come to The Pas."

In retrospect, I should have reported him, but I didn't. If he was a rotten apple, the system probably weeded him out. In any event, the evidence at the trial had been taken down by a Court Reporter and would have been available if the Force wanted to know why the case had been dismissed.

Committed Clients

The City of Brandon, Manitoba's second largest city, is known as "The Wheat City." The fertile land, the farms and the volume of No. 1 Northern Wheat that has been harvested in the area for over a hundred years, easily justifies the title. Lighter land is devoted to raising feed and cattle. The presence in the community of a large hog processing plant and the production of fertilizer by Simplot has broadened the manufacturing component of the community.

Brandon University, its School of Music, Assiniboine Community College, and the Regional Hospital are other large contributors to the life of the city. The Keystone Centre is the home to the Brandon Wheat Kings, and the Manitoba Royal Winter Fair held every winter draws crowds from across the prairies.

Brandon straddles the Assiniboine River and its broad valley.

A person coming from the east on the Trans-Canada highway who wants to enter the city, has a choice of entry - descending the north hill of the valley and driving past the former mental hospital and crossing the river onto First Street at the east end of the business section, or going a mile further west on the Trans-Canada highway and descending the hill at 18th Street. That is also highway No. 10 which goes south to the United States border and north to Dauphin, Swan River and Flin Flon.

The descent down the hill passes new homes and condos facing south to take advantage of the spectacular view. Restaurants, motels, manufacturing businesses and large farm implement and automobile dealerships line the area between the top of the hill and the C.P.R. tracks on the southern rise.

When I practiced law in Brandon, I had some cases where the outcomes now seem unbelievable. John Mortimer's Horace Rumpole had the Timsons to provide a continuing source of fame and petty profit, but mainly personal enjoyment from the lawyer's point of view. He and Hilda, 'SWMBO' hardly lived the life of the lofty QCs who graced the High Court of Justice and lived and travelled in opulent circles; but he did have fun defending the undefendable and a win over Head of Chambers Ballard or Claude Erskine-Brown was sweet indeed.

The pittance paid for Rumpole's time and efforts would not even keep Chateau Thames Embankment on the table but he was happy with his station in life and his wins in The Old Bailey or before one of the 'Old Darlings' in England's High Court. Rumpole's fictional life at the bar provided the enjoyment a junior barrister would die for. Some of my most enjoyable cases also involved repeat offenders and often there was no payment for my time and effort. The fun and games made up for that mundane omission.

Instead of Rumpole's Timsons, I had the McIvors who added similar spice to my life. They regularly got into scrapes with the law and had a unique ability to pretend or plead innocence. They enjoyed the challenge of the law as much as I did. It was impossible for me to tell whether they were easy targets for the police to suspect or whether they were likeable scoundrels after all.

It may be that some success should be credited to my 'luck of the Irish' rather than to any magic or courtroom expertise but the considerable defence work I did can be credited to one simple fact. No other lawyer in town would act for the questionable characters who became my stock in trade. Some lawyers were inclined to tell their clients to plead guilty but it was much more fun for me to follow their instructions and try to get them off.

Guilt is, of course, in the eye of the finder of fact, whether that be a jury or the presiding judge. I learned early in my practice that judges and jurors are nice people. They have their own belief in human nature and a further belief they can correct the errors and wrongs inflicted by society on the less fortunate.

My greatest successes also seemed to revolve around the McIvor brothers and their imaginative exploits that excited the interest of the local police and others with whom they had to deal. Lest my readers think I was protecting offenders in a string of lesser or greater crimes, let me say that my approach to the world of criminal defence law was that every person charged with a criminal offence was entitled to the best defence I could provide.

It was not my responsibility, I decided, to question my clients to death to get at the 'truth'. I was not there to judge them or to decide their fate. Unless they volunteered that they had done the dirty deed and were guilty as charged, I accepted their case either to prove their innocence or to put the Crown to the test and to seek an acquittal if the Crown fell short of its objective. In simple terms, I saw the contest as one where the Crown tried to prove guilt and I tried to challenge that assumption.

Following the training of our revered Criminal Law Professor in fourth year, Deputy Attorney General John Allen, Q. C. I believed that if the Crown could not prove the guilt of an offender beyond a reasonable doubt he was entitled to go free. I also believed the law would be stronger if it could stand the testing I tried to bring to bear. It wasn't a game. It was serious business, but the rules of cricket nevertheless applied. Good old British Justice. There was no better guide.

I was never one who could break a witness down or have them reverse their testimony, as could the great protagonist at the bar, the bulldog and entertaining advocate, Harry Walsh, Q. C. Harry was feared by Crown Counsel and expert witnesses alike. Part of his stature was that he looked like Edward G. Robinson and had an equally fierce visage. His prowess in the courtroom was legendary. It was said that by the time he finished his cross-examination of a complainant they would be lucky to recall their own name. Expert 'hair and fibre' scientists and breathalyzer analysts would shudder at the thought of being questioned by him and could only hope to hang on until the last question was answered so they could drag what was left of themselves back to the witness room.

There were indeed a few Crown Prosecutors like my former Chief Justice, Archie Dewar and Brandon's Frank Meighen who looked forward to a joust with Harry and often came out on top. Most were no match for the master and lived to regret their attempts at bravado. I knew I could never cross-examine and destroy a witness like Harry Walsh so I had to develop a softer, less threatening, more devious tact which sometimes worked.

When I practiced as defence counsel, there was no such thing as the compulsory disclosure of the Crown's case, as there now is. In Provincial Court I found what the evidence against my client was as the witnesses gave their evidence. In jury cases I learned more during the Preliminary Hearing. It was my practice, however, not to ask too many questions at a Preliminary as I didn't want the prosecution to learn the approach I would take at trial. I did not really see what all the fuss over disclosure was all about. It delayed the commencement of a case by months and dragged the process out as every confusing avenue of evidence was explored. I don't think more accused are either acquitted or convicted by the long drawn out proceedings of today. A trial in the 'olden days' provided the accused with all the protection he needed. I say "he" as I can't recall defending any women.

Most of the accused I acted for, whether they were charged with murder, rape or drunk driving, seemed to have a philosophical approach to their plight and that was comforting when their case was lost. They wanted to get the trial over as soon as possible and if they were convicted they wanted to keep the sentence to a minimum and get that over with quickly as well. Appeals against convictions were sometimes taken, but they too were not prolonged. I don't remember having a criminal appeal in our Court of Appeal that lasted more than an hour or two.

A Court of Appeal appearance was a frightening experience for me at first. The first time I appeared was before the compulsory retirement age of 75 was introduced. I was deflated when one of the old judges turned to another and quite audibly asked, "What did he say his name was?"

I have digressed and must get back to the McIvors. The first time I was engaged by them they had been charged with the theft of a quantity of lumber and other building materials from a lumberyard. I elected to have them tried before the recently appointed County Court Judge Kerr, so there was a Preliminary Hearing in the old police station and lock-up before the highly respected judge, Bill Stordy.

The theory of the Crown was that, during a noon hour, the brothers drove into a lumberyard in their truck. The Crown believed that while one brother talked to and distracted the only staff member on duty, the other loaded up their truck with a variety of 2 x 4s, plywood and a couple of used doors. The lumber yard in question was on the busy No. 10 highway I described.

The Crown had no witness that saw the accused at the lumber yard and no one saw them steal anything. In any event, for some unknown reason, the police went to the boys' storage shed and seized a massive supply of lumber. Out of an overabundance of caution, the newly appointed full-time Crown Prosecutor brought every stick of wood the police had seized into the courtroom for the Preliminary.

The room was not large and it was difficult to move around and almost impossible for the witnesses, when giving their evidence, to go over to a door or sheet of plywood to try to identify it. Even the owner of the lumber yard couldn't identify the lumber as his. All he could say was that he thought he might be missing some lumber and two old doors similar to those in the courtroom. No witness saw my clients take anything, let alone drive off in a truck. They were nevertheless committed to stand trial in County Court.

The Crown Prosecutor finally obtained a date for the trial and it took place in the old fashioned courtroom on the second floor of the Brandon Court House. The room had two jury boxes, a remnant of the days when Grand Juries existed, and a formal wooden bar or fence in front of which the lawyers sat and behind which the spectators sat in rows of squeaky theatre style wooden seats.

There was no elevator to the second floor so the massive quantity of lumber we saw during the preliminary hearing was nowhere to be seen. All I could see were two old wooden doors leaning against one of the empty jury boxes. The case began with the owner of the lumberyard saying how he thought his property had been removed. My cross-examination did not require any particular skill. He admitted he was not in the lumberyard at the time of the alleged theft and could not identify any of the lumber as his. He did say that the two doors were similar to ones he had on hand that were no longer in the shed when the police came to investigate his call. He said they were not new and had been taken off a shed in the yard sometime previously.

The judge had his decision ready as soon as the last witness testified and the Crown and I had completed our final arguments. His verdict was basically "not guilty" but he did find my clients guilty of being in possession of the two doors. He ordered that the doors be returned to the lumberyard and imposed a suspended sentence on my clients. My clients were delighted with the outcome.

The Motel

A rural couple had sold their farm and, wanting to get into business in Brandon, bought a large motel. They proceeded to renovate the interior and to have the driveways and parking lot paved with asphalt.

They engaged a local company to do the work and were still arguing about its sizeable account when they came to see me. Their complaint was that the tar had tracked into the motel and had ruined the carpeting in the hallways and in some of the rooms. I accepted their assessment and sent the company a letter saying something was wrong with the material they used or with their workmanship as the tar had been tracked into the motel.

The company did not reply but I finally heard from a firm of insurance adjusters. They denied liability and said their expert had visited the hotel. They said his inspection showed no tracking of the recently laid asphalt. Further, they said the carpets were filthy and looked as though they hadn't been cleaned for a long time. Their expert witness also said he couldn't find any trace of tar inside the motel.

My clients were not impessed with the reply. They were sure the company was just trying to get out of paying for the damage it had caused and was looking for an excuse not to reduce their bill. They asked me to sue.

Before considering that, I said we would have to get an analysis of the rugs to prove that the new tar had damaged them. We had a technician come from Winnipeg to examine the situation. He took samples of the new tar and took pieces of carpet the owners said were contaminated. It took some time for his laboratory to run tests but he eventually sent me a report. It was not very strong. There were dark markings on the carpets but the tests were inconclusive as to whether the staining of the carpets was caused by the new tar or by other dirt people had tracked into the motel.

My clients said they had inspected the floors before agreeing to buy the motel and that the dark marks now on the carpets were not there at that time. They said they could each testify to that. Again, they asked me to sue. Before doing that I made sure the lab's bill was paid and found out what it would cost to have their technician come to court in Brandon for a day. I collected that amount from the clients.

As my clients were so insistent about going to court and the good evidence they could provide, I filed a Statement of Claim at the Court House and had it delivered to the contractor. After some delay, I received a copy of the Statement of Defence that had been filed on behalf of the contractor by another of my classmates, Keith Turner.

Keith was doing a lot of court work and was reputed to be a good litigator. We exchanged letters setting out our positions and what our witnesses would likely say. Mine would say the tar damaged the carpets and his would say it didn't. I told him we would be calling an expert to corroborate my clients' position. It was agreed we would proceed directly to trial, eliminating examinations for discovery. We were some distance apart so the possibility of a settlement had not been discussed.

I called my man as our first witness and he told of buying the motel after carefully examining it. He said he and his wife paid particular attention to the carpeting and it was in good condition. He then told about opening for business and how the carpets started to look dirty. He said he was convinced the newly tarred area was the culprit. He expained that a great deal of the carpeting in the hallways had been damaged beyond cleaning and beyond repair. He had looked at samples of sturdy carpeting and the cost of replacing the damaged areas. He said it would cost $40,000.

When we took the morning break, Keith Turner approached me and said: We'll settle for $5,000 if your clients will accept that amount right now."

I put the offer to my clients. They were incensed and told me to reject the offer. The case continued. When my first witness had been cross examined I called his wife. She was quite combative and said she was insulted by the attitude and questions being put by Mr. Turner. He was, in fact, challenging her veracity and suggested they were just trying to get out of paying the rest of his client's account.

He also suggested the carpets were in the same condition today as they had been during her first examination of them.

He was calling her a liar but his voice was never raised. She got the message just the same. When we adjourned for lunch, Keith approached me again. He said, "We'll pay $4,000 if you settle now."

I had never been faced with that sort of bargaining before, where an offer of settlement kept going down. My clients were outraged and the wife thought she had done a better job than her husband. She hadn't. In any event they told me to reject the offer.

After lunch I called the expert who had examined the carpets and the tar from the driveway. He did pretty well on the stand but wasn't quite as positive as I thought he would be. It was impossible to tell whether the judge had been persuaded by our witnesses or not. It would depend on the witnesses Keith Turner would call. I assumed the person who had done the tarring would testify and probably a defence expert who had examined the carpets.

Keith spoke to me again. Without saying why or arguing his position, he said: "This is my last offer. We'll pay you $2,000 if you take it now."

I spoke to my clients: "I think you should take the offer and get out of the case while you can. If we go ahead, Mr. Turner will call the people who laid the driveway and they will say it was properly done and that there was no tracking into the building. They probably have an expert witness as well, and while he may not be absolutely sure, he will probably say he couldn't find any staining he could connect to the recent driveway material. He may also say the dirt on the carpets he examined had been there for a long time. Our expert wasn't as positive as I thought he would be and Mr. Turner has already cast some doubt on his conclusions. If we lose, you will have to pay costs to the other side."

"We've gone too far now. Turner is just trying to turn the pressure up. I've been in business before and I know the games some of these contractors play" said my man. I asked his wife and she agreed with her husband and told me to carry on.

We went ahead and finished the evidence. A written judgment was received later. The judge said the plaintiffs hadn't proved their case to his satisfaction. He dismissed their claim and awarded a modest amount of costs to the defendant.

The result for me personally was that I lost money on the case. I had some advances to engage the expert witness but I was unhappy with the result. I never did send the clients a bill to pay me for my time.

I decided to be more careful in deciding when a case was likely to be a winner or a loser. When I thought I might be faced with a case that had a limited chance of success, I decided I would inform the client of that in writing. If the client insisted in proceeding, I should write again saying that was against my advice. I should then get a substantial payment on account so I would get paid whether the case succeeded or not. In the alternative, I should decline to take the case.

I might still agree to write a demand letter in any event, to see what the response of the prospective defendant might be. In some cases an insurance company, or one of its adjusters, might consider the claim in the nuisance category but offer a limited payment nevertheless. Some clients were happy to receive even a minimal payment. It made them feel that their concern was justified and that they had prevented the "offender" or "the big bad insurance company" from denying its responsibility as the client saw it.

In this case, we went to court and I was embarrassed by the result. It did little good to my ego or to the happiness of the client to remind the client and say "I told you we should have settled." It's not that easy to withdraw from a case after you get started.

The Easy Judge

When I first visited Shoal Lake, the gravel highway between Minnedosa and Russell curved around a small lake and the town of the same name. The rich farm land, hills and winding roads by-passed the sloughs and marshes that attracted hunters in the fall.

I can't recall why I had to stay there overnight, but I stayed in the ancient Shoal Lake Hotel across the tracks from George Lauman's law office. My room on the second floor of the three storey hotel had no running water but it had a toilet bowl under the bed and a basin in a wash stand. When I went into the hall in the morning I was surprised to find a warm bowl of water on the floor along with a small pitcher of hot water for shaving. There was no dining room in operation so I was directed to a café in town.

George Lauman's small two-room white brick law office was as unprepossessing as its owner. It faced the railway tracks with its line of grain elevators. In earlier times the view from the office would have displayed horse-drawn grain boxes delivering grain to the elevators. By the time of my visit they had pretty well been replaced by larger grain trucks which drove into the elevators to have their grain weighed, tested for grade and dumped into the elevator's hopper for movement to its storage towers. Empty box cars stood idly by until a train load could be made up with other points along the line to transport the grain to flour mills or shipping terminals at Thunder Bay.

The law office would always have been convenient for the farmers who combined their trip to town with a visit to their favourite coffee shop to catch up on the farm news, crop prospects, weather and the local gossip. Before going home they would likely visit the bank, the drug store and one of the grocery stores as well as George Lauman, their counsellor and friend. On later trips to Shoal Lake I also visited Bill Wherritt, a political warhorse who used to drive Senator Crerar and members of Parliament like Gibb Weir and Stuart Garson, to catch up on the latest political news.

In addition to running his office, George Lauman was a part-time Provincial Judge who sat on criminal matters in the old Court House in Minnedosa from time to time. Don St. John, a Minnedosa lawyer and a President of the Law Society of Manitoba at one time, practiced with his father after law school and on his own after his father passed away, but kept away from criminal law. I was therefore called on regularly to drive the thirty or so miles from Brandon to Minnedosa to represent people charged with drunk driving, assault and other relatively minor scrapes with the law. I also went there for Preliminary Hearings in death by criminal negligence or murder cases, most of which were heard by Judge Coward from Brandon.

When I started to go to Minnedosa, the resident County Court Judge was Judge Lindal who lived in Winnipeg but stayed in the judges' quarters in the Court House on a fairly permanent basis. Unfortunately, probably because of that exception to the rule that County Court Judges were supposed to live in the district to which they were appointed, Minnedosa lost its full time County Court Judge and its County Court seat when Judge Lindal retired.

The Crown Prosecutor, when I first went there, was William Ferguson, until he was appointed a Judge of the Court of Queen's Bench and moved to Winnipeg. He was succeeded as Crown Prosecutor by his partner, Bill Burgess. Ferguson had been a decisive and aggressive prosecutor. On one occasion I went to his office on Main Street and asked him to give my young client a break. He responded, shaking his finger at me, "Young man, every person I prosecute has already been given every break before I decide on the charge to lay. Don't ever come to me again looking for something else." I didn't.

In spite of a strong submission from the Crown, George Lauman could usually be counted on to impose a modest penalty when an accused pleaded guilty. It was therefore quite a shock when I had a case where a middle aged man was charged with having intercourse with his two daughters over a period of years. The evidence was made up of statements from the girls and was quite strong. The father, to his credit, didn't want to put them through a trial.

After the charges were read to him in court, my client entered a plea of guilty to each charge and sat down beside me. I rose and said that while my client's conduct was inexcusable, he had apologized to his daughters and was placing himself at the mercy of the Court. I suggested a suspended sentence would suffice, particularly in view of the public scorn that had been directed at him and his isolation from the community.

Judge Lauman listened to my submission seeking leniency and to Crown Prosecutor Bill Burgess' suggestion of a substantial sentence. I was shocked when Judge Lauman, without an adjournment or further discussion said: "Your treatment of your innocent children has been abominable. No doubt, if the circumstances had not come to light, you would have continued to abuse them. I sentence you to five years in the Penitentiary."

Many judges consider some crimes more severe than others. Judge Lauman's kindly nature was not to be taken for granted or treated lightly, and I was witness to the limit of his patience. My client understood and accepted the verdict. No appeal was contemplated and I never heard from the father again.

Juvenile Justice

My involvement with juveniles was limited. Most charges against them were dealt with in a compassionate way by Youth Court judges and Probation Officers. The few cases I did have were nevertheless sufficient to bring back memories of my father, a Juvenile Court Judge from 1925 to 1945, who used to discuss his cases over supper when I was growing up. He worried about the youth and about finding a penalty or solution that would keep them away from a life of crime and encourage them to become productive citizens.

Apart from a kindly approach to those who kept getting into trouble with the law, he required the parents to attend court where he sought their cooperation. At the same time, he believed in the adage "spare the rod and spoil the child," and he practiced what he preached. It seems to me I was always getting spanked by either my mother or my father, for some long forgotten sins of omission and commission. His other focus was to try to find an alternate form of punishment, rather then sending the delinquent boys to the Manitoba Home for Boys in Portage la Prairie or the girls to the Home for Girls in East St. Paul. The Home of the Good Shepherd and the McDonald House were other supportive institutions.

My father made sure that I was introduced to the serious authority of the Juvenile Court. One Saturday morning after I waited for him to complete a short docket, we went to our car to drive home. It was parked behind the Vaughan Street Detention Home in the area where convicts were once hanged when the building was the Winnipeg jail.

As I stood waiting for my Dad to unlock the car, I heard cries and screams coming from the top floor of the court building. When I asked what was happening, my father pointed to the small barred windows under the building's eaves and said: "That's where the worst boys get strapped. Their pants are pulled down and the Probation Officer paddles them, giving them a lesson they won't forget. I don't want to send them to jail so I hope this will make them change their ways."

I think my father must have arranged to have me in the courtyard at that particular moment. The cries and howls of pain let me know that my father and the Juvenile Court meant business.

Juvenile, later Young Offender legislation has changed over the years. The ability of teachers and law enforcement authorities to apply corporal punishment, meaning punishment inflicted on the body, is now forbidden. Parents are advised not to touch their children and warned they could be charged with a criminal offence if they beat them. The paddle, let alone the cat-o-nine-tails, became a thing of the past in Penitentiaries, even for the most severe rape. Even the word "rape," which once made individuals and gangs think twice, was removed from the Criminal Code of Canada, to be replaced with various types of sexual assault.

The Canadian Council of Women spearheaded the movement to do away with the term "rape," as it appeared that women were reluctant to come forward and complain if attacked. The unfortunate result of the change was that sexual assault cases weren't tried by a judge and jury and the penalties applied by judges became less severe. I am not convinced the changes have benefited those who are attacked, and the changes have certainly affected the manner in which abusers are prosecuted and the penalties they receive. Those who seem to need extraordinary measures to help them turn their lives around are not helped by the reduced level of punishment.

In the 1960s in Brandon, I acted for only a few delinquents. One was a loveable rascal whose caring parents just couldn't control him. The mother and father had a loving relationship and a stable home. Two of their three children were married and settled in productive careers, but the youngest was a happy but incorrigible child. Billy just couldn't stay out of trouble with the law. It was as though he was jousting to see what sort of mischief he could cause and get away with.

His earliest escapades occurred long before I started to act for him. He had his first run-in with the police when he was seven years old. The street on which the family lived ran north and south, sloping to the railway tracks and the river beyond. Bill saw a truck parked on his street one day and got into the driver's seat, where he started to move the various controls. The truck started to roll and Bill steered it at an ever increasing speed for a couple of blocks until it ran over the curb and into a tree in a vacant lot. The police arrived and escorted Billy home by the scruff of his neck. His parents were shocked and apologized for their son's behaviour. I don't know whether they spanked him or whether they just talked to him, but they were concerned.

The next incident happened when he was a few years older. He walked into the Crystal Brothers clothing store on Rosser Avenue one day, picked a hat from a shelf, took it to the cashier and said: "My Dad told me to bring this back. It doesn't fit." The tag was still attached to the hat so he was given the purchase price in cash.

In his early years there wasn't much the police could do, so they were happy to leave his discipline to the parents. The parents came down hard on Billy and confined him to his bedroom on the second floor of their home. That is where they thought he was when the police arrested him for break, enter and theft. They took him home to the shock and surprise of the parents. He had gone out the bedroom window, down the roof and onto an adjacent tree, on his way to the scene of the crime. As witnesses had seen him in the store that had been robbed, it was difficult to prove he was at home at the same time. About the same time, one of my neighbours told me Billy used to sing in their church choir and had the most angelic voice.

About all I could do in my several appearances on his behalf was to tell the Judge he came from a good family and that they would supervise him more closely in future. On one occasion I said he was going to live with his brother and on another, to work in a quarry. As time went by, the penalties changed from a reprimand to a suspended sentence and then time in the provincial jail. As time went on I saw less of Billy, probably because he was spending most of his time in jail.

Billy told most of the stories on himself in later years. He didn't mind bragging about his exploits and the attention he was gaining. I don't think he paid much concern to what I did in trying to keep him out of jail. It was always his parents who engaged me.

In later years when I went to the jail to see other clients, Billy would find out I was coming and would get permission from the

Warden to speak to me. I never knew how he managed that but he probably said I was launching an appeal from his last conviction. If so, he would get permission.

The last time I saw Billy in the old Brandon Jail he told me he had been brought up to see me from "the Hole" where he had been for a week. Most prisoners begged to be released after a single night. I knew exactly what the hole was like because I had recently obtained permission from the Attorney General of Manitoba, Sterling Lyon, to take a church group on a tour of the jail. There was some local and government interest at the time in having the old jail replaced with a modern facility on the North Hill. A guard took us on a complete tour of the building. The first thing that struck the visitors was the trouble the guard was having with his large key in trying to open the barred doors through which we had to pass. The keys kept sticking and refusing to work but the guard kept wiggling until the doors opened. The visitors wondered what would happen in the event of a fire.

We visited the Hole that was used to punish inmates who were causing trouble in the institution. Those on the tour were appalled at the barbaric sight. The basement was dark and dank. The Hole was a room with a solid metal door except for a metal window that would allow a guard to look in or pass in food without having to unlock the door. There was a cot in the room but no mattress, and a pail for a toilet. There was one dim light bulb that could only be turned on in the corridor. There was no window. A tin pipe that disappeared into a wall was supposed to supply fresh air. We couldn't detect any.

When Billy came into the interview room he was blinking and could hardly see during our chat. He told me he had been in the Hole for yelling and swearing at the guards and the warden. He said the warden told him he could return to his cell if he promised to behave, but Billy refused. He was enjoying the notoriety. He was tough and wanted all the prisoners and the guards to know it.

The next time I saw Billy was one day when I was hearing Chambers applications as a Judge in Winnipeg. He had been brought to court from Stony Mountain Penitentiary and was representing himself and several other inmates. In preparing for the hearing, I read the material that had been filed in support of the application but

I hadn't noticed his name. The application challenged the manner in which the institution was calculating the time before inmates were entitled to apply for parole. The inmates had no lawyer but Billy stood up to argue the application on their behalf. As soon as I recognized him I said I knew him and had been his lawyer in Brandon. As it would have been improper for me to hear the case, I adjourned it for a week so another judge could deal with it.

I never saw Billy again but it was obvious he was still challenging authority and had graduated into more serious crimes, as the Federal institution housed only prisoners who were sentenced to two years or more. It was also obvious that his associates considered him to be a person of some importance as he had earned the bogus title of a 'jailhouse lawyer.' Unfortunately, in spite of the best efforts of his devoted parents, he remained incorrigible.

I represented two other juvenile offenders at the request of their parents. The difference between the parents was dramatic and the manner in which the boys and young men developed was equally astonishing. Both were 15 or 16 years of age and both had been charged with driving while under the influence of alcohol.

John, who lived with his mother, admitted his conduct immediately. He was given a suspended sentence. No one made any excuses for him and he went to court and accepted the punishment handed out by the judge. He was a promising athlete and some men who were connected to the team came to his assistance. They took him under their wings and provided the male support he was lacking. They supported him as he graduated from team to team and became an international player. The boy learned from his run-in with the law. While his mother showed her love and concern for him, she insisted he admit what he had done and plead guilty to the charge.

Tom, the other boy I represented, had the same charge and he lived with his mother and father, both of whom had good jobs. The difference was that his parents were insulted when their son was charged with driving under the influence. They insisted on a plea of not guilty and they gave evidence that their son hadn't been drinking.

The police constable who had pulled the boy over said there was a strong odour of beer in the car and the boy couldn't walk straight when asked to do so. He was convicted and was given a suspended sentence and probation. In less than a year he was in court again facing the same charge. Again, his parents insisted he plead not guilty and that I get him off. The father supported everything he said and criticized the RCMP officers who testified that the car was weaving on the road and that when they got him out of the car he was unsteady on his feet and his breath smelled of alcohol. He refused to walk a straight line as requested. His parents could not accept the fact that their word had not been accepted by the police or by the judge.

They didn't think much of my performance either, and fortunately, I was never called upon to defend their son again. From reports I received over the next few years I concluded that the boy was just drifting through life with no permanent job and nothing to commend him. Unfortunately his parents continued to shelter him and to protect him from reality. The parents were clearly implicated in their son's attitude and development.

Often, the manner in which a young offender is dealt with the first time he or she comes into contact with the legal system, determines how he or she will act in the future. Youth Court judges have an opportunity to steer young people away from a life of crime the first time they appear in court. Unfortunately the influence diminishes dramatically if the youth or his or her parents continue to challenge the system. The parents who have the best chance of keeping their children away from crime have to become involved in supporting the police and the courts as they try to discourage youth from joining gangs and from illegal activity.

If courts feel compelled to incarcerate a first time young offender, the government should provide separate facilities so the young offender will not become influenced by the hardened youth who are in the same institution awaiting trial on yet another charge.

Although I didn't think of it at the time, these experiences may have helped me deal with a ticklish situation that arose within six months of becoming a judge. Someone had broken a window in Grosvenor School, right behind our house, and the police were keeping an eye on it. One day I had a call from a police officer saying he would like to interview one of our sons who had been seen throwing something at the school. I asked to be present at the interview.

When two officers arrived at our home, Lorna and I and our son met them in our living room. They had seen our son throwing something at the school. Our son admitted doing that as part of a game he and another boy were playing but said they hadn't hit any window. The police had nevertheless obtained a summons requiring our son to appear in Juvenile Court.

When my son and I arrived at the Juvenile Court in one of the Fort Osborne Barracks buildings in Tuxedo, the place was crawling with young people and young lawyers. One said, "What are you doing here My Lord?" I don't recall the non-committal reply I gave him.

We were ushered into the office of a Probation Officer. She heard my son's story then said we could leave and that would be the end of the matter. I wasn't satisfied and asked if we could see a Judge. A few minutes later we were ushered into the office of Judge Ray Harris. After he heard my son's explanation, he spoke to him in a fair but firm way and advised him to be careful not to do things that might cause others to think he had done something illegal.

Having to go to court was embarrassing and a shock for both our son and me, but we both agree to this day, it was a worthwhile experience.

Politics

I had a setback in business when I ran for parliament as the Liberal candidate in Brandon-Souris in the 1963 federal election. The sitting member was the popular Walter Dinsdale, a son of a Salvation Army preacher, a member of that church himself, a war hero and a Minister in the Diefenbaker government. The main object of having a Liberal candidate was to keep Walter at home as much as possible rather than having him travel the country supporting other candidates. My Conservative friends and clients weren't happy with my venture and I lost some business to other firms. Fortunately my criminal clientele and civil litigants weren't concerned about my political preference.

It was no surprise that I lost; in fact I only won one poll. That was in Deleau where I said a few words in French and recited the first part of Lamartine's Le Lac which I remembered from Victor Leathers' teachings at United College. I was in trouble though when some of the ladies at the meeting started to speak to me in French. There were only two redeeming features to the election. I won the Deleau poll and Lester Pearson became the Prime Minister.

Some have asked if political activity helped my appointment to the bench. I don't know but I can say "It didn't hurt." Actually my later political activity put me in touch with more political leaders. In my capacity as president of the riding association, I introduced Jean Marchand in French when he made his exploratory circuit of the west and was part of a small contingent of Manitobans who supported Pierre Trudeau from the beginning when he became one of the contenders to succeed Pearson at the leadership convention in Ottawa in April 1968.

The convention was the most exciting meeting my wife and I ever attended. In the months before the convention, the various candidates crossed the country, addressed meetings of delegates and supporters in every city and town of any size. They visited farms and agricultural meetings and their comments were reported by the local media.

The candidates for the leadership were quite outstanding. Mitchell Sharp was a Manitoba favourite as was Paul Hellyer. John Turner had a loyal following of younger delegates, partly because his wife was from Winnipeg. The majority of the delegates seemed to think that John Turner, who later became the Minister of Justice and briefly Prime Minister, would make an ideal leader but most decided he was too young. Unfortunately for him, being considered for 'the next time' didn't help his chances in 1968. Paul Martin Senior, who had been the Minister of Health in Pearson's cabinet, could work a room like no other. He seemed to be able to call everyone by name even though he hadn't met them before. He was well respected but didn't offer the excitement of some of the other candidates. Mr. Winters from eastern Canada had a strong background in finance and was the choice of many delegates.

As the date of the Ottawa convention approached, some candidates withdrew and urged supporters to vote for another candidate. By the time we reached Ottawa, Jean Marchand was the chief strategist and organizer for Trudeau. Jean Chrétien, who few of us had heard of, would sit cross-legged on the floor of a room in the Chateau Laurier hotel and speak as the 'little guy from Shawinigan.' His homespun approach and support for Trudeau was a valuable addition to the Trudeau campaign. Another plus was the presence of Joey Smallwood, sitting beside Trudeau, who had recently brought Newfoundland into Confederation.

All the campaigns were well organized and every supporter of one candidate or another was assigned a task. I was a 'floor man' responsible to keep track of the delegates from rural Manitoba. I, and the other liberal floor men, wore an orange stove-pipe hat so we could be identified and distinguished from other workers. If some of the Manitoba delegates were doubtful who they would support, I was to meet with them and urge them to support Trudeau. He had been the Minister of Justice under Lester Pearson so I used some of his work in that office in my discussions with voters. The greater responsibility was during the numerous votes. As one candidate after another was eliminated, my job was to approach that candidate's supporters from rural Manitoba to try and persuade them to vote for Trudeau on the next ballot.

Mr. Trudeau won the convention and became the leader of the party and the Prime Minister to succeed Pearson. Shortly after, the national election campaign began. One of my tasks as the local president was to drive Trudeau from the airport at Rivers to his hotel in Brandon. During the trip he questioned me on the condition of the crops and local issues he should address. His approach to politics was novel when compared with the serious approach of western speakers, like Jimmy Gardiner, of earlier days. He made converts but also shocked many of his own supporters. I was present in the Winnipeg Auditorium when he made one of his shocking remarks, only part of which was reported by the media.

When he was talking about the grain industry and Canada as the breadbasket of the world, he said at one point, "Why should I sell your wheat?" A gasp went through the crowd and many apparently didn't hear his next words, "You have the Canadian Wheat Board." Remarks like that and C.D. Howe's comment, "What's a million," shocked many westerners but 'Trudeaumania' prevailed and he won the election handily. The remarks would however come back to haunt him later on when the Liberals had a hard time holding on to the western vote.

My less partisan involvement in politics was as an elected School Trustee of the Melita School District, the Brandon School District and then as chairman of the Brandon Division Board when the Larger School Divisions were established by the Roblin government in 1965. I had the privilege of being the Chairman of two provincial boards. I was the last President of the Urban School Trustees Association of Manitoba and the first President of MAST, the Manitoba Association of School Trustees.

The main thrust of the new organization was to try to provide students throughout Manitoba with a similar education and a similar variety of courses and programs. That was particularly important as some communities were unhappy about losing their one or two room schools which kept the children close to home, and the loss of local control over education. The new board intentionally had a limited number of members from the several Winnipeg School Divisions and a substantial number of Trustees from other regions of the province. National conventions enabled the Trustees to keep abreast of developments in other parts of the country.

The Minister of Education in Duff Roblin's provincial government at the time of the change, was Dr. George Johnson from Gimli. He worked tirelessly to bring the various factions together. MAST and the MTS (Manitoba Teachers Society) had joint meetings as well and they were the most positive and cooperative ones I ever saw between the two organizations, as they were too often on opposite sides of bitter salary negotiations. How to get rid of the occasional incompetent teacher was another disrupting issue that was never properly addressed during my tenure. It was unfortunate that teachers and trustees were seldom on the same side of issues affecting the education of children.

All these political activities ended when I became a judge. Politics could no longer be discussed and I couldn't even hear a case if I knew one of the parties. On a few occasions a person I had met would be called as a witness. If I knew the person well I could not continue to hear the case. If I didn't know the person well I would still have to advise counsel in open court that I knew the person. The lawyers then had the choice of asking me to step down or, if they thought the evidence of that witness would not be vital to the outcome of the case, they could ask me to carry on and hear the case. Sometimes I made up my mind in advance. One of my good friends and classmates even asked me once why I would never hear a case involving one of his clients. I said, "I can't. We've skied together in the past and I consider him a friend." I don't think my explanation was accepted but I couldn't debate it any further.

I had to ask myself what I would do if a witness I knew said something I didn't accept or didn't believe. It wasn't a difficult decision for me not to hear some cases to be sure that possibility never arose. There were enough judges on the court so another judge, with no knowledge of the case or its witnesses, could hear the case and all the witnesses. I also had to be careful not to hear a case where any of my former political friends were involved. There was only one case where that arose. A former supporter was unexpectedly called as a witness. As soon as he was called I advised the lawyers I knew him well. They discussed the matter, said his evidence would not deal with any contentious matter, and they asked me to hear him and remain with the case. I was still uncomfortable having to hear him and that further strengthened my resolve not to be put in that situation again.

The Cabinet Maker

The only other case involving one of the McIvors I will relate started when I received a call from a friend who was having some work done by Willie, saying Willie had been charged with impaired driving and leaving the scene of an accident after he had left his house the day before. He said he could vouch for him being sober and he wanted me to defend him.

The topography of the north hill came into play once again. It appeared that, after work, Willie had taken the cross-street at the top of the hill, turned south onto 18th street and headed down the north hill. He apparently caused utter confusion and came to the attention of the police when he tied up the rush hour traffic on 18th Street for an hour or so. His car had run into a steel guard rail at the north end of the bridge over the Assiniboine River.

When the police arrived they found a damaged old car in the centre of the road blocking traffic in both directions. Confusion reigned as drivers got out of their trucks and cars to see what had happened. It took an hour for a tow-truck to remove the car and for the police to get traffic moving.

As I later learned, when the police got the situation under control they started to look for the driver of the car to find out what had happened. They were approached by an irate citizen who announced in a booming voice, "I was right behind the car as it came down the hill. It was weaving from side to side, and then it hit the bridge. The driver was drunk out of his mind. Where's the driver? I presume you have him under arrest."

In an apologetic voice the officer had to admit, "We don't have anyone under arrest and we don't know where the driver is."

Another person in the crowd spoke up: "The driver was Willie McIvor. His arm was bleeding and a friend took him to the hospital. I saw them walking towards the south end of the bridge."

The irate citizen said he was going to see the Chief of Police.

Willie came to see me after he received a summons to appear

in court. He told me how the accident happened and what he had been doing that day. When we got to court a month later, the Court Clerk read the charges of drunk driving and leaving the scene of an accident. Judge Coward asked: "How do you plead, Guilty or Not Guilty?"

"Not guilty," Willie answered, forgetting to add 'Your Honour' as I had instructed him to say.

"We'll let you know the trial date when it's set Mr. Hamilton. In the meantime the case is adjourned for a month."

When the trial date arrived my client, dressed in his Sunday best, and I took our seats at the counsel table. The Crown Attorney came in with a man who looked vaguely familiar.

"Order," called the Clerk as he ushered the Judge to his place on the bench. To my surprise, it was not Judge Coward, but Bill Pearson, a respected local lawyer and part-time judge. It dawned on me that Judge Coward might have declined to hear the case as he had tried my client on another charge a few months earlier. While he was a tough Judge, he was meticulous in applying the legal procedures intended to give every alleged offender a fair trial.

Without any preliminary comments, the Crown Attorney began: "I call William P. White as the first Crown witness."

I remembered who the man was and I shivered.

"Tell the court your place of residence and your occupation please Sir."

"My name is William White, I live in Winnipeg and am the Director of the Licence Suspension Appeal Board for the Province of Manitoba." My suspicion was confirmed.

The Prosecutor began: "Without going into detail for the moment, I understand you witnessed an accident on 18th Street in Brandon, Manitoba, on November 25th of last year."

"Yes I did. I was directly behind the car that crashed into the bridge. The driver was obviously drunk and a menace to everyone on the road," the witness offered without being asked. "I've never seen such dangerous conduct in all my years of driving on Manitoba streets and highways. The man should be barred from driving for life."

The witness was in charge. He wasn't waiting for the Prosecutor to ask him questions. He knew what he had seen and he wanted justice done immediately.

"We'll come back to that," the Crown said, "but first tell the court about your work. What is the License Suspension Appeal Board?"

"I am the Director and I have a large staff. If someone has had their driving licence suspended by a court, they may apply to me for a restricted licence that will allow them to drive back and forth to work or from place to place while they are working. When the paper work is done, I examine it and assign the case to one of my Hearing Officers. I meet with them regularly to make sure we all apply the same standards."

"The people usually come to the hearing with a lawyer, and the circumstances of the offence are discussed. It is important a person admit his or her fault. The Hearing Officer then hears the reasons why the person is asking for a limited driver's licence. They usually say they can't earn a living without being able to drive. Their previous driving record is examined with care. If they have had a suspension before, they won't likely get another chance. If they breach the conditions of any conditional license we have granted, their licence will be automatically cancelled. We turn down the majority of applications as we see our responsibility as keeping drinking drivers off the road."

The Crown moved on: "Were you in Brandon on the day the accident in this case occurred?"

"Yes, we had decided to establish an office in Brandon to hear applications from western Manitoba and a number of people had applied to become Hearing Officers. I was here to interview them and to speak about our service at a luncheon meeting of the Chamber of Commerce. At my request, the city and RCMP had been invited to send their senior officers. My topic was Keeping Drunk Drivers Off The Road."

"Going back to the day of the accident, when did you first see the car you were following down the north hill?"

"I first noticed the car when it pulled in front of me onto the highway from the street at the top of the hill. As it went down the hill in front of me it was weaving from side to side. The driver was obviously drunk."

"I object your Honour," I said, rising to my feet. "Perhaps the witness would limit his comments to what he saw and leave conclusions to the court."

"Very well," the Prosecutor conceded. "Please just tell His Honour what you saw."

Obviously frustrated at having his monologue interrupted, the witness restrained himself and said, "Well, he was swerving all the way down the hill. At one point I was sure he was heading for the ditch and the next minute I thought he was going to drive into the traffic coming at him. There is only one lane in each direction."

"What did you think about the safety of others?"

"I was afraid someone was going to get killed. It was the worst driving I've ever seen in my life. I'm not surprised he ran into the end of the bridge. The car spun across the road and the traffic was blocked in both directions."

"What did you do after the collision?"

"I got out of my car as quickly as I could and waved to cars coming down the hill to pull over and stop. It looked as if the highway would be blocked for some time, so I ran toward the bottom of the hill and directed other vehicles to turn onto the street that would take them across to the First Street bridge. When the police arrived I asked if there was anything else I could do."

The prosecutor was finished with the witness and it was my turn to cross-examine. I treaded as gently as possible because I knew this was a dangerous witness who wanted to see my client convicted. He probably thought he could deliver a deathblow to any mitigating excuse the driver might come up with. He might also have been thinking what he would do to him if he ever applied for another conditional driver's licence. Everyone but the judge knew my client already had a conditional licence. That fact could not be disclosed to the judge unless there was a conviction.

"Was the car being driven within the speed limit?" I asked.

"Speed had nothing to do with the situation."

"I take it then you agree the car was not speeding?"

"Yes I guess I do," he almost whispered.

I decided to move on. "Did you speak to the driver of the car after the accident?"

"No," was his blunt reply.

"Did you see him walk?"

"No. There was chaos and cars all over the place. I don't even know where the driver went."

I thanked the witness and told the judge those were all the questions I had and sat down. The obviously disappointed witness abruptly left the courtroom.

Two city police officers were the final witnesses for the Crown. They said that after the damaged car had been pulled away and traffic was beginning to move they went to the hospital, intending to speak to the driver.

"What did you learn at the hospital?" the Crown Attorney asked.

"A nurse told us Willie had been there but had left. The doctor who had seen him said he needed a few stitches and a bandage on one arm.

"I asked the doctor if he had given him an anaesthetic and the doctor said, "No, he didn't need any."

I jumped to my feet. "I object Your Honour. This witness can't speak for the doctor. If my learned friend wants to know what the doctor did he can call the doctor as a witness."

"Objection sustained," the Judge declared without calling for argument.

"What did you do next?"

"We were told he was walking when he left the hospital so we drove up and down a few streets till we saw him plodding along a sidewalk towards his home. There was a lot of snow on the ground and he was moving slowly. We grabbed hold of him."

"Did he say anything?" the Crown Attorney asked.

"He said: Unhand me youse guys." It was hard to keep a straight face but you have to do that in court no matter how humorous a situation or comment may be.

"What then?" the Crown continued. "He smelled of alcohol, so we asked if he'd been drinking."

"He said 'Yeah'. When we asked where and how much he had to drink he said, (the officer looked at his notes), I found a bottle of rye in the car after the accident and put it in my parka. I was still sore after I left the hospital and it was cold. The rye helped with the pain and helped to warm me up."

"Then what did you do?"

"We asked for the bottle and he said he threw it away when it was empty. He said he had thrown it into a hedge or an empty lot a couple of blocks back. We told him to go home and we started looking for the bottle."

"Did you find it?"

"No, it was getting dark and we couldn't find it so we quit looking but went back the next day but still couldn't find it."

The second constable took the witness stand and confirmed what the first one had said but was steered away from repeating the doctor's comment. I didn't ask him any questions and the Crown closed its case.

"Your Honour, I would like to consult with my client before continuing, would it be possible to take a break at this point?"

It was close to noon so the Judge adjourned court until two o'clock. Over a quick lunch at the Bus Depot, I told my client things looked pretty bleak and that he should be ready for a conviction and the suspension of his driver's licence. I said I was concerned about the effect the Director's evidence might have on the Judge. I wasn't really telling Willie anything he didn't know but I wanted to prepare him for the worst.

"What would you think of pleading guilty and having me ask for a low fine and a short licence suspension?"

That settled the matter. Willie came to life and bluntly said: "No way. I'm not going to plead guilty. I just can't afford to lose my licence. Put me on the stand so I can tell the Judge my side of the story."

"And what exactly is that?" I asked.

"Never mind. I'll tell it. I know I'm in deep trouble at the moment so what have I got to lose?"

"OK it's your funeral. I'll lead you through the day."

"I want to talk about the work I was doing and why the car was weaving."

"OK, I'll ask you about that and about why you left the scene of the accident."

When court resumed and I called my client to the stand, I could almost feel the Crown Prosecutor rubbing his hands in anticipation of a productive cross-examination. Accused people seldom take the witness stand when there is so much evidence against them, but Willie was determined and the Crown was in for a surprise, and so was I.

"Willie, were you working on November the 25th, the day of the accident?" I began.

"Yeah, I was making cupboards."

"Was there anything unusual about that?" I asked, having some idea of what he would say.

"Yeah it was cold out and all the windows were closed. I was gluing all these pieces of wood together and the smell was getting to me."

"What do you mean by that?"

"The glue was making me dizzy but I wanted to finish the job by five so I kept going."

"Anything else?" I asked, not wanting to shut him down.

"I left the house at five and headed home. I turned onto 18th Street and started down the hill. I had trouble controlling the car." He paused.

"Why was that?"

"There was three reasons."

"What were they?"

"Well, I was a bit dizzy from all that glue. You're not supposed to use it unless there's good ventilation. The other thing was that the street was slippery. If it wasn't ice, there was hoar frost on the road." He paused again.

"You said there were three reasons."

"The main problem was that I had my table saw and all my tools in the trunk and back seat. It felt like the front wheels were up in the air at times. I was going slow and trying to control the car but it slid and I hit the end of the bridge."

"Anything else about the accident?"

"Nope."

"You heard the police say they couldn't find you at the scene of the accident. Did you leave?"

"Yeah my arm was bleeding and Harry Schemki dropped me off at the hospital."

"What did you do there?"

"A doctor bandaged me up then said I could go, so I started walking home."

"What happened next?"

"These two cops drove up in their car, got out and grabbed me. They asked me if I'd been drinking and I said 'yeah.' They asked where I was drinking and I said between here and the hospital. They wanted to know how much I had to drink and I said about half a twenty-six. They wanted to know where I got the bottle and I told them it slid out from under the seat of my car when the accident happened. One of my kids must have left it there. I was cold and hurting when I left the hospital so I drank it to warm me up and settle me down."

"Was that the end of your conversation with the police?"

"No, they wanted to know where the bottle was. I said I threw it in a hedge or bush a couple of blocks back."

"Then what happened?"

"That's it. They told me to go home, that they'd be in touch."

"Is there anything else you want to say?"

"Nope."

"Your witness," I said to the Crown Prosecutor.

The prosecutor went over the events of the day as described by the Director and the police, but try as he might, he couldn't get Willie to change his story. He did ask one question that hadn't been covered, "What did you have to drink at work?"

"I had a beer with my sandwich at lunch."

"Are you sure it wasn't three or four?"

"Nope, just one."

The Crown Attorney had a whispered conversation with the police. Apparently they couldn't think of anything else that needed to be asked. Addressing the judge he said, "Those are all my questions, Your Honour," He shrugged his shoulders, and sat down.

I said, "That completes the case for the defence Your Honour."

The Judge called for final arguments. As I had called the accused to testify, I went first. I referred to the reasons Willie had given for the swerving of the overloaded car and explained that he had not run away from the scene and did not deny he was the driver of the car. He waited for some time before a friend took him to the hospital. He didn't try to escape, but was quietly walking home when the police caught up with him. My final comments were contained in two sentences: "There is absolutely no evidence that the accused was under the influence of alcohol at the time the accident occurred. The Crown has not discharged its onus of proving the guilt of the accused beyond a reasonable doubt."

The Crown Attorney suggested my client's story was a far-fetched pack of lies. In effect he asked the Judge to ignore everything my client had said. He referred repeatedly to the independent evidence of the senior civil servant. He argued that, taking all the facts into account, the Judge should infer that Willie was under the influence of liquor when the accident occurred. He conceded he was not concerned about the lesser charge of leaving the scene of the accident. In effect he was agreeing to a finding of 'Not Guilty' on that charge. On the drunk driving charge he pressed for a conviction.

The Judge adjourned court but was back in half an hour with his verdict: "I find the accused Not Guilty on both counts," he said. "There was no evidence to refute the evidence of the accused that the car was heavily loaded and difficult to steer; and secondly, the onus is on the Crown to prove beyond a reasonable doubt that the driver was under the influence at the time the accident occurred. It has not discharged that onus."

I wasn't home when the friendly employer phoned to find out what had happened to Willie in court. When Lorna said, "He got off," his reaction was, "I don't believe it. It must be some kind of miracle."

Apparently the Director of the Licence Suspension Appeal Board was furious with the outcome. He "knew" his first impression was right and he insisted on an appeal. The Crown must have disagreed, as there was no appeal. For my part, I had one of my associates go with the next client who had to appear before the Licence Suspension Appeal Board. Who knows who might have been presiding!!

Reasonable Doubt remains the foundation of our system of criminal law. Without it people would be convicted and punished on the basis of what someone thought must have happened, might have happened, or probably happened. The need for real proof would not exist.

This case is a perfect example of reasonable doubt. The story of the accused even sounded far fetched to me, but let's examine it. If he was building cupboards and using glue he might well have been affected by it, but there was nothing to suggest that caused the accident. The car was apparently laden with heavy tools and equipment. The police would have examined the car and the Crown Prosecutor didn't challenge the accused on the point when he was in the witness box.

The only other issue of consequence was whether the accused was under the influence when he hit the railing. There was a suggestion that the accused might have been under the influence when he got to the hospital but the Crown didn't call the doctor to describe his condition. Having a bottle of booze slip out from under the seat seemed unusually convenient, but the prosecution could have challenged that if the doctor said the accused was under the influence when he saw him. The Crown could have asked the judge for an adjournment so it could call the doctor as a witness in rebuttal, but it didn't. If there had been evidence of drunkenness before the accused started to walk home that would certainly have produced a different result.

The judge might have wondered about these matters but, there being no evidence to clear up some of the questions he might have had in his mind, he had to give the accused the benefit of the doubt and find him not guilty.

Preventive Medicine

An unusual call to our home early one Sunday morning diverted me from our usual ten minute drive to church to a two hour drive to Kirkella, by that time only a railway siding on the trans-Canada highway near the Saskatchewan border. The caller was in a state of panic on the phone. He told of having shot and killed a stranger who had threatened him on a remote country road. He asked if I would come to see him as soon as possible, so he could explain what happened and show me the area where the shooting occurred.

When I arrived, the client and I drove a few miles north and turned onto a narrow gravel road. My client explained that he had been checking some sloughs to see where the ducks were accumulating so he and a couple of buddies could go for an early Monday shoot. He said that as he was walking back to his truck he saw two rough looking characters coming towards him from the east and another from the west. One was carrying a baseball bat. He called to them and asked what they wanted. There was no response so he ran to his truck, grabbed his rifle, put in a clip, pointed at the pair and told them to stop. They didn't stop. He was sure he was in for a beating and probably the theft of his truck. He was also worried about what they might do with the rifle if they got hold of it.

When the man with the bat and his associate were about 30 yards away he put the rifle on his hip and fired a shot into the road. Immediately, one of the men fell to the ground. The other, who had been walking with him, stopped, examined the man and ran off in an easterly direction. The man to the west had disappeared. The one lying on the road wasn't moving and appeared to be dead. My client drove home and called the RCMP at Virden and told them what had happened.

The client told me he fired his rifle to let them know he was armed and that he meant to protect himself. He said he had lots of experience with firearms and specifically aimed for the road in front of the two who were closest to him. He made a point of saying he wanted to scare them away and never had any intention of hurting anyone with the shot he fired. He was convinced the bullet must have hit the road and ricocheted.

After the Mounties got the call from my client, they called their cars on their radios, told them of the report they had received and asked them to be on the lookout for two scruffy-looking strangers who were on foot and might be looking for a ride or trying to steal a car. Two highway patrol officers who happened to be driving on #1 highway east of Kirkella, apprehended two men trying to catch a ride. As they couldn't give a good explanation of what they were doing and where they were going, they were taken into custody and placed in the detachment's cells in Virden.

When I finished looking at the scene and my client took a few pictures, I phoned the RCMP office in Virden and spoke to the officer in charge. I explained that I had been retained to assist my client. I also said he was very upset by the incident and would cooperate with the police in every way. I also said I would phone the Superintendent in charge of the Brandon Region the next day, to extend the same offer of cooperation to him.

The next day I phoned the Superintendent and asked if the possibility of laying a criminal charge could be put on hold until the autopsy had been completed and his forensic experts had examined the bullet to see if there was any evidence of a ricochet. He said he was aware of the case, the statement my client had given, and that I was representing him. He also said he would be discussing the case with the Crown Attorney shortly and would pass on my comments and request. He wouldn't commit himself.

When I saw the Crown Attorney a few days later, he confirmed that the marks on the bullet supported my client's story. The fact that both apprehended hitch-hikers had criminal records and were wanted in Regina also lent credence to my client's belief that he was going to be attacked or worse. No charge of any kind was ever laid against him. I never heard anything about the third man or what happened to his body.

My client might not have been charged in any event, but I was pleased to have a client who believed that a lawyer might be of some assistance in delaying the possibility of a criminal charge or the need to appear in court charged with a serious crime. From my perspective, though I had a good relationship with the police generally, it was nice to be able to actively cooperate with them instead of always being on the opposite side of contested cases.

The Paddle

The most dramatic case I had before Judge Cy Buckingham in Virden involved a charge of robbery with violence. I was about to find out how tough he could be. Two men in their early 20s, who had appeared in his court on a number of occasions, engaged me to defend them.

They had been in the Virden beer parlour, followed a farmer when he left and headed for his truck. When he put the case of beer he had purchased in the back of his truck and got into the cab to drive home, he saw the two thugs reaching into the box and grabbing the case of beer. He got out of the truck and asked them what they thought they were doing. A scuffle ensued. The farmer was hit and he fell to the ground. The thieves took off with the beer. The farmer was shaken but sustained no serious injuries.

The local RCMP were called. The description of the offenders and a description of their car enabled the Highway Patrol to apprehend them. The stolen beer was recovered and saved in case it had to be identified in court. The Crown prosecutor was getting tired of these offenders and charged each of them with 'Robbery with Violence.' The accused contacted Legal Aid in Winnipeg and I was asked to represent them.

There wasn't much I could say or do in their defence. We entered a plea of guilty and the Crown told Judge Buckingham what had happened. I said the boys had been drinking and, while they tried to steal the beer, they had no intention of fighting with or harming the farmer.

The shock came when the judge pronounced sentence. He reviewed their record of offences the Crown had given him, said how despicable their theft was and that they would have to change their ways. He sentenced each of them to two years in the Penitentiary and to be paddled. They must have heard from others how severe a paddling in Stony Mountain was because they were shivering from fright. I told them I could appeal the severity of the sentence if they wished.

They both wanted to appeal, but for different reasons. One said, "I don't care how long I get in the Pen, I don't want the paddle. I was talking to my uncle and he said several guys got the paddle when he was in the pen a few years ago. They hit you so hard and so often, they need a doctor present to fix up your injuries. They can't strap you within six months of your release as they don't want the injuries to show. He said the guys were screaming and the screws were piping the thing through the loud speakers."

The other one said, "I've been in Headingley too often and I don't want to go to jail."

"Well, you're sure going to jail." I said.

"What I meant was, I can take all the paddling they can hand out. I'd rather have the paddle and keep the sentence as short as you can."

As my clients wanted a different outcome, I couldn't act for both of them. Willie wanted me to keep acting for him and Tom asked me to find him another lawyer to argue his position. I asked Nate Nurgitz, my Winnipeg agent to find someone to join me in the Court of Appeal. I can't recall who the lawyer was but we made our presentations based on our respective client's preference. After the hearing before a three judge panel of the Manitoba Court of Appeal, the Chief Justice said they were reserving their decision and would let us know their decision when it was ready.

In the meantime our clients had to wait in the Brandon jail. When the written decision finally arrived, my co-counsel and I were both surprised and our clients were delighted. The decision was written by Chief Justice Cal Miller and he settled the concerns of both clients. He found that the theft and the assault on the farmer were separate incidents and therefore the accused were guilty of two offences – theft of beer and assault. He said the conviction for robbery with violence would be set aside and replaced with one offence of assault and another charge of robbery. The two year sentence would stand. The result was that each accused would go to the penitentiary for the length of time Judge Buckingham had stipulated, but neither of them would be paddled. Our clients were delighted.

For years I thought this was a very imaginative finding. Looking back on it now, I think there may have been other forces that caused the court to take the approach it did. Cal Miller had been a successful and popular lawyer in Portage la Prairie. He and his brother Joe practiced together. They had a general practice and were also instrumental in the establishment and operation of the Portage Mutual Insurance Company, which had its home office in their home town. In later years two of his sons took over the practice of law and one became a County Court Judge and a Queen's Bench Justice when the courts amalgamated in 1964.

About the time the Virden paddling case reached the Court of Appeal, John Diefenbaker of Prince Albert, Saskatchewan, was the Prime Minister of Canada. He had been an effective courtroom lawyer and an outstanding orator. When in that office he introduced a number of changes to Canada's legal system. An amendment to the *Federal Judges Act* required all federally appointed judges to retire at the age of 75. Capital punishment was suspended and my guess was that public discussions were taking place about other viscous practices of the past.

The cat-o-nine-tails had been replaced with a leather strap and that had been replaced with the wooden paddle. I don't recall the dates those changes took place, nor do I recall when the paddle was outlawed. My assumption was that the courts were responding to these parliamentary initiatives; and the decision of Chief Justice Miller and his fellow judges may have been, at least in part, responding to impending changes.

We see a similar and often confusing change in the law today. The use of conditional sentences, house arrests and suspended sentences for fairly serious offences has many members of the public and police officers concerned that sentences are not severe enough. The Supreme Court of Canada and the Federal Department of Justice are struggling to find an appropriate balance, but the issues are far from settled. Judges today react to what they think the law is, what the Supreme Court of Canada has said, and the changes Parliament may or may not make.

Judge Bruce McDonald

Judge McDonald was another good rural judge as far as I was concerned but he did have a temper and his treatment of Aboriginal people and the RCMP continually got him into trouble. In my opinion he was not racist but the manner in which he tried to lecture and improve the lives of offenders didn't go over well. His angry outbursts against people from a local Indian Reserve or First Nation Community, who regularly got into trouble and regularly appeared in court, were intended to encourage them to change their ways but were still not understood or appreciated.

He was equally hard on the RCMP. Some said the reason went back to an encounter when he had been stopped and given a ticket which he thought was unjustified. Whether that was the case or not he dealt with police officers in the same way he dealt with Aboriginal people and others who appeared in court. He would fly off the handle and dispose of cases in a manner the police did not appreciate. He was strict at trial but lenient when it came to imposing a sentence.

The only contested case I had before him involved a farmer charged with crossing a yellow line while driving east on Highway No. 4 near Gladstone. My client pleaded not guilty and the trial was held in Portage la Prairie. The Crown Attorney, Mr. Gilroy, asked the police officer what he had observed.

He said "I came onto the highway from a side road and turned east. I was in the right hand lane going east and the accused was in the left lane, also going east. There was a solid yellow stripe for the right hand lane and a dotted line for traffic going west. The accused turned across the solid line in front of me."

In cross-examination, I asked, "Had you seen where on the road the car was before you pulled onto the highway?"

"Not exactly," the officer replied, "but he was heading east."

"When did you first notice the yellow line?" I asked.

"As soon as I saw him he was on the wrong side of it," he replied.

"You didn't see my client cross the line from south to north then." I suggested.

"No I did not," the officer replied.

After a few more incidental questions, I called my client to the stand. "Please tell His Honour the sequence of events that led to your being stopped by the police."

"I was heading for Gladstone and there are a few small hills on No. 4. As I came over a hill I saw a police car on a cross road to the right that was partly turned to go east. I pulled over to the left in case he wanted to go in front of me. He didn't move so after I passed him I pulled into the right lane."

"You heard what the officer said about you crossing a yellow line. What do you say about that?"

"I did cross one, but only to get back onto the right hand side of the road. The line hadn't started until I was almost up to the police car. I stayed on the north side of the road until I was sure the police car wasn't going to pull out in front of me. I tried to explain all that to the officer but he wouldn't listen."

The Crown Attorney argued that my client had crossed a yellow line and it didn't matter what the reason was or whether the line was in his lane of travel or not. I took the position that my client was acting in a responsible manner. In addition, I said the law was intended to prevent people from crossing a yellow line onto the wrong side of the road where there might be oncoming traffic. I said there was no law against crossing a yellow line in the opposite direction when a person was not in breach of the law before the line appeared.

Judge McDonald agreed with me and dismissed the charge. In my opinion he applied a more reasonable interpretation of the law than the RCMP officer was prepared to. No doubt the decision added to the complaints that had been levelled at him over the years.

Unfortunately the judge died before having an opportunity to face his critics. On the other hand, from what I knew of him, he might have chosen to say nothing. He might have been content to feel the system was either against him or failed to understand the positions he took and the results he sought to attain.

The Suitcase

The most horrendous case I handled as a lawyer was the murder charge in *Regina v. Drysdale.* A couple of hunters, plowing through the bush in the rolling Brandon hills ten miles south of the city, stumbled on a grass covered suitcase that appeared to have been there for some time. Out of curiosity, one of them opened it and nearly passed out when he saw a small skeleton covered in a flowered dress. He showed it to his partner and they wondered what to do. They made a note of how to find it again, then drove to the intersection of highways 2 and 10 and phoned the Brandon Detachment of the RCMP.

They were told to sit in their car on the shoulder of the highway with their headlights on and to flag down the police car that would arrive in fifteen minutes with its siren on and its lights flashing. They led the Mounties to the suitcase, then returned to their car where an officer took a short statement. They agreed to give a more detailed statement and subsequently went to the RCMP office in town where it was recorded.

The police initially assumed that an unwanted child had been left in the bush by a parent. The theory was quickly abandoned when an autopsy revealed a strange but violent death. It was impossible to tell exactly what happened but the police knew they had a murder case to investigate. The doctor who performed the autopsy estimated that the child had been dead for five to ten years.

The police checked their records and asked other detachments and the city police to examine their records to see if there was any outstanding report of a missing child. None was found. There were no leads and eventually the investigation came to a dead end. The skeleton, clothing and suitcase, were placed in storage and information that had been gathered was placed in an 'unsolved' file. In accordance with their normal procedure, the file was re-examined every year, but nothing new was discovered.

It would still be several years before I became involved and that wouldn't likely have happened if a young man named Brad hadn't committed a minor offence and ended up in the Winnipeg Remand Centre and was required to speak to a probation officer. As he hadn't been in trouble with the law before, the officer said she wanted to understand him and why he had committed the offence. She was considering recommending a suspended sentence. She spoke to him about his past and how he came to get into trouble with the law. He was asked about his parents and his early years. He said he had left his unhappy home at an early age and lived with his sister in Brandon for many years. When asked if she was married, he said she was divorced and had two little children.

The counsellor must have thought he was holding something back so she asked if there had been any violence in the home. He said his sister was very kind but that she had lived common-law with a violent man for a few years, and that he was cruel.

"How was he cruel?" she asked.

"He would hit me and my sister for no reason. When my sister asked him to leave he punched her in the stomach and hit her in the face with the back of his hand. He said 'I'll leave all right, but not 'til I want to.' He used to hit her little kids and make them stand over a heat duct till their legs were red."

At that point Brad broke down and cried. "He killed my little niece," he sobbed. "He was mad because she was making a noise while he was sleeping. He hit her in the face and pounded on her head till she passed out. My sister tried to wake her up but couldn't."

"What happened then?"

"He put her in a suitcase and made me go with him. He covered the suitcase with some mud and branches, then we drove back to the suite. He threatened me and my sister. He said, 'if you ever tell anyone what happened I'll kill you both and I'll kill the other kid too.' He left a couple of weeks later and we've never heard from him since. We keep moving cause we're afraid he'll find us again."

The counsellor reported what she had learned to the Winnipeg Police and they advised the Brandon Police what they had learned. The Brandon police spoke to the Mounties and it didn't take long before they opened their dormant file. When Brad's sister was found and was told what he had said, she confirmed what had happened to her daughter. She was still afraid for her life if he found out she had spoken to the police. She was promised protection, and now that the details of the killing were out she cooperated with the police in spite of her fears.

It didn't take long to locate Drysdale. He was in the federal penitentiary at Prince Albert in Saskatchewan where he was serving time for a violent offence.

After he was charged with murdering the little girl, he was transferred to the Brandon Jail. Someone from the Warden's office phoned my office and said a prisoner wanted to see me. I was asked to go to speak with the Superintendent before I saw the prisoner. He was not happy about having a violent offender in his institution and he didn't want me to see him on my own. I said I had to speak to him privately and reminded him that was the law.

He finally said, "All right. I'll have a couple of guards let you into his cell so you can talk to him. I'll tell them not to listen to what you're saying but they'll be close enough so if you get into trouble you can yell and they'll come running."

I was a bit nervous but I didn't want my client to notice. One thought that made me feel somewhat secure was that a lawyer may be the only ally an accused person has. In any event, I had to find out what he had to say about the murder charge, and if he had killed the child, whether there were any mitigating circumstances.

"Tell me what happened," I said.

"Nothing," he said.

"Okay," I said. "I haven't spoken to the Crown yet so I don't know what information they have. I'll be back in a couple of days."

"The cowboys tell me I'm charged with murder. The guys in here tell me you're okay. Have you handled any murder cases?"

"A few," I said.

"You're my man then," he said.

I called the guards and they let me out. The Superintendent was pleased to know no problems had arisen. We agreed to use the same procedure whenever I would have to come back to talk to him.

We went to court in a few days. My client was brought in to the courtroom by several Mounties. He was in handcuffs and leg chains. The formal charge of murder was read by the Judge. It alleged he had killed the child on the 8th of December, 1966. When the judge asked him how he pleaded, I answered: "My client pleads not guilty your Honour."

It was obvious that the Mounties were handling the case and not the city police. The province had assigned one of its Winnipeg Crown Attorneys, Al Sarchuk, to conduct the trial. At one of the adjournments when he was in town he asked me if my client would be willing to give an oral statement which the Mounties would record. I put the request to my client, expecting him to refuse.

Instead, my cocky client said, "Sure, I'll give a statement. I'm not afraid of no f'n cop or Crown lawyer. I'll tell them a thing or two."

The taping took place in a witness room on the second floor of the Brandon Courthouse. Only the technician, a guard and the two lawyers were present. Other officers were, I am sure, standing guard in the hall.

My client enjoyed the attention he was receiving and answered every question immediately and in considerable detail. He denied any knowledge of the death of the child and denied hitting or mistreating her at any time. No matter how deeply the Crown Attorney probed, he didn't deviate from his story. For all intents and purposes it was an exculpatory statement. It didn't seem to help the Crown case at all.

The trial before Mr. Justice Roy Matas and a jury was very difficult, even though the Crown had plenty of evidence implicating the accused. The first witness was one of the hunters, then the RCMP who arrived on the scene and the pathologist who described the injuries to the child and the cause of death. The prosecution made sure the jury was continually reminded of the tragedy. It had the skeleton of the child lying on a table in front of the court reporter where it was also in front of the jury and close to the witness box.

"My Lord," I said after the doctor finished his testimony, "might I ask that the remains of the child be removed from sight unless it becomes necessary for another witness to identify them."

Without even asking the prosecutor to respond, the judge had them removed. His order came just in time as the next witnesses were the child's mother and Brad. They avoided looking at Drysdale as they gave their evidence. They were very emotional and probably frightened. There was little doubt about the impact of their evidence. They did say they couldn't swear the accused deliberately set out to kill the child, but their descriptions of his continuing acts of cruelty left the impression he didn't care whether the child lived or died.

The clear and honest manner in which they gave their testimony left no doubt in my mind they were telling the truth. You could tell by the looks of anguish on the jurors' faces that they felt the same way and had already made up their minds about the accused. While the witnesses kept their eyes away from him, the jurors would have noticed the way the accused glared at them as they told their story. He was still trying to intimidate them.

The Crown introduced Drysdale's statement, then produced witnesses to show that it was a pack of lies. It certainly did not impress the jurors who seemed to have their minds made up.

The Crown probably over did the attack on the statement of the accused. They called additional witnesses to show that much of it was untrue. They refuted his suggestion that he loved children and dogs. One witness the Crown called told of witnessing his cruelty to and killing of a dog on one occasion. I didn't notice the significance of that evidence at that time, probably because I had given up all hope of an acquittal.

Mr. Sarchuk and I summed up the evidence and urged the jury to convict or to acquit. He asked the jury to bring in a verdict of murder and I asked them to convict him of manslaughter.

It was then time for Justice Matas to instruct the jury on the law and direct their attention to the evidence they should pay particular attention to. His concluding remark was that they could convict Drysdale of murder if they found he had deliberately beaten the child and caused her death. If they believed his statement that he had never touched the child, they should find him not guilty. The other option he left with the jury was to find Drysdale guilty of manslaughter. That would only be possible, he said, if the accused hit her by mistake or never intended to cause her death. His taped statement, the judge pointed out, hadn't even suggested that possibility.

The jury retired to consider their verdict and were back within an hour. They found him guilty of murder.

My client immediately told me to appeal. I said it would be better to have another lawyer and I recommended Mel Myers. The Court of Appeal panel was Chief Justice C. Rhodes Smith, Justice Sam Freedman and Justice Brian Dickson, as strong a court as you could get.

The appeal was allowed and a new trial was ordered. The judges said that in prosecuting someone for a criminal offence, the Crown may not introduce evidence of prior acts of violence that have nothing to do with the current charge. Justice Freedman, who wrote the decision, said that evidence of prior acts of violence to the dead child could be introduced, but acts of violence to other children or to a dog were not admissible.

The accused changed lawyers again. Paul Walsh took over the case and started to prepare for trial. He also discussed the advantages of pleading guilty with the accused. My guess is that they discussed the fact that a sentence for manslaughter would be shorter than one for murder. Eventually Drysdale agreed and the Crown also agreed to settle for manslaughter rather than go through a full trial all over again.

The irony was that, during my discussions in the Brandon jail, I had tried to persuade Drysdale to plead guilty to manslaughter in the first place. I didn't know whether the Crown would agree but I thought it was worth trying. I was correctly apprehensive about the result of a trial for murder. He wouldn't even consider pleading guilty to manslaughter at that time.

In spite of the terrible circumstances of the case, it showed the extent of responsibility that rests on the shoulders of defence and prosecuting lawyers. It also showed that even the worst and most heinous crime and criminal is entitled to the same rights and protections other citizens enjoy.

As far as my client was concerned, I don't think he cared one way or another. He may even have been missing Prince Albert, where he had friends and more freedom than he had in his spartan cell in the antiquated Brandon jail.

Defend Your Castle

Judge Coward sat mainly in Brandon but from time to time in other courts in the Western Judicial District. He was tough, from the standpoint of defence counsel. His factual findings were solid and he was a good student of the law. One of the cases I had before him arose in Elphinstone, a small town on the 'turkey trail' which wends its way from No. 10 highway to Russell south of Clear Lake and the Riding Mountains.

A storekeeper at Elphinstone was at work one day when two rough looking characters entered his store and, after poking around for some time, approached him and demanded he fork over all the money in the till. After some hesitation, and a few excuses, he did as he was told and the men left the store and ran down the street. The proprietor grabbed his shotgun, ran outside and fired, bringing one of the robbers to his knees. The men were arrested by the RCMP and charged with theft, but to the proprietor's amazement, he was also charged. The charge against him was 'the unlawful use of a firearm.'

We entered a plea of 'not-guilty' and the trial was heard in Minnedosa. One of the burglars was called as the first witness.

"Did you rob the Stephenson General Store in Elphinstone on July 13, 1968?" the Crown began.

"Yes, Wilber and I did."

"And have you both been charged with that offence and sentenced to 18 months in jail by Judge Lauman?"

"Yes, we pleaded guilty cause the Mounties nabbed us after I got shot."

"And are you now in Headingley?"

"Yep."

"Where were you shot?"

"I was hit on the back of my legs and I fell down."

"Do you know who shot you?"

"It was Mr. Stephenson. I didn't see him shoot but he came

running after us with a shotgun in his hand."

"What happened to the money you stole?"

"The Mounties took it from us after they arrived to take me to the hospital in Erickson."

"You admit you stole the money from Mr. Stephenson?" the Crown continued.

"Yeah, we pleaded guilty."

"Did you fire a gun of any kind at Mr. Stephenson?"

"No, we didn't have a gun."

"Those are all the questions I have," Crown Attorney Bill Burgess announced.

In cross examination I tried to paint the robbers as pretty rough characters.

"Isn't it true that you threatened to kill Mr. Stephenson if he didn't give you all the money in his till?"

"Yeah but we didn't really mean it."

"There was no way he would know that was there?"

"I guess not," was the reply.

"Why did you think an honest business man would just hand over his money to you?"

"I don't know. We had been drinking and we needed money to buy some more beer."

"Were you surprised that Mr. Stephenson would come after you with a shotgun?"

"No, I suppose not."

"Don't you think he was entitled to shoot at you?"

Mr. Burgess was on his feet. "I object your Honour. That is for this court to decide."

"Objection sustained," Judge Coward said.

I called Mr. Stephenson to tell his side of the story. "Why did you shoot at the robbers?" I asked.

"They had just stolen $75 from me and I thought I was entitled to protect myself and my property. If I hadn't winged one of them they would never have been caught or brought to justice."

"Did you recognize the robbers or know their names?"

"No, I don't think I had ever seen them before, although it's hard to say. I didn't know their names or where they were from. All

I know is they were Natives." The Crown Attorney went over the same issues, then it was time for argument.

My argument was that the actions of the storekeeper were justified and were taken in self defence and in the defence of his property. I pointed out that was the only way to apprehend the offenders and the only chance there would be to recover his stolen property. The Crown argued the measures he took were extreme and were not justified in law.

Judge Coward gave his decision immediately. Although he said he could understand my client's reaction he said the law doesn't permit citizens to take the law into their own hands. "Mr. Stephenson could have phoned the RCMP and they would hopefully have been able to catch the offenders. On the other hand, he could have chased the robbers to see where they went. In any event he had no right to shoot them."

"The law of self defence permits a person to use reasonable force to repel an assault upon them. It also permits a person to use reasonable force to prevent another from illegally taking their property. The deciding factor in this case is that Mr. Stephenson did not attempt to stop the theft by any use of force. Nor did he take the shot gun and use it to chase the robbers away. He didn't take the shotgun into his hands until the robbers had left his store and were running down the street. Therefore the possible defence of 'self defence' doesn't apply in this case."

The only break my client received was that, although he had been convicted of the improper use of a firearm, the Judge gave him a suspended sentence. I couldn't argue and there were no grounds for appeal. My client still felt he had done what was necessary and that the law was unevenly balanced in favour of the real offenders.

In practical terms, although there was no publicity or reporting of the case in the local newspaper, the case was intended to send a message to the public that people shouldn't take the law into their own hands. They should call the police.

I wondered if the law was fair, but I couldn't think of an amendment that wouldn't upset the law's intended balance.

The Poor Percheron

Mr. Smith had a law practice in Oakburn, ten or fifteen miles north of Shoal Lake. He was, like Judge Lauman, a mainstay of his community. He was a good friend of Marie and Mike Kotyk who had come from Oakburn but were living in Brandon when we knew them. Mike had been a farmer and lived a quiet life. Marie, on the other hand, was a ball of fire and active in a variety of activities in Brandon. She was a teacher and involved in everything contentious or political. She spoke her mind.

She had Lorna and I go to Oakburn one Saturday to see its magnificent churches. I think she was hoping I would open a branch office there as Mr. Smith, their resident lawyer and friend, was planning to retire. I didn't establish an office but did take over some of Mr. Smith's work and clients, particularly those who had moved to Brandon.

One of them had a business near my office in Brandon and he and his brother still operated their farm near Oakburn and bred Percheron horses. While the horses were sizeable beasts and could handle the most strenuous farm chores, modern machinery had taken over their work and the remaining pair were groomed and trained as show horses who strutted their stuff at agricultural fairs throughout western Canada. They had earned a number of trophies and brought in some income as well.

One winter day a call came into the office from Joe Michalyshyn who had just spoken to Mr. Smith who suggested I be contacted immediately. Joe's brother had been exercising the Percherons along the side of a secondary road near Oakburn when one of them stumbled and fell. Its leg had gone through a rusted culvert and it looked as though it might die. Joe wanted to know if they would have any recourse against the municipality where the accident occurred. I said I would look into the matter and gave him some instructions on what he or his brother should do in the meantime.

When I contacted the municipality where the accident occurred, the Secretary-Treasurer agreed to contact their liability insurer to see what they had to say. The brothers and I went to the scene of the accident the next day and took measurements. Joe's brother took pictures of the snow-covered gravel road and the culvert with its jagged hole. The measurements showed that the hole was at road level and not over the ditch. Most importantly, the culvert was badly rusted around the hole and must have been in bad shape for some time. One picture clearly showed its condition. It was impossible, however, to tell how long the hole had been there or whether it was created when the horse stepped on the rusted area.

The municipal official got back to me within a week and advised that the Provincial Department of Highways, and not the municipality, was responsible for the maintenance of the road in question. I then sent a letter to the Department explaining what had happened and the damage that had been caused to the horse's leg. I told the Province we could discuss damages later but asked it to admit liability, as the highway was in an unsafe condition.

There was a considerable delay but I finally received a letter from another country lawyer, saying he had been engaged by the Department and was instructed to deny liability. The cause of the accident, his letter alleged, was the failure of the driver to look where he was going and his failure to keep the horses on the road. A further exchange of letters failed to produce any compromise, so I filed a Statement of Claim in the County Court office in Minnedosa.

We appeared there in due course and obtained a date for trial. At my suggestion, the trial would be held in the theatre in Hamiota, which was within easy reach of Oakburn and interested farmers. My clients and the Veterinary Surgeon were our only witnesses and the Department had a senior departmental person and the local employee who was in charge of maintaining the road, as their witnesses. Farmers, neighbours and a few others who seemed to be connected with the government, made up the audience. The presiding judge was His Honour Judge Lindal and he was assisted by his senior Clerk from Minnedosa.

As the Plaintiff, we had to go first. Our first witness was Joe Michalyshyn's. brother. "Were you driving a team of horses on the Provincial Road near your farm on December 4th of last year?"

"Yes, I was."

"I understand something happened to one of the horses."

"That's right, it badly damaged a leg."

"And did that happen in the Province of Manitoba?" I said, having learned my lesson from Cy Buckingham.

"Yes," he replied.

"I assume my learned friend admits that the maintenance of the road in question is the responsibility of the Province of Manitoba," I said turning towards him.

"Yes, there's no issue on that point your Honour. The position of the Province is that the road was in good condition and it denies any responsibility for the accident or the damage to the horse."

"Very well," the judge intoned, making an entry in his note book. I was pleased to have the Judge hear the real issue so early in the case.

Turning back to the witness, I asked "How often did you exercise these horses as a team?"

"A couple of times a week in the winter," he replied.

"Did you always take the same route?"

"No, I have a number of ways to go but on the day it happened it was very cold so I took the short way around the farm."

"Had you exercised the horses on that road before?"

"Oh sure," he said.

"Do you know how wide the road is where the accident happened?" He pulled a folded paper from his pocket.

"I object," my friend said rising to his feet.

"Norman, please tell the Judge what you are looking at." I interjected.

"These are measurements my brother and I made the day after the accident."

"Have you made copies of your notes and can you give a copy to His Honour and to my learned friend?"

He reached into a bag and produced several copies which I distributed.

"I would like to file the measurements as Exhibit 1" I said, handing a copy to the Clerk. That seemed to bother the government people. No doubt they had made their own plans and would be introducing them later. I, of course, was not interested in letting them introduce their plans and their explanations just yet.

"Now will you please refer to the exhibit and explain what all the marks and distances you have on it mean." He did that in a slow and deliberate manner.

"Please describe in greater detail, if you can, where the hole in the culvert was in relation to the road and the ditch."

"It was on the right hand side and on top of the road, where a plough had recently cleared the snow." I took time to make a careful note of that and to give the judge time to do the same. I was following the McGirr approach.

"Do you have any pictures of the area?"

"Yes I took pictures after taking the measurements with my brother."

"Please give copies of them to my learned friend."

"This one shows the way the road was ploughed. You can see the edge of the hole there and this is a close-up of the hole in the culvert."

"How soon after the accident did you take the pictures?"

"The accident was in the morning and the pictures were taken in the afternoon, after my brother spoke to you. More pictures were taken the next day."

Both the judge and the opposition looked at me, but I just carried on.

"I tender the photographs as Exhibits 2A through 2J your Honour."

"Very well," the judge said, accepting them.

"Using the sketch and the photographs, please explain where on the road you had the horses and what happened to one of them."

"I drove them like I always do. The roads around our farm often have stones or bumps on them, even in the winter, so I always go along the right hand side of the road where there is less traffic and where there is looser snow. I can't go too far to the right of course or I would go into the ditch."

"If you had driven this stretch before, can you explain why you never saw the culvert with the hole in it?"

"I can't really explain it. I didn't actually see a hole, but maybe the road was ploughed a little wider that day. Maybe a snowplough had made the hole or the horse may have made the hole when she stepped on the rusted culvert, I don't know."

The government lawyer objected to the speculation.

"In any event, are you saying you had never seen the hole until after the accident?"

"That's right."

I moved on. "Please tell His Honour what happened."

"The horse lurched and stopped. When I went around in front of her I saw the hole in the culvert and that her right front leg was bleeding. It looked like the skin was stripped down to the bone. As I drove the team back to the barn, she was limping all the way. The Vet came right away and bandaged the leg. Today she still has a limp and we're afraid to put her in a show. She has an uneven gait and would never pass an appearance test, let alone pull a wagon. We'll keep her but she's done as a show horse."

"How long had you been training her?"

"For ten years anyway."

"Do you have another horse that can take her place?"

"No, we just have the two show horses."

"Do you know how much it would cost or how long it would take to train a new pair?"

"Not really, but my brother keeps the records."

Counsel for the Highways Department cross examined but was unable to shake the witness. If anything, he became more comfortable in the witness stand and more positive about what he had done and where the dangerous culvert was located. I then called Joe to the stand. He was the brother that looked after the finances for the farm. He also had, and produced, detailed records of all the fairs at which the horses had been shown. With pride, he recited the long list of trophies the pair had won. The brothers had groomed the horses themselves and were the drivers of the wagon at all performances over the years. He spoke of how the damage to the lame horse had brought an end to their annual tour of agricultural fairs where they took pride in showing the animals and winning major awards.

As a businessman, he was able to provide an accurate accounting of the monies spent on the animals each year. He was also able to give a carefully calculated estimate of the value of the damaged horse. He went over several photos and explained the injuries that were easy to see. He explained they couldn't just buy another horse. To remain in business they would have to acquire two young horses and train them together.

He estimated it would be at least five years before they could even hope to start winning purses with them. He assumed their days of raising and training Percherons were over. He confirmed that he had spoken to me on the day of the injury and had instructed his brother to take measurements and photographs immediately. He pointed to the dates on the photographs indicating they had been developed within three days of the accident.

Our final witness was the Veterinary Surgeon.

"I understand you are the Vet for the Michalyshyn brothers of Oakburn, Manitoba."

"Yes, that's right."

"Were you familiar with their team of Percherons?"

"I had looked after them and the cattle on their farm since I came to Oakburn five years ago."

"Did you examine an injured Percheron on December 4th last year?"

"Yes and I have a copy of my findings."

"When did you prepare them?"

"Some were notes I made on the day of the injury and my prognosis was made later, after I'd treated the injury and tested the ability of the horse to walk."

"Have you seen the horse recently?"

"I saw it yesterday."

"Did anything you saw change your diagnosis?"

"No, the horse isn't improving. Its health is OK but it won't be able to work or to appear as a show horse again."

"Can you advise the court what injuries you observed?"

"The fetlock was scraped down to the bone and the bone itself was badly damaged."

"Did you examine the place on the road where you were told the accident occurred?"

"Mr. Michalyshyn showed me the rusty culvert with a hole in it the day after the accident. Tissue from the leg was still sticking to the jagged metal when I saw it."

"Could you tell how deep the hole in the culvert was?"

"It looked as if the leg had gone down to the metal at the bottom of the culvert. I didn't measure it but it was a foot or two."

"I show you a series of photographs. Can you see the culvert in any of them?"

He identified a number of them and I passed them up to the Judge as he spoke.

"What if anything can you say about the relationship of the hole to the surface of the road?"

"The hole was on the right hand side of the road just inside the area that had recently been ploughed. I could see the rusted hole in the culvert quite clearly but I can't say if it was enlarged when the horse went into it."

The witnesses for the province didn't have much to say. The snowplough operator said he never saw any hole in the road or in a culvert. He also said he had examined the culvert some time after the accident and that it was not at the level of the road but was down in the ditch. He hadn't seen the photographs and couldn't explain why they showed the hole within the area he had ploughed some time earlier. He had no record of when he last ploughed the road before the accident.

When it came to argument, I quoted from a couple of cases I had dug up showing the responsibility of the government if its employees negligently maintain its highways. I argued that the rusted culvert must have been in bad shape for some time and should have been observed by some maintenance crew member and repaired. The onus, I suggested, was on the government to show it had not been negligent and it had been unable to do that.

The evidence was strongly challenged in argument, the government lawyer arguing that if the hole could be seen by the camera, the driver should have seen it and should have steered the horses away from it.

Judge Lindal reserved his decision but ended up accepting our evidence. He quoted from the cases I had given him and from the evidence given by the plaintiffs and the Veterinary Surgeon. He rejected the evidence of the grader operator.

He found in favour of the plaintiffs and awarded them a reasonable amount in damages and costs. They would likely have received a larger award if they had sued in the Court of Queen's Bench but their main concern was to have the province admit its fault. No doubt grader operators were instructed to watch for deteriorating roads in the future. The Province did not like to be sued.

Sometimes people have to take a stand and demand fair treatment.

The Furious Fireman

An unusual phone call was received one morning by the Desk Sergeant at the Brandon Police Station. A male voice said: "I thought I should let you know, I just killed my wife."

"Who's calling?" the Sergeant asked.

"It's me, Bernie Hill. I'm a fireman and work in the fire hall across the street from the police station."

"Where are you now, Bernie?"

"I'm at home and my wife's here too."

"What's your address?"

"27 Barnett Crescent."

"Okay. Stay there, we'll be right over."

The sergeant notified the chief, gathered up a detective, a couple of officers and a photographer and headed out. When they arrived at the house they opened the door, called to Bernie and went up to the bedroom. Bernie was sitting quietly in an arm chair holding a '22 rifle by the barrel. He handed it to the detective. The woman lying on top of the bed seemed to be covered with bullet holes. She was dead. There was no doubt about that.

"Was it an accident Bernie?" the sergeant asked.

"No, I meant to kill her."

"Okay fellows, we'd better not go any farther. Do you have a lawyer Bernie?"

"No, but I hear Al Hamilton down the street handles things like this."

"We'll give him a call and ask him to come and see you at the station. I don't think we have to take you to jail."

When I arrived I had a chat with Bernie and found out why he shot his wife and where he got the rifle and ammunition. I called the Fire Chief, told him what had happened and asked if any of Bernie's pals would post bail. In the meantime the police had been in touch with the Crown Attorney who said Bernie would have to be charged with murder. Bail was agreed to and Ed Alder, a part time magistrate, walked over from his office and did the paperwork. Bernie's sister took him home to her place.

Sylvia and I went to the store where Bernie told us he had bought the gun and ammunition the previous week. We talked to the clerk who handled the transaction and got a copy of the sales slip, and obtained some other information as well.

We went to trial rather quickly, after the preliminary hearing covered the work the police had done and a Coroner gave the cause of death. I was not too concerned about jury selection but I did try to select those who looked as if they might be compassionate. I rejected a couple of scowling farmers and a small business operator who seemed unhappy about being taken away from his usual work to sit on a jury.

The Crown Attorney called the police officers as his first witnesses. They told of the phone call, going to the house and what they observed. The only questions I had of them in cross-examination were intended to show that the accused was quite calm and cooperative when they saw him. I cross examined the Coroner to make certain seven bullets had been fired at the wife from short range. He said most of them were fatal. There was no sign of a struggle, in fact no sign the woman had even moved during the shooting.

When the Crown finished its case, I called the employee from Sears who sold Bernie the gun a few days before the death. She said she sold him the gun and two clips of ammunition. She also said he didn't know how to load the gun so she showed him how to insert the clips and cock the gun.

I then called the Chief of the Fire Department who said Bernie was a good fireman who had been with the department for twelve years. He described him as a steady employee who wasn't excitable and did his work in a careful and deliberate manner. He was unaware of any marital strife.

Finally I called Bernie to testify. "You heard the lady from Sears say you bought the gun several days before your wife's death. Is that correct?"

"Yes it is."

"Please tell the jury the experience you had with a rifle."

"I didn't have any. I never owned a gun and had never shot one before."

"Is it true, nevertheless, that you used the rifle and shot your wife to death?"

"Yes it is."

"How many shots did you fire?"

"I don't know. Quite a few I guess."

"Did you mean to kill your wife?"

"Yes."

"Please tell the jury why that was."

"She had been running around with other men for some time. When I asked her where she had been when she came home late, she would say she was in a truck or elsewhere with someone she had picked up in the pub."

"Did she say what they did in the truck?"

"Wherever it was, she would tell me how great the sex had been. She told me that every time and she told me about her fun and how stupid I was. She didn't want to separate and didn't want a divorce but she wouldn't stop rubbing it in. I just couldn't stand it anymore. I got the gun out on Monday morning when she was still sleeping and I killed her."

The Crown Attorney tried to get Bernie to admit to other motives but he wouldn't budge from his story. When the Crown Attorney asked if he was sorry for what he did, he said, "I don't know what else I could have done."

During my address to the jury, I asked them to consider the reason he acted as he did. I said this wasn't a case of murder.

"If he had just wanted to kill his wife, he could have done that with one or two shots, but he didn't stop after she must already have been dead. He was not himself. Instead of being the steady fireman you heard about, he was out of control. He was reacting to her hurtful actions and her continual taunting. She drove him to it. It was as if he was trying to stop her from tearing his life apart."

I ended by telling the jury I wasn't trying to justify his actions but I asked them to find him not guilty of murder but guilty of manslaughter. That is what the jury did.

The client had to pay for what he had done, but an understanding jury tempered their decision with mercy.

It's Not Cricket

From time to time a case or an individual involved in a case can teach lawyers and judges some basic principles about justice they have overlooked or forgotten. Many Aboriginal people have a solid belief in the Creator and 'Justice' is an important part of their culture. Basically it means having people do what is right and what is fair. They apply the principle in their daily lives and they expect others to do the same.

More than 3700 Dakotas came to Canada and settled on nine reserves after the 1862 Minnesota Uprising. They now live on five reserves in Manitoba. Several thousand of Sitting Bull's Titans crossed the Canadian boundary seeking sanctuary after Gen. George Armstrong Custer's Battle at the Little Bighorn in Montana in 1876. Although the Canadian Dakotas or Sioux are status Indians, they were not entitled to sign treaties because they had no lands to surrender. They were nevertheless granted reserves by the Canadian authorities and are governed by the *Indian Act*.

One of those reserves is the Sioux Valley reserve, thirty or so miles west of Brandon on the north side of the Assiniboine River. When people from the reserve come to Brandon some drive their own vehicle, if they have one, but many without transportation hitchhike or walk to the Trans-Canada Highway and hail a Greyhound bus. The bus depot in Brandon, at the time, was on the corner of Princess and 11th Street, across from the courthouse.

An elderly Sioux gentleman was waiting outside the Bus Depot for a ride home. As he waited, he was approached by a couple of young fellows who demanded some money. He refused, saying he needed the money to get home, but a struggle ensued and he was thrown to the ground.

Two Brandon City police constables, driving their cruiser, saw the skirmish and took off after the youths as they ran north down an adjacent lane. They split up and the police lost them. Their description however matched a couple of young ruffians who were frequently in trouble with the law. They were arrested later that day and I saw them when they were in custody.

The Crown agreed to bail without sureties because they had no one who could put up cash bail or who owned any property. We appeared in court before long, where they entered a plea of not guilty to the charges of assault and attempted theft. A trial date was set for the middle of the next month.

When the day arrived, my clients and I showed up, ready to go to trial. When the case was called, the Crown Prosecutor rose to his feet and said: "Regretfully your Honour, I have to ask for an adjournment for another month. I am having trouble locating an important witness."

"Very well," the Judge said, setting a new date.

When my clients and I arrived at 10 a.m. for the trial to commence, the Judge said he had one or two short matters to attend to before we could start. As the time dragged on to 11:30, the Judge finally announced that we would start the trial at 2 p.m. My clients and I left the courtroom and I told them I would see them back in court at that time. We went in to the courtroom together. I sat at the counsel table and had my clients sit in the public area behind me.

As the accused had already entered pleas of not guilty, the case began with the Crown calling one of the constables as its first witness. The other constable was not in the room. The prosecutor asked the witness what he had seen from the police car and the view he had of the men he chased down the hill.

He said: "I didn't get close enough to make a positive identification, but they looked a lot like the men sitting behind their lawyer."

"Did you arrest them?"

"Not right then, but I knew where they lived and I arrested them at 6:35 p.m."

"Did you question them?"

"Not formally, but they said they didn't know what I was talking about when I mentioned the beating and attempted robbery of the older gentleman at the bus depot."

"Can you identify the accused today?"

"Yes, that's Brian Fisher sitting to the left of Mr. Hamilton, and

Robert Fisher sitting to his right."

With that Robert raised his hand, waved, and said, "That's me."

Everyone in the courtroom was surprised and the Judge glared at Robert.

As the questioning continued, every time Robert's name was mentioned, he hollered, "That's me."

Judge Coward directed his next comment to me. "There seems to be something wrong with one of your clients. Please ask him to stop interrupting the proceedings, Mr. Hamilton."

"Yes your Honour, I replied, leaning over to tell Robert to keep quiet."

My attempt was ineffective. Robert, obviously intoxicated, kept interjecting and disrupting the trial.

"Mr. Hamilton," the Judge said. "If you can't keep your client quiet I'm going to remove him from the court."

"I'm attempting to do that Your Honour," I replied.

We tried again and Robert said, "That's me."

"Mr. Clerk, please remove Robert Fisher from the court."

Robert left without resisting. The Clerk returned and the trial continued. The officer completed his testimony by saying he had seen the old man being roughed up and thrown to the ground. He said the two ruffians ran away when they saw the police car coming.

The Crown Attorney then called the second constable to the witness box and he was sworn to tell the truth. He told how he and his partner had seen a struggle when they were about a block away from the bus depot and he told of chasing the two youths down the lane between 10th and 11th and told of arresting them later in the day.

"Do you see the people you arrested in the courtroom?"

"That's Brian Fisher setting behind Mr. Hamilton." He said, "but I don't see his brother."

"Will the defence admit the identity of the other accused?" the Crown asked.

"No Your Honour," I said. "I think he should be identified in the usual way."

"Bring in Robert Fisher," the judge ordered.

The Clerk and a police officer went out the door to the hall.

We waited for a considerable time but no one showed up. Finally the Clerk came in and whispered something to the judge. He said, "We'll take a short recess," and left the courtroom.

Not knowing what was going on, the Crown Prosecutor and I just waited. After a while the first police officer came in and whispered something to the prosecutor.

At about the same time, the Judge returned to the bench and announced, "It appears that the accused Robert Fisher has left the building. We'll have to adjourn the case for another week. When we start again it will be at 10 a.m."

When I questioned Robert later in my office, he said, "The judge said to get out. There was no one in the hall to tell me to wait or anything else, so I went home."

The case didn't proceed the next week as the Crown Attorney was again having trouble getting hold of a witness. We did however get started about three weeks later.

The Crown began by calling the second officer again and he asked, "Do you see the other person in the courtroom you saw at the bus depot?"

"I can't be sure but he looked like Robert Fisher. We chased the two down the lane but they split up and we lost them. When we went to the Fisher home, the boys denied being anywhere near the bus depot."

I didn't ask any questions and the prosecutor called the older gentlemen to the stand. After getting his name, the Crown Attorney asked: "Were you attacked by two youths outside the bus depot on the 10th of July?"

"Yes I was."

"Did you know them?"

"No."

"Do you see them in the courtroom?"

"No."

It was obvious my clients were Aboriginal and I knew there were Fishers living in Sioux Valley, so I was surprised when the witness said he didn't know them.

The explanation for his denial came to light later when a City of Brandon detective told me the reason there had been so many delays in getting the case to trial. It was because the older gentleman didn't want to testify. To get him to court the Crown Prosecutor had to arrest him and put him in the Brandon jail three times.

Without saying a word, it was obvious the gentleman was telling the prosecutor and the legal system that their conduct in arresting him wasn't proper. If he didn't want to have the boys prosecuted, what business was it of the prosecutor and the police to do so? I'm sure each arrest stiffened his resolve not to play the white man's game.

The Fisher brothers were often in trouble with the law and became repeat legal aid clients, but they were less imaginative than the McIvors. When they were caught red handed we pleaded guilty.

On one occasion they were in police custody on suspicion of having broken into Bernie Coleman's law office. Someone had been in his office and had been rifling through his files. The boys denied it was them, as they always did. When I advised the police I would be acting, they were released and weren't charged.

They seemed to be in the category of "round up the usual suspects" of Casablanca fame.

Part Two

Prelude

Having been asked many times how I came to be appointed to the Court of Queen's Bench, I will answer the question as best I can. The simple answer is, "I don't know." I can however describe the appointment process as I saw it.

The Manitoba Court of Appeal, Court of Queen's Bench and the County Courts were all established by the Province of Manitoba, but all their judges were appointed by the federal government. The Prime Minister appointed all the judges of the Supreme Court of Canada and all the Chief Justices and Associate Chief Justices in the provinces. The other, or *puisne* judges, of those courts were appointed by the federal Minister of Justice.

As I understand the process, the Minister would seek suggestions or obtain information on possible appointees through one of his staff people and from people they called on for all sorts of advice in the provinces. I didn't know who the influential advisors were, but the word would get out that a new judge was to be appointed and people passed on their suggestions to those they thought might be influential.

From what I saw, the government in power usually appointed people who had been recommended to it as good lawyers. They wanted judges who would do a good job. Every once in a while a person who had not supported the political party in power was appointed, so the government could say it did not only appoint those who supported it.

It wasn't widely known or discussed but I had heard of some Chief Justices in Canada exercising a veto. If the government asked them if a certain person would be an acceptable judge in their court, and the Chief Justice didn't think they would be, he could say no.

A lawyer's performance in court was probably a major factor in whether he or she was selected or not. Were they considered to be a good lawyer? Would they bring any particular expertise to the court? Neither Brian Dickson nor Roy Matas were known to have a lot of courtroom experience but they had outstanding qualities the courts needed. Both had extensive experience in commercial matters and commercial law. Both became outstanding judges and Brian Dickson ended up as one of the best and strongest Chief Justices the Supreme Court of Canada ever had.

I had a few things going for me, I was told. I had done a lot of civil and criminal work in the trial courts, the Court of Appeal, and had two cases in the Supreme Court of Canada. I regularly attended the Manitoba Bar meetings and annual conventions. I was a Q. C., had been a Bencher of the Law Society for a number of years, and was the Chairman of its Discipline Committee when I was being considered.

The most important factor, I believe, was that there had not been a 'country appointee' on the Court of Queen's Bench since Justice Ferguson of Minnedosa died a few years earlier. Several names were being mentioned in the weeks leading up to Justice Frank Bastin's retirement. Two of them were outstanding Winnipeg lawyers and my name was being mentioned as well. I was the only one who lived and practiced outside Winnipeg.

It was a thrill when I received a phone call from Justice Minister John Turner on December 23, 1971, during which he said I was appointed to the Supreme Court of Manitoba. The slight slip in nomenclature didn't bother me.

Within minutes, Chief Justice Tritschler phoned, congratulated me and asked me to be in his office the next morning. Almost as soon as he hung up, another call came in. The speaker only said "My Lord." It was Chief Justice Sam Freedman extending a welcome to the bench.

In the morning I was greeted by the other Q. B. Justices; Israel Nitikman, Louis Deniset, Jimmy Wilson, John Hunt, Roy Matas and John Soloman.

The Chief and I agreed that my swearing in would take place in Brandon a few days after New Years and that my first assignment would be to hear whatever was on the Brandon docket the following week. I rushed down to Malabars to have a judge's gown made. If it was not ready for the swearing in, Justice Nitikman had one I could borrow. As it turned out, the gown was ready.

My swearing-in took place in the Brandon courthouse. Justice Nitikman represented Chief Justice Tritschler and chaired the proceedings. Chief Justice Freedman represented the Court of Appeal and Lieutenant Governor Jack McKague swore me in. Other judges filled one of the jury boxes and Lorna, judges' wives and our children were in the other jury box. Lawyers and their wives were there from all over the province. Some city dignitaries said a bit and my partner, Ozzie Hirschfield, brought congratulations from the Bar.

A reception followed. That allowed me to thank the people who came from all over Manitoba. The McIvor brothers were there and I was delighted when they gave me a little box with a new golf ball in it. When I showed it to a friend, he said, "Wouldn't you know, it's an English ball and it's illegal."

A few local parties followed on the weekend that enabled our friends to chant 'Here come da judge," whenever I moved to another group.

A Change of Pace

As a judge, my approach to the law had to change. No longer did I represent a client and try to achieve the best result I could for him or her. No longer would I concentrate on finding points of law that would ensure a win for a client. My task as a judge was to be totally independent. I would have to listen to and assess the testimony given by all the witnesses in every case, listen to the arguments of the lawyers and make findings of fact, in other words, decide what happened.

After that I would have to read the cases the lawyers asked me to consider, and possibly others I might think were relevant. My decision might turn on who I believed and who I did not, or it might turn on my interpretation of the wording of a statute or the decision of another court in Canada or abroad where judges had considered the effect of the law in similar circumstances. My decision would bring the proceedings in the Queen's Bench to an end. A dissatisfied litigant could appeal my decision to the Court of Appeal.

The change from being a lawyer to becoming a judge was neither dramatic nor difficult because of the time I had spent in court, but it was challenging and a lot of work none the less.

In making findings of fact I might accept all the evidence of one party and reject all the evidence of the opposing party, but as cases came before me, I found that important facts or explanations were found in the evidence of both sides.

I quickly came to realize that a major factor in many of my decisions was the arguments presented by the lawyers and the principles of law they adapted and applied to the case. Some lawyers are stronger than others. Some examine and cross examine witnesses better than others and some are better at legal research. Some specialize in certain types of cases and others limit their work to a specific area of civil law. Some lawyers do only criminal law and Crown Attorneys do nothing else.

It is natural for witnesses to exaggerate the facts that support their or their friend's position and to gloss over the facts that are not as favourable to their cause. I found I had to reserve my decision in every case of any length. I would have to read over my notes and compare what the various witnesses had said. I don't think any judge can say his assessment of every witness is always 100% correct, but every effort has to be made to come to what, as a trial judge, you consider to be an accurate conclusion.

Trials, while they present serious issues to be resolved, are also a mirror of human nature. Very often the parties and their witnesses are nervous and uncomfortable with the trial process and the limitations it places on what they are permitted to say. Many doctors and engineers, unless they have been properly prepared by their lawyer, become frustrated when a lawyer interrupts them to object to an opinion being outside their area of expertise or because it has no relevance to the matters in dispute. Some witnesses will snap at aggressive counsel or turn to the judge for a ruling that will let them say what they want. I had to explain the reason for a valid objection or tell the witness he or she could give their evidence in their own way.

Some of these exchanges could be quite humorous, but I learned early on that I should never laugh out loud. I laughed in one case in which I was presiding in Court Room No. 5. The case involved the demolition of a rundown building by the City of Winnipeg and the owner was suing for the loss of the building and anticipated profits.

When the owner was giving evidence he asked me to turn around and look at the wall behind my chair. He persisted in saying, "My Lord, you have to look at the wall."

I ignored his request and just kept looking at him. After several futile attempts to get me on his side, he said, "My Lord, there's a big crack in the wall behind you. If I owned the Court House it would be declared uninhabitable and the City inspectors would tear it down."

I wasn't ready for the remark and I laughed. Fortunately, the witness laughed too. After I stopped laughing it took about ten minutes to get everyone to return to a proper degree of decorum. Because of that experience I never laughed in court again. Cases are too serious and too important to the contesting parties. I found that if I, as the presiding authority, didn't laugh, others would contain themselves as well.

Eight person Queen's Bench, taken in 1973

Tradition

From the blank stares that sometimes appeared on the faces of jurors and witnesses, it was clear that many do not understand court practices. Nor do they understand many of the traditions courts follow. At times the lack of understanding is embarrassing. The titles applied to judges are also strange and unfamiliar. They certainly differ from what a viewer would learn from watching Perry Mason on TV. The gowns the various players wear are different. They can't be English, some think, because no one is wearing a wig. The judges never think it necessary to explain and I can't recall doing so either.

The manner in which judges are addressed *is* based on English tradition, although that country has made some changes over the years that haven't been adopted in Canada. At the time of the cases described earlier, a Justice of the Peace was addressed as Your Worship in court. He probably wore a suit and tie and seldom heard contested cases. People would plead guilty to a ticket they had received and the 'judge,' who did not have to be legally trained, would apply a fine. A magistrate heard pleas of guilty and tried minor criminal charges as well.

As the authority to hear cases expanded, a Provincial Court was established and the former magistrates became provincial judges and were called Your Honour. They heard criminal cases involving adults and juveniles. Over time their jurisdiction was expanded by the *Criminal Code of Canada*. They can now hear most cases with the consent of the accused or, if the accused wants to be tried by a judge and jury, a provincial judge will conduct a Preliminary Inquiry to see if there is enough evidence to warrant a trial in the Court of Queen's Bench with a jury.

Murder cases still have to be heard by a judge and jury in the superior court of the province where the alleged crime took place. Some provinces call that court the Court of Queen's Bench, while others use Superior Court of Justice, Supreme Court (of the province) or Cour supérieure. Each province has its own Court of Appeal.

In Ottawa there is the Federal Court which deals with cases involving federal legislation and the Tax Court, each with their own Courts of Appeal. The Supreme Court of Canada hears appeals from all the Courts of Appeal. In most cases the Supreme Court of Canada chooses which cases it will hear. If it declines, the decision of the Court of Appeal is final and binding.

Provincial Judges are addressed as 'Your Honour'. The judges of the superior courts are referred to as My Lord, Your Lordship or Mr. Justice---. Women judges are addressed as Madam Justice --- or My Lady. The same titles are used in Courts of Appeal and the Supreme Court of Canada.

Someone once took me to task for being called a *Superior* Court Judge. The term 'superior' only refers to the superior or more extensive jurisdiction the federally appointed judges have. For example, the Court of Queen's Bench has jurisdiction to hear almost all civil (non-criminal) cases and the criminal trials that are to be heard with a jury. Until abolition of the County Courts (1984 in Manitoba) and its amalgamation with the Queen's Bench, the County Court Judges heard criminal cases without a jury and managed the administration of all wills and estates.

Some confusion and embarrassment results when a lawyer refers to a judge as My Lord or My Lady on the street or at a social event. I found it odd if I was at a hockey game and a lawyer said 'hello my Lord'. England, from where our traditions came, has cured the problem with the establishment of less formal rules outside the courtroom.

When visiting the High Court in England in the '80s, I met a Superior court trial judge, then sat in his courtroom as he dealt with a case. When the case was adjourned to his private Chambers he asked me to go along. The counsel on the case wanted to give the judge some information in private so the next witness would not be embarrassed. The lawyers, who had addressed the judge as 'My Lord' in court, called him 'Judge' in his private Chambers. At noon the judge invited me to his Inn of Court. As we gathered in an ante room before going in for lunch, I noticed that lawyers and judges were calling him "George."

When I spoke to him about my confusion, he said the present practice is to use the title 'My Lord' in court. On other occasions judges are referred to as 'Judge,' and if the lawyers know the Judge well they will use his first name. He said the Canadian practice was abolished long ago. I like the English system. There were only two lawyers who always called me 'Judge' when out of court. Both were first class barristers – Darcy McCaffrey Q. C. and George Dangerfield Q. C. who had spent some time as a barrister in England.

While on the topic of lawyers, they are referred to as 'Counsel' in court and refer to one another as 'my learned friend'. While England maintains a distinction between a Barrister and a Solicitor, that distinction has never applied in Canada. On being called to the bar (becoming entitled to practice law) lawyers are designated as barristers and solicitors. Those who practice in the courts may call themselves barristers if they wish and those who do only commercial work may use 'barrister and solicitor' or 'solicitor.'

The title "Queen's Counsel" is an honour bestowed by Provincial Attorneys General, supposedly to recognize some degree of proficiency. The practice of awarding the designation is less in favour today than it used to be. Some provinces have done away with it altogether and in others it depends on the attitude of the government of the day. Manitoba does not name Q. C.s at the present time. In England, barristers choose to 'take silk'. That entitles them to use the designation Q. C. but their manner of practice is, or used to be, curtailed. They do civil and criminal trials, but the last I heard, the client has to be referred to them by a solicitor.

In criminal cases, the prosecution is always conducted in the name of the sovereign, thus the government lawyer is referred to as 'the Crown Prosecutor' or 'Crown Counsel.' The lawyer who represents or acts for the person on trial is the 'defence counsel' or 'counsel for the defence.' In civil cases the lawyers are referred to as 'counsel' for the plaintiff or defendant.

The dress worn by judges in the various courts in Manitoba varies. Justices of the Peace usually wear business suits. Magistrates often wear a black gown over a business suit and Provincial judges wear a red and white gown over a barrister's vest. Justices of the Court of Appeal and the Supreme Court of Canada wear a Q. C. type black gown, although the Supreme Court Judges have more ornate red and ermine gowns for formal occasions.

When he was Chief Justice of the Court of Queen's Bench in Manitoba between December 1946 and January 1962, E. K. Williams introduced a colourful gown to his court. It is similar to the gown worn by some judges in England. It is a zippered purple robe with a red sash, black scarf and cummerbund worn over a white shirt with a separate winged collar and white tabs. Its large rose taffeta cuffs can be replaced if stained or worn out from constant note taking. Queen's Counsel wear black silk gowns and other lawyers wear ordinary 'stuff' black gowns, vest, wing collar and tabs.

Rules of Evidence

The rules of what a witness may say while giving testimony in the witness stand are quite restrictive. A person giving evidence may say what he or she did, saw or heard an accused or the other party to the case say, but little else. They are not supposed to say what someone else told them. If a lawyer wants to know what another person said, he is supposed to call that person as a witness. One reason for the rule is that a judge or jury cannot see the other person and consider whether they are being truthful and persuasive or not.

This limitation certainly prolongs a trial. Every witness who attends the scene of a killing, for example, must only say what he did and saw. There are some exceptions but a trial is structured to hear from a succession of witnesses who paint a picture the judge and jury can understand.

If a witness starts to talk about something that is not within his own knowledge but will have no bearing on the outcome of the trial, opposing counsel will often remain silent and not object, but if they start to discuss a matter that is in dispute, the lawyer will say: "I object my Lord."

When that happens the judge may say, "Objection sustained," if he agrees with the challenge or he may ask the lawyers to present their opinions and arguments. The judge must be careful not to allow inadmissible evidence to be given. If he permits inadmissible evidence to be heard by a jury, the Court of Appeal, if asked to review the case, may overturn the verdict and order a new trial.

Occasionally, a judge may have to take a chance and allow some questionable evidence to be given. If the witness goes too far, the judge will have to tell the jury to ignore the improper evidence when they are trying to arrive at a verdict.

I had to bend the rules in a murder trial I heard with a jury in The Pas. The Crown prosecutor called several police officers and a succession of people who had been in a house where a death had occurred. An Aboriginal witness was being questioned and when he started to reply, defence counsel said "I object. He can't tell us what others said." I agreed and the Crown attorney asked another question.

The question dealt with what various people were saying.

The witness started "When I came in Johnny told me ..." (Johnny was a bystander and not the accused.)

"I object," defence counsel said.

I told the witness he couldn't tell us what someone else told him and urged him to tell only what he saw or did. I ended by saying, "Just tell us what happened in your own words."

The witness replied, "I'm trying to, but they, pointing to the lawyers, won't let me."

He had a point. I suggested the witness be allowed to continue uninterrupted and said I would stop him if he went too far. As it turned out he didn't breach any of the rules of evidence but he thought he had to describe the scene and tell what others were doing and saying, so the jury would understand why he really hadn't seen anything of importance. He said he knew the deceased and the accused but he didn't see what happened.

Rights of the Accused

A charge of murder is often laid by the Crown in cases where a death appears to have resulted from an assault, a shooting, or some other illegal act. My task as the presiding judge in a trial with a jury was to monitor the proceedings, see that the procedural rules were followed, see that the accused had a fair trial, and to instruct the jury on the law and tell them their possible verdicts.

One of the first jury cases I presided over dealt with a death that occurred outside the hotel in Elie. An argument had developed over a cheque in the beer parlour where the accused, the deceased, and most of the witnesses had been drinking heavily. The argument continued outside the hotel until the deceased ended up lying on the sidewalk with blood oozing from an ear.

One witness said he saw the accused lift the deceased and drop him on his back on the sidewalk. Other witnesses said they had no idea how he got onto the sidewalk or what caused the head injury the Coroner said caused his death. The accused took the witness stand and denied lifting or dropping the man.

An RCMP corporal interviewed the accused the next afternoon. After asking a few questions the Crown Attorney asked that the jury be excluded so a *voir dire* could be held to determine whether his conversation with the accused was admissible. A *voir dire* ("the truth to speak") enables a judge to hear evidence a party wants to introduce, in the absence of the jury. It is a mini-trial within the trial but without the jury. After the judge hears the evidence he has to rule on whether it can be heard by the jury or not.

During his investigation, the RCMP corporal suggested to the accused that he had been in a fight with the deceased. He said the accused replied: "Not a fight," then added, "well he was drunk. I had an argument with him about a bad cheque."

"Did you touch him?" the Mountie asked.

His answer was "just like that," indicating a brushing aside motion with one hand. He added, "To be honest with you I was pretty drunk."

The constable then asked, "Did he hit the ground?"

The accused answered, "Yeah."

The Mountie then said "Did he get up?"

He said, "No, they carried him away."

"At this point," the Mountie continued, "I gave him the standard warning. I advised him that he possibly would be charged with a criminal offence of assault, or manslaughter, murder, that type. I advised him that he didn't have to say anything, he had no hope from any promise or favour and the usual police warning. I asked him if he understood the warning."

Defence counsel asked him his exact words and the officer replied: "You have nothing to hope from any promise or favour. You need not say anything. Anything you do say may be used in evidence at your trial."

The officer then asked, "Do you want to give a statement?"

He answered, "I'd rather see my lawyer."

I ruled that the statement was not admissible and could not be presented to the jury. The questions and answers given before the warning, were not to be heard by the jury and the comments made after the warning were not admissible as the accused said he wanted to talk to a lawyer. The comments of the accused were not crucial to the case but an accused must be given the opportunity to seek the advice of a lawyer.

After the Crown had finished with all its witnesses, the defence counsel called the accused to testify. He said the deceased grabbed him by the shirt and continued arguing about the cheque. He said all he wanted was to get free of him so he pushed him away. He said the deceased stumbled and landed on his back on the sidewalk.

The jury took some time to reach a verdict but finally found the accused not guilty. I assumed they had trouble knowing how drunk the various witnesses were and whether the allegation of one witness that the accused had picked the deceased up and threw him to the ground was true or imagined. The other possibility was that the deceased merely fell and hit his head. I don't have a record of what counsel said in their addresses to the jury, but the jury's decision settled the case. Personally, I seldom disagreed with a jury's decision. Juries are made up of people from the judicial district where the incident occurred and they are the ones who have the responsibility for deciding who to believe and to decide, as best they can, what happened.

The jury's delay in arriving at a decision may have been based on my caution to them that accused persons do not have to prove their innocence. They are entitled to be found not guilty unless the prosecution has established their guilt beyond a reasonable doubt.

Reasonable Doubt

The Drunk Driving Case and The Case of the Mighty Moose were both borderline, where the accused might easily have been convicted. They were not convicted and it will be noted that in each case, as defence counsel, I had suggested to the trial judge that the Crown had not proved its case beyond a reasonable doubt. Under our legal system a person cannot be convicted just because the police think or are even convinced the person is guilty. Nor can a person be convicted just because a judge thinks they probably committed the crime with which they are charged. A person is entitled to go free unless or until the Crown, representing the Queen, has proved their guilt to the point where no reasonable doubt of their guilt remains.

At some times and places people accused of a crime and even a misdemeanour have been convicted and put to death on a suspicion of guilt. People might be pilloried or stoned to death or drowned. Women suspected of being witches were dumped into water. If they floated they were branded as a witch. If they sunk, that was taken as a sign they were innocent.

In some church courts, people had to convince those who were trying them that they were innocent. If they couldn't do that they might be imprisoned indefinitely or fined or publicly shamed. At one time in England people were thrown into 'Debtors Prison' if they couldn't pay their rent, a loan, or some other debt. Charles Dickens, born in 1812, brought that sort of case to the attention of the public in the many novels and short stories he wrote prior to his death in 1870.

Canada became a semi-independent nation as a member of the British Commonwealth of Nations after various Canadian provinces were annexed or ceded their jurisdiction to England. The Dominion of Canada was formed with the passage of the *British North America Act* by the British Parliament in 1867. That document defined the federal and provincial areas of jurisdiction. The administration of justice was left to the provinces but the federal government retained the authority to enact criminal law. That included the authority to deal with young persons, thus the former *Juvenile Delinquents Act* and the more recent *Young Offenders and Youth Criminal Justice Acts*. The provinces had control over education and the right to establish municipal governments and school boards.

Canada based its court system and its basic laws mainly on those in Britain, and to a lesser extent on those established in France under the *Napoleonic Code*. Canadian courts used to rely heavily on decisions of the various courts in England. That is less so today as Canadian statute law and the Canadian common law generally supplies sufficient precedents to enable trial courts and the Supreme Court of Canada to continue to refine Canadian law.

One British decision of the last century that has been adopted by the Canadian justice system still provides the basis for the Canadian law requiring proof beyond a reasonable doubt before any citizen can be convicted of a crime. The principle is the same whether it is being applied by a trial judge or by a jury.

The English case of *Woolmington v Director of Public Prosecutions* [1935] Appeal Cases 462, confirmed the principle of reasonable doubt, which applies to most situations where a citizen is accused of having committed a crime.

The famous comment of Lord Sankey in that case explained the principle:

> *Throughout the web of English Criminal Law one golden thread is always to be seen, that it is the duty of the prosecution to prove the prisoner's guilt (subject to what I have already said as to the defence of insanity and subject also to any statutory exception.) If, at the end of and on the whole of the case, there is a reasonable doubt, created by the evidence given by either the prosecution or the prisoner, as to whether the prisoner killed the deceased with a malicious intention, the prosecution has not made out the case and the prisoner is entitled to an acquittal.*

Applying that principle to the case of the swerving cabinet maker, he was acquitted because, in spite of any doubts the judge might have had, the Crown had not been able to prove his guilt beyond a reasonable doubt. The same principle will be seen in other cases I describe. Some people don't believe in that approach, but it remains a cornerstone of our system of justice.

Contempt of Court

When sitting in Chambers one morning, something occurred that took my mind back to the troubled Mayor McBride, trying to keep order in the courtroom during the trial of the marksman who had downed the moose. It took many years but as they say, 'What Goes Around, Comes Around.' I was tested when an inebriated or ill spectator continuously disrupted a hearing by interjecting disruptive and obscene remarks. I couldn't concentrate on the submission of the lawyer who was looking for some sort of order.

'Chambers' in this setting means a hearing devoted to a variety of relatively short applications based on affidavits where lawyers seek an interpretation of a document or some procedural direction. A small courtroom is used for the purpose. No witnesses are called, but a dozen or more matters may be on the list.

Ken Price, a friendly giant of a man, was my clerk. He sat at a desk in front of me and had all the files in front of him. After I had recognized and called on the Q Cs in their order of precedence at the bar, Ken called the rest of the cases in the order they appeared on the list. Occasionally a party would ask to have his or her case heard last, and the Crown Attorney in this case had done that. He knew that a person who wasn't represented by a lawyer had an interest in one case.

Ken's task was to receive additional documents from the lawyers as they argued, stamp them and pass them up to me. If people in the audience started to talk to one another when a lawyer was making his or her submission, he would holler 'Order'. It was up to him to maintain order and decorum during the hearing.

I was wearing my black Q. C. gown with the traditional wing collar and white tabs and Ken wore a black gown but without the fancy tabs and collar. The lawyers were not gowned.

It took quite a while for the lawyers to present their applications but everything was peaceful until about 11:30. I had noticed a woman squirming in the front row but she had been quiet. An older man with a clerical collar was sitting next to her and kept trying to calm her down. She finally came to the end of her tether. She staggered to her feet, brushed the clergyman aside when he tried to restrain her and said "Hurry up," looking at the lawyer who was speaking. When the clergyman tried to get her to sit down she spoke even louder, "I haven't got all day you know."

She certainly caught my attention. I could no longer hear the lawyer and certainly couldn't concentrate on what he was saying, so I said, "Madam, will you please be quiet."

That didn't solve the problem. The clergyman was still doing his best but she turned on him and pushed his arms away. I asked the lawyers to wait a minute and whispered to Ken Price to go and speak to the woman and ask her to be quiet.

Ken nearly fainted on the spot. In spite of his size, he was apparently a pussycat and I hadn't realized that. He squirmed, looked pleadingly at me, but was still in his seat behind his desk. It took repeated urging on my part to get him to leave his protected spot and go towards the woman. He still didn't speak to her directly but sought the help of the clergyman next to her. The two spoke, then Ken hurried back to his protected seat.

The woman was quiet for a few minutes but as the lawyer was gathering steam she looked at me and said in a voice everyone in the room could hear: "Who's that guy up there in the choir gown?"

"Ma'am" I said in as quiet and controlled a manner as I could muster, "you're making it impossible for me to hear the lawyers. Will you please be quiet. We'll get to your case before too long; by the way, which is your case?"

Ken, now back on familiar ground, spoke up, "number 11 my Lord, estreatal of bail."

Estreatal is an application by the Crown for the forfeiture of bail. When accused people are awaiting their trial it is common for them to be released on bail. Those with a prior record or a history of not showing up for court when they are supposed to, may be denied bail. Those let out on bail often have to put up money to guarantee their attendance when required. In questionable situations, an accused person may have to get someone with property to pledge it as security. If the person shows up and is tried, the bail automatically expires. If the person fails to show up or can't be found, the Crown may apply to have the money or property forfeited and turned over to the government.

As soon as I heard "bail estreatal" I said "Oh Oh" to myself and assumed the woman was a prisoner who had been on bail and was now in custody. In any event, trying to ignore the interruption, I nodded at the lawyer to continue. It sounded as if he was winding up his submission. The woman was apparently not as optimistic as I was and she spoke up once again.

"I'm sorry, but if you don't leave I'll have the clerk remove you," I said in as firm a tone as I thought appropriate. She wasn't impressed and Ken nearly fell off his chair when I said, "Mr. Clerk, remove that woman from the courtroom."

"I'm sorry ma'am" I said, "I'll have to ask you to leave the courtroom. You can come back when we get to your case."

"The hell with you, I'm staying, and I want my case heard right now. I've been here for an hour and a half and that guy, (pointing to a Crown Attorney) told me it would only take ten minutes. What is this, a dentist's office?"

"Mr. Clerk" I repeated so no doubt would remain about my resolve, "remove that woman from the courtroom."

Ken got up and headed for the offending female. You could see the wheels turning as he considered his options and whether there was any escape from this impossible task. He reached out to take her arm and she batted his away. He seemed to be considering his options. "How will I get hold of this wildcat? What if she moves and I touch a part of her I shouldn't?"

He tried to persuade the woman to be quiet. He then decided he had to remove her but every time he extended his arm to grasp hers she would turn away. Ken, always the gentleman, obviously couldn't figure out how to grab hold of the woman and he clearly wasn't prepared to manhandle her.

At that point the man sitting next to her spoke up and shed some light on the situation. He said he was a Prison Chaplain at Headingly Gaol and had come to court to give the woman some moral support. He said she was on "medication," and was inclined to get upset. I had some doubts about his diagnosis, but his next explanation struck a familiar chord. He explained that she had gone bail for an accused. She wanted her bail money returned to her and not taken by the Crown, because the reason the accused couldn't make his court appearance as required was that he was in jail at that time on another charge. I asked the Crown Attorney to go into the hall to discuss the matter with the woman and see if her allegation was correct.

The woman wasn't listening, as she was enjoying keeping Ken Price at bay. She was doing very well at keeping from being forced out of the courtroom and Ken was still wondering how he could carry out my directive.

His dilemma was fortuitously settled and his secret prayers were answered when Alfie Weeks charged into the room. Alfie, a survivor of the Korean War, was a Sheriff's officer who was always looking for another battle to be won. He was the protector of the courthouse and the guardian of its law-abiding occupants. Woe betide anyone who thought they could cause trouble or disrupt a sitting of the court. Someone who had seen what was happening must have called him.

Alfie was certainly the judges' guardian and loyal friend. He was at his best when jury trials were in progress. He could detect dangerous supporters of a prisoner and would search them and confiscate knives and other potential weapons. He was in heaven when someone gave him some lip. One of his favourite pastimes was pinning someone to the wall and giving their arms a twist while he frisked them. When he was around, after these preliminaries which I presume were intended to convey a message, no one would dare disrupt a trial or a judge in the performance of his duties.

He preferred action to words. In his bulldog manner, Alfie marched up to the woman, grabbed her by an arm and had her in the corridor before she knew what had happened. She did however take time, as she was leaving, to give me a parting shot. She turned towards me and mouthed what I should do to myself. Ken saw, but others may not have. As the clergyman left, he apologized, saying his friend was not herself today. We heard a few whimpers through the closing door, then silence reigned once more.

I called a recess so we could compose ourselves before returning to complete the list. Ken escorted me out of court but didn't say a word. He was still in a state of shock. Nothing like this had ever happened to him before. When we were back in court he called number 11 on the list, but no one responded. The Crown Attorney must have left as well.

There were enough spectators in Court to relay and embellish the incident. Reports of what happened in Chambers circulated like wildfire. The court staff revelled in the humour and novelty of the situation. I know that Ken was the target of some good-natured kidding. The staff and lawyers were too polite to tell me what they thought of my part in the vaudeville show but I enjoyed it immensely.

Ken later asked me if I was going to hold the woman in contempt of court and I said I was not going to do that. Ken looked relieved. I don't think he ever wanted to see her again. The "Chambers lady" was either drunk or on medication of some sort, and she probably had good reason to be upset with her faithless friend who had flown the coop and placed her hard-earned bail money in jeopardy. I was also sure I couldn't make the impression Alfie had made. Her insults hadn't hurt me and hadn't really placed the administration of justice in disrepute, but any punitive action I could have taken might have. I decided to let the matter drop but it has remained one of my most interesting experiences with the living law.

Judges do occasionally hold people in contempt of court, but I only did that once and it was a woman I sent to jail. Although I had ordered her to do so on several occasions, she refused to tell me the location of a child her estranged husband was entitled to visit. I sent her to the Jail for Women in Portage la Prairie to remain there until she purged her contempt. She made the disclosure after a week and was released.

My First Drug Case

In May of 1972 I heard a jury case involving Hersh Wolch. He later became well known as an effective defence counsel but in that case he was the Crown Prosecutor. The charge was drug trafficking. Most of the evidence dealt with the manner in which the police, with several vehicles, followed the accused from the airport to a hotel and other places in the city. It was clear to the police the driver was running amber lights and speeding to make sure he was not being followed.

Several bags of MDA were seized from his room in the Fort Garry Hotel. The police were in an adjacent room and monitored those coming and going from the room where the accused was. They finally entered and seized a supply of narcotics. The case was interesting as it showed the coordinated work of a number of police officers but, looking back, it was significant because of the sentence I imposed. I sentenced the accused to nine years in the Penitentiary, consecutive to a five year term he was still serving on another conviction.

Drug cases were few and far between in the early 70s. It didn't take many convictions and sentences like this one before defence counsel and the clients they represented decided it was safer to avoid a jury trial and take their chances before a judge alone.

Hersh Wolch became a household name when he became involved in the release from prison of David Milgaard who had been wrongly identified as the killer of a nurse in Saskatchewan twenty or so years before. With scientific developments, it had become possible to re-examine evidence found at the scene of a murder and test it for DNA. Milgaard had to be released, as have other prisoners, when the evidence that was used to identify and convict them at their trial didn't match their DNA. Compensation for Milgaard's wrongful conviction has been paid.

Juries

It is unclear where and when the use of juries began. They were certainly in use in medieval England and used people from the community to decide what happened and whether the accused was guilty or not. In the 1800s, there was quite a bit of legislation in England that regularized their use. In more recent times England has further revised its system. One of those changes has been to permit a judge to accept a verdict from ten or eleven jurors where the jury has failed to reach a unanimous decision. It is in the discretion of the judge to say how long a jury should spend trying to reach a unanimous verdict before the lesser numbers will do. Judges usually wait at least two hours before agreeing to accept a less than unanimous verdict.

In Canada at the present time, if a jury returns to the courtroom and advises the judge they cannot agree on a unanimous verdict, the judge will likely ask them to keep trying and may continue to do that for a day or more. He will certainly remind them that if they don't agree, the trial and presentation of the evidence will have to be done all over again before another jury. Judges will normally not release a jury until everything possible has been done to get them to agree. While I followed that practice myself, I always felt I was being unfair to the majority of the jurors. I had the feeling at times that I was putting too much pressure on them to agree.

Hung juries, those unable to agree, are not a major issue in Canada but the delay in empanelling a new jury at a time when a judge and all the lawyers are available, results in lengthy delays and additional cost to the system. I recommend that Justice Canada examine the reasons for the change in England and bring the Canadian law up to date. If an accused is in custody but thinks there is a good chance of being acquitted, he or she will likely resent having to wait another year for a new trial.

In the United States, jurors may be questioned about the case after it is over but Canada has never permitted that to be done. It is against the law to question a former juror. We don't know what those who have been discharged without rendering a verdict think of our system. I like to think there must be some way of asking members of hung juries, without revealing their identities, what they would think of a less than unanimous verdict being allowed.

Another problem with the jury system in Canada is, in my opinion, the way in which the judges' charge to the jury is subject to minute analysis by the higher courts. The purpose of the judge's charge is not to turn the jurors into lawyers but to help them with their deliberations. They are told to determine the facts, namely what happened and who did what. Then they are told to apply those facts to the few legal options they have. Has the guilt of the accused been established to their satisfaction? If it has, do they believe his conduct amounted to murder or manslaughter? If the facts don't satisfy the jury beyond a reasonable doubt they should find him not guilty. The parameters are fairly simple and the judges' role is to keep the charge as simple and understandable as possible.

If a judge goes on at length he will lose the jury, either out of boredom or because too much legalese is impossible for the jury to absorb in the hour or so the judge spends talking to them. Some charges take a day or more to deliver. When the Supreme Court of Canada says the judge should have given a more precise description of a principle of law, trial judges are obliged to follow their wording when dealing with the matter when it comes before the next jury they instruct. The result is that charges have become longer and longer and more convoluted than necessary.

In my opinion, if the higher courts think it necessary to use very specific wordings, the wordings they recommend should be incorporated in a booklet to be distributed to all jurors as soon as they are selected. That of course might not achieve the desired result. The judge must still address the jury in language they will understand.

In a case in Winnipeg some years ago, a jury was in the jury room trying to decide upon their verdict. They sent a note to the judge asking him to explain what 'reasonable doubt' meant. He repeated what he had said earlier but after a while another note was delivered to him by the sheriff, asking the same question. Mr. Justice

Louis Deniset of our court decided he had to reply in language they would understand.

While I may not have his exact words, he said in his delightful Franco-Manitoban accent: “You know in baseball if the batter is running to first base and the base umpire isn’t sure whether he got there before the ball or not, the doubt goes to the runner. That’s reasonable doubt.” The acquittal of the accused was not appealed. If it had been appealed to the highest court, I’m not sure what it would have thought of his very practical description of an important legal principle.

From my experience, both as counsel and as judge, I know a jury can quickly lose track of the message the judge is trying to convey and become confused, and some will doze off as the judge goes on and on talking about the evidence they have already heard and the intricacies of the law.

The problem is in the system. Many serious cases that have been decided by juries go on to the Court of Appeal and then to the Supreme Court of Canada. The appellate courts examine the law in great detail and the judges, if they find fault with the charge to the jury by the trial judge, suggest lengthy wordings that should have been used and should be used in future cases. Long, repetitive and confusing charges have accordingly become the model trial judges follow.

In my opinion it is time for another look at the jury system. I was part of a panel appointed by the Law Reform Commission of Canada which was involved in a study on the jury in the 1970s when Frank Muldoon, later Mr. Justice Muldoon of the Federal Court, was the Chairman. The ultimate report of March 1982 recommended the retention of juries.

In the part dealing with judges’ charges to juries the report recommended that the Canadian Judicial Council prepare standard jury instructions. I don’t think that is the appropriate body to do that but someone in the administrative branch of government, such as the Minister of Justice, should. It also recommended that the requirement that juries be unanimous remain. Those findings need another look.

The cost of re-trials and the resulting delays should be re-examined and the results of the change in England should be examined. What benefits have been achieved by the English changes? Has there been any diminution in the principles that protect an accused? What problems has it overcome? It is time to examine the English system again to see if our system is antiquated. Do other jurisdictions have features that would improve our antiquated one?

The Bank House

Between 1972 and 1983 I had fifty-four jury trials and innumerable civil trials and applications. My first contested civil trial was fascinating and challenging at the same time.

Portage la Prairie is an old town by prairie standards. It and Winnipeg were trading posts in the fur trade era. Fort Garry was established at the forks of the Red and Assiniboine rivers in the days of the Hudson's Bay Company and Portage la Prairie was originally Fort Lorraine. Towns with permanent residents grew as the Canadian Pacific Railroad and branch lines brought new settlers to their soon to be constructed sod huts. The western survey, dividing 200 million acres of land into Sections and Townships, began just west of Headingley on the tenth of July 1871.

Portage, as it is usually called, existed when the Red River ox carts transported prospective farmers and their belongings to their homesteads on the prairie. A remnant of the oxcart trail is its main street, as wide as Portage Avenue in Winnipeg, which permitted the squeaking oxcarts to be dragged through the mud and clay and leave room for others going in the same or opposite direction. The broad streets were twelve oxcarts wide.

The nearby Assiniboine River had occasional shoals or gravel ridges that permitted a crossing after the spring floods had passed. In the spring of the year transportation was available by paddlewheel steamers as far upstream as Brandon. In the 1930s I recall crossing the river near Portage on a cable ferry that carried cars and passengers from one shore to the other. The ferry got stuck in the middle of the river. Our car stayed on board but my parents, with skirt lifted and pants rolled up, waded across while my second oldest sister carried me on her shoulders.

Portage lays claim to spawning one of Canada's prime ministers, Arthur Meighen, and Chief Justices McPherson and Miller. It is the Head Office of Portage Mutual Insurance Company, once maintained a large mental hospital and still has Manitoba's only jail for women.

It is on the fertile Portage plain in the midst of the best farmland in Canada. It has an old style Court House with creaky wooden floors and stately tailored stairs. Its traditional courtroom has a brass bar separating the public from the lawyers, witnesses and the judge. The long leather-inset counsel table with massive legs is probably the most ornate in the province.

When I had a sitting there that lasted for more than a day, I had to stay in the creaky old bed in the dark and dismal judges' combination office and bedchamber. (The use of hotels and motels wasn't permitted for several years.) At night I was alone in the massive edifice, save for the unseen caretaker and his family who had a suite of rooms in the basement, two floors below. It was from the door between the chambers and the courtroom that I emerged in the morning to take my turn conducting the monthly sitting of the court.

The building's law library is an antiquity in its own right. Although its supply of law books is not always up to date, it has a rolling ladder supported on a railing at the top of the upper shelves some twenty feet above the floor. I liked to find an excuse to climb it in search of an obscure case among the English Reports or Meeson and Welsby on the upper shelves.

The massive high backed judge's chair, more like a throne, was so heavy it took some exertion to hoist it to the writing desk after you sat down. The judge and lawyers were fortunate if they could hear one another as their voices disappeared into the domed ceiling thirty feet above their heads. The building equalled the grandeur of the stately homes that were being built when it was erected in the 1890s.

It was in this setting that I heard my first full civil trial, less than three weeks after my appointment to the court. I had no lessons, no instructions and no preparation, except what I had learned in law school or as a trial lawyer. There was no one to consult. I was on my own.

The case didn't have the aspect of civil disobedience of the moose fiasco but it was similar because it indicated how members of a community can become upset and involved when the world around them is not unfolding as they think it should. The case in the stately courthouse involved one of the city's other stately structures.

At one time, every town in Manitoba had at least one bank and many of them maintained a company house or a suite of rooms above the bank. The manager was not only provided with fine accommodations, but the houses were among the best in town to make certain the manager maintained a position of prestige and influence in the community. Bank managers were looked up to and their advice was regularly sought on matters of business and town affairs.

The Bank of Montreal house in Portage was a two and a half storey red brick mansion, surrounded by other stately homes, and looked across an inland lake at a quaint wooden bridge and Island Park on the other side. It was certainly one of the best homes in town.

Due to a change in policy that required managers to provide their own accommodation, the bank had to sell the home and the local manager gave a multiple listing to a local realtor. Some confusion then set in. Two offers to purchase were received and both appeared to have been accepted. The question before me was: Which is the legal and binding offer, or did both have some legal effect?

I was not given all the details, and it didn't matter in the legal context of the case, but a suggestion crept into the evidence that the "first buyer" was not as well known to the manager or the realtor as the "second buyer." It appeared they preferred to see the second, who was better known in the business community, become the new owner. Some of the antics to secure the sale for him were unorthodox, to say the least.

The bank manager, the listing agent and the first buyer had agreed that he would have until 6:00 p.m. to accept a counter offer the bank had made. In the meantime the second buyer had presented his offer to buy. When the first buyer, accompanied by a sub-agent, tried to find the manager and the listing agent so they could accept the counter offer, neither could be found. It was only after 6:00 that the manager and the agent showed up, and when they did, they took the position that the first buyer was too late and that the offer of the second buyer, which had by then been accepted, was the binding one.

Unknown to them, when the banker could not be located, the first buyer and the sub-agent notified another employee of the bank and the wife of the listing agent that the first buyer had accepted the bank's counter offer fifteen minutes before the deadline. I decided that notification amounted to sufficient compliance with the bank's terms. I found that a person cannot make a sale conditional on acceptance by a certain time and then absent himself so compliance becomes impossible.

Unlike the Moose trial, this was not a happy one, but a serious and hard-fought one, with a sense of tension in the air. None but the parties and their lawyers remained in the courtroom. The reluctant witnesses testified and abruptly left. The lawyers were left to present their arguments in peace and quiet and to try to persuade me to their particular points of view. They argued the effect of the evidence and how it related to the laws of contract, agency and real estate. As I wanted to be sure my tentative interpretation of the law was correct, I reserved my decision so I could read the authorities counsel had given me, do some further research of my own, and provide counsel with a written opinion. I found that the first buyer was the legitimate owner of the house.

That was not the end of the case. It was re-opened and expanded to include the second buyer who the bank had permitted to take possession of the house. His own lawyer became involved and sought to have him keep the house or be compensated for renovations he had made. I chose the latter remedy and ordered the bank to pay damages. The shenanigans of the bank manager and his agent had proved costly, particularly when the bank was required to pay the legal costs of both 'buyers'.

From my own perspective, although I could not express it at the time, the case had its humorous moments as the architects of the convoluted plan tried to support its validity. I expect the case was a local *cause celebre* as neither side was willing to concede defeat. The imposing presence of the house, in itself, warranted an all-out joust with all the legal ammunition counsel could muster. In the end the house won the day and calmly retained its place overlooking the lake.

As with many cases, when stripped of the trappings and the debate, justice and the case law, at least as I interpreted it, prevailed. The moral of the story and the principle of law were the same. You can't sell the same house to two different people at the same time.

The case introduced me to Harvey Pollock who probably had more civil cases before me in Winnipeg than any other lawyer. He was as fierce a competitor as there was. If I urged him to move along when I thought a number of witnesses had covered a particular point *ad nauseam*, he would just ignore me. I finally tried to keep quiet. It is the lawyer, after all, who must keep his or her eye on what a court of appeal might consider important.

The Broken Bed

The Court House in The Pas was also the local jail. Its two-storey unprepossessing brick building was prominently located at the main intersection in the centre of town. It had a large jury-style courtroom and other court-related facilities on the main floor. The second floor was entirely devoted to jail cells, and there were more cells, reserved for the most difficult prisoners, in the basement.

When we were in town to hold court on circuit, the Queen's Bench judges were expected to sleep in the 'Judges Quarters' behind the courtroom. The suite, if you can call it that, included a bathroom, desk, two chairs and a bed. If the judge needed to talk to counsel during a trial or when court documents had to be signed, the lawyers on the case and the court clerk would come in. Someone always had to sit on the bed.

Darcy Bancroft was a large and effective lawyer who resembled Nero Wolfe of TV fame. He was a bachelor and lived above his law office in a former bank building a block north of the courthouse. When a visiting judge was in town, he would invite the judge, his partners and the out-of-town lawyers to his suite for a drink before supper. I would attend as long as Darcy had no case or applications before me at that sitting of the court. Jimmy Wilson was a personable and well-liked judge and he went to at least one of these gatherings where Darcy's ocelot chewed his gloves to pieces.

Jimmy had been one of our professors in law school and was second only to Sam Freedman as an after-dinner speaker when lawyers held graduation or other large dinner meetings. Before appointment to the bench, Jimmy was also the counsel of choice by lawyers who were caught with their fingers in the till – more particularly in client's trust accounts.

Although five members of my law class ended up in Stony Mountain Penitentiary, that didn't diminish their choice of Jimmy Wilson as long as he was a practicing lawyer. When appointed to the Court he continued to be highly regarded as a pleasant, practical and knowledgeable judge.

Whether it was on the same visit to The Pas or not, I don't know, but on one occasion Darcy had to see Mr. Justice Wilson in his office to have a document signed. He was invited to sit on the bed as Jimmy didn't think he'd fit into one of the chairs. Darcy was just leaning back and looking forward to a chat, when the bed collapsed.

Darcy wasn't hurt but the sound of the two of them laughing had the court clerk rushing in. She too broke up at the sight of Darcy on the floor and the bed in pieces. Both Darcy and Jimmy became heroes to the other members of the bench as the incident put an end to the practice of requiring judges to live in utter isolation when on circuit. Jimmy, of necessity, moved into a motel and before long Chief Justice Tritschler sent a memo to us all saying we could stay at any hotel we wanted in any of the circuit towns.

Chief Justice E.K. Williams had ignored the rule long before, at least for himself. When he sat in court in Brandon he always had a suite in the Prince Edward Hotel. "E. K." as he was called, was a tough taskmaster in court. He demanded perfection from the lawyers who appeared before him and didn't mind giving a public scolding to any who didn't meet his standard.

When still a lawyer, I felt elated when, after a case I was on before him finished, I receive a note from the Court Registrar saying the Chief Justice would like me to join him at the hotel for a drink at five o'clock. He only drank two fingers of Scotch whisky with no ice and no mix, and that is what I was handed after I got seated in his luxurious two room apartment. I can't remember what we talked about but he made me feel that I had finally become a full-fledged lawyer. Nor can I recall appearing before him again. He took early retirement from the court after assurance that his choice of the next Chief Justice would be accepted.

The court house in The Pas also contained the only jail in the north. The name, carved in stone over the entrance and the steel bars on the basement and upper floor windows, left no doubt this was a place of confinement. I assume the courtroom was established on the main floor to be convenient for its clientele. The courtroom containing a jury box and a small law library supplied the basic criminal and civil reports for the judges and local lawyers. Sheriffs' and Registry offices assisted the court process and contained the records of court-related matters. The jurors' room was behind the judges' quarters and although the judge could tell that discussions were in progress, unless there was an outburst of some sort, the details of their discussions could not be discerned.

It was not uncommon for prisoners on the upper floor to jump from their bunks and send a crashing bang to those at work during a jury trial. No doubt the prisoners were unhappy about being in jail and they liked to vent their frustration when the court was in session, particularly if a jury was trying one of their friends. With the heavy boots they wore, the sound was like a thunderclap and the proceedings ground to a halt while the presiding judge directed the sheriff to quell the disturbance. The sheriff would enter the cells, yell at the prisoners and make some threats but could do little when they all denied making any noise at all.

There had been demands to build a more modern jail and court facility for years and finally a new jail was built on the outskirts of town, along with a new courthouse. They were connected to one another by an underground tunnel. There was also an outdoor fenced in recreation area for the prisoners.

Judges could park behind the building and get into their office without going through the public registry area. The court clerk would have the files arranged on the judges' desk so he could sign documents and grant ex parte orders. If he had to see a lawyer, the clerk would bring them in and wait in case the judge needed anything else. The courtroom, easily accessible from the judge's office had the usual jury box and a large public seating area.

The court sitting would start with ex parte applications the lawyers were making, then uncontested divorces. Contested motions and divorces were usually heard next and civil trials would be given the anticipated number of days either before or after the empanelling of a jury for a criminal trial. The Court Registrar would have met with counsel to obtain their estimates of how long their matter would take.

The Sheriff's office was also moved to the same building. They would escort any prisoner who had to be present in court, back and forth through the tunnel. The judge would stay in one of the two motels with a good restaurant.

A question of protocol arose on one occasion when I was staying in the motel closest to the old courthouse. Its restaurant often had lawyers, with or without clients, eating there as well. One morning when I was waiting for breakfast to arrive, one of the local lawyers approached my table and said, "Good morning My Lord, may I join you?"

"Don't you have a matter before me in court this morning?" I asked.

"Yes I do." He said.

"In that case it would be improper for us to eat together or to talk to one another." I said.

I don't recall whether he apologized or not, but he had breached one of the basic rules of conduct expected of the bar. Lawyers don't talk to judges they are about to appear before. So I won't appear to cast aspersions on the whole bar in The Pas and although I won't name the lawyer, I can say he was disbarred by the Law Society many years later over some infraction of the rules he had committed.

The Perfectionist

Alfonso Weeks came to Canada after having worked for the Chief Justice of Barbados. He was proud of being a court reporter in the Brandon courts and extremely conscientious. His escape was the tennis court where he and his wife were fierce competitors. I mention that activity as he could, if challenged about the quality of his work, apply similar aggression to a critic.

The transcripts of evidence given by witnesses during a trial are vital documents when decisions of trial judges are appealed to the Court of Appeal, to say nothing of a further appeal to the Supreme Court of Canada. The difference between winning and losing an appeal may turn on the accuracy of the transcript. It is not unusual for a lawyer to argue that a reporter has made a mistake.

If a transcript has a witness saying, "He did fire the gun," a lawyer may tell the Court of Appeal: "The reporter made a mistake. The witness actually said: "He didn't fire the gun." Generally speaking, the courts accepted the transcript as accurate, but that didn't stop Mr. Weeks from telling all and sundry that any lawyer who questioned his work insulted him and that his professionalism had been maligned.

I knew him when I was a lawyer and later as a judge. When I first had him on a case, he recorded the evidence of the witnesses and the comments of the lawyers and the judge in notebooks in pen and ink. If a copy of the evidence was required, he would type a formal transcript from his notes. He had always been a pen and ink reporter.

A local lawyer once challenged the accuracy of his transcript in the Court of Appeal. He told me how upset he was. When he next appeared on a trial I was involved in he had a back-up system. He still recorded the testimony in pen and ink but he also had a tape recorder going at the same time. He felt comforted knowing he could produce the tape if there was any doubt about the accuracy of his transcript.

As his transcripts continued to be challenged on occasion he would complain to me about the conduct of the complaining lawyer. There was nothing I could or should do, but I assured him I never had a problem with his work or his transcripts. It was impossible to console him.

Whether there were other complaints about his work or not, I don't know, but he was still not satisfied. At the last trial I had with him as the court reporter, he had added a second back-up system. He now had a steno-mask.

It was an unusual sight to see Mr. Weeks carrying out his important task. He sat at his usual table just below the judges' bench, close to the witness box and in front of the counsel table. He was now taking the evidence in pen and ink while speaking into the steno mask and the tape was running at the same time.

When I hadn't run into the likeable Mr. Weeks for some time, I asked the court clerk why I hadn't seen him in court. He had retired from the public service but continued to play a mean game of tennis. I was sorry to see him leave. He was basically a happy person and certainly a dedicated servant of the judges and the lawyers. It was too bad he was a sensitive perfectionist as well. We were good friends and he was highly respected.

I Put the Boots to Her

The most memorable murder case I heard in my first year on the bench was replete with humorous witnesses and hilarious situations. It was also pathetic but it showed how normal people can become caught up in a situation they don't intend.

The hilarity of the case was augmented by the participation of two colourful lawyers. Jack Montgomery, the Crown Prosecutor, was extremely polite as he dealt with his witnesses and the court, but he could explode if defence counsel took exception to something he did. As a strong advocate, he believed in the position the Crown had taken and was bent on achieving a conviction.

Max Isaacs was counsel for the accused. An older gentleman, he examined the witnesses in a quiet but positive manner. He had a knack for surprising and upsetting the Crown Counsel by arguing vague procedural issues as the case progressed. The theatrics of both counsel would have earned Oscars. I am not criticizing the lawyers but describing the roles they assumed while attempting to get the jury on side.

The first foray occurred when a Crown witness, a twenty year detective with the fingerprint and photography branch of the Winnipeg Police Force, was giving evidence. He introduced a book of photographs showing the suite where a fight had occurred, the closet where a body had been hidden for a while and the riverbank where it was later found. When he started to describe the injuries he saw during the autopsy of the deceased, Mr. Isaacs rose to his feet and objected.

"That matter will be covered by the medical evidence. My learned friend is just trying to enflame the jury."

"I am insulted," Mr. Montgomery yelled as he leapt to his feet. "I am merely having the witnesses tell the jury about the care that has been taken to let them know how careful and independent the police have been in their examination of the case."

There was nothing I needed to say. Mr. Isaacs moved on to

another point.

The next witness was the Coroner and Medical Examiner, Dr. Denton Booth. He had gone to the banks of the Assiniboine River with the police and saw a body ten to fifteen feet from the water's edge. When he later examined the body he found it severely traumatized and concluded the person had been dead for several days before being placed in the river. He had also examined a closet in the suite to which he was taken and was able to say there had been a body in it. It was empty but smelled of decomposing human flesh. Under cross examination he said the marks of blows on the body could have been caused by a human fist. The autopsy was done by Dr. McMorris who described all the marks on the body and his finding that the blood alcohol level at the time of death was extremely high. His conclusion was that the woman had died as a result of lacerations to the head and hemorrhage in the brain. The injuries had all been sustained before the woman died.

A University of Manitoba student called the police after seeing a man break a window and crawl into a ground level suite. Three police officers entered the suite and found the accused asleep on the bed. They said they could tell he had been drinking, although he was not intoxicated.

The man said he had forgotten his key and had to break the window to get in. A conversation with the caretaker confirmed that he was a lawful tenant. He said he and his female friend had a fight and she had gone to Vancouver.

When the police were satisfied with his explanation and were ready to leave, Acting Detective Ostash asked one more question, "in jest" he testified. He said: "I asked the accused - What did you do, take her out back and kill her or something?"

"He replied, yeah I killed her and threw her in the river."

The officer asked him to go to the river with them and show where he put the body. He pointed to a spot about two feet from the bank. On the way to the station in the police car when he was under arrest he said: "Yes it's true. I want to turn myself in."

Although objected to by the defence, I found the comment had been volunteered. In cross examination each of the officers agreed the accused was very upset and very emotional after he admitted his fault.

Detectives Jack Taylor and Peter Vander Graaf, who I would hear from in other homicides over the years, spoke of examining the suite for evidence. The most significant item they found was a frying pan with hair from the deceased adhering to it. Other marks of a violent struggle were found on a chesterfield. After a *voir dire* to prove his subsequent statement to the detectives was voluntary, it too was admitted into evidence. This *voir dire* in the absence of the jury, satisfied me that the statement had been properly taken without pressure or any improper solicitation. I was satisfied and the statement was read to the jury.

The various pieces of hair and other samples the police had gathered were tendered as exhibits. Mr. Montgomery presented each vial and described what was in it before it was marked as an exhibit by the court clerk.

As the vials were passed to Mr. Isaacs for examination, he said, looking closely at one. “This one seems to be empty.” In a sonorous long drawn out tone he added “Strange.”

Mr. Montgomery was on his feet in a flash. “My learned friend knows very well it’s empty. He knows it contained some hair of the deceased that was analyzed by Dr. McMorris. I reject my learned friend’s implication that I’m doing something underhanded.”

I couldn’t imagine Mr. Montgomery being upset but he certainly appeared to be. It may be he thought he had to be certain the jury didn’t think there was a missing link in the evidence. In effect, by interjecting as he did, he was giving evidence, but he got away with it.

That was the only case I presided over that my wife and daughter Irene attended, but it was that exchange they thought was the highlight of the case. Lawyers in court can easily be confused with actors on a stage but they are usually the ones who make trials as entertaining as they usually are.

After the Crown closed its case, Mr. Isaacs called his client to the stand. He questioned him about all his actions, his love for the deceased and the degree of intoxication he was in when their fight turned physical. He expressed his regret and his sorrow and blamed his intoxicated state for what happened. He admitted telling one officer "I put the boots to her."

After counsel made their closing addresses to the jury, I described the law that might apply and the choice of verdicts open to them.

Both counsel would have been able to claim a victory. Mr. Isaacs was no doubt pleased the jury convicted the accused of manslaughter rather than murder. Mr. Montgomery would, I think, have been satisfied with the sentence of seven years.

I don't recall the length of sentence either counsel suggested but that would have had a bearing on the length of the sentence I imposed. I was also probably impressed by the accused' sincere expressions of regret when he gave evidence. The fact that both were heavily intoxicated probably convinced me and the jury that the accused never meant to kill.

He Didn't Mean to Do It

Jack Montgomery was again the prosecutor acting for the Crown in a pathetic case where intoxication and booze was again the real culprit. By that time I was aware that many of his friends called him 'Hollywood Jack', in tribute to his striking good looks and his mastery of the courtroom stage.

Lawrence Greenberg, acting for the accused, had his own unique style that often served clients well. He spoke slowly, was liked by juries, and exuded a belief in his unfortunate client. In contrast to Jack Montgomery, he was low key. Listening to his calm and even casual questioning of a witness would almost cause me and the jury to wonder if there had been any wrongdoing at all. It was a treat to see such masterful counsel at work.

The suite where a body had been discovered was in shambles. The deceased legs were tied together with sheets and the injuries to the upper part of his body were consistent with a beating. Blows to the head and neck ruled out the possibility of suicide. The pathologist who did the autopsy found fractures of the skull and injuries to the brain. He estimated death had taken place about an hour after the injuries had been inflicted.

The stage for the murder trial was set by the first witnesses, the police photographer and the Medical Examiner, Dr. Denton Booth. They showed and told what they saw in the suite. The jury was left in no doubt about the severity of the traumatic death and the fight that must have taken place.

The first civilian witness told of the stupidity of the accused, but all murderers aren't vicious killers, as the previous case also showed. He said he met the accused, who he knew, in Central Park. "He told me he had just killed a guy. It was such a casual statement I didn't know what to think but after a few minutes, I said I didn't believe him."

He said, "I'll show you, and we went to the apartment. He opened the door with a key and I saw a dead man lying in a pool of blood.

He didn't say anything and neither did I. We went back to the park, then he and the young guy who was with him left and went into the YMCA. That's when I phoned the cops. When they came I took them to the 18th floor."

Several police officers testified about the condition of the suite. They said it looked as if a violent fight had occurred. Furniture had been broken and everything was turned upside down. They told of the injuries they could see on the body, of leaving everything as it was and calling for the police photographer and a medical examiner.

Other officers told of going to the YMCA and talking to the clerk who had registered guests for two rooms earlier. When asked if they were drunk, the clerk said he smelled some alcohol on the older man but decided he wasn't drunk or he wouldn't have rented him a room. The police arrested the pair and took them downtown for questioning.

When they apprehended the accused they saw dried blood on his boots and his clothing. His fingerprints later matched some found in the suite. He had a key in his possession which opened the door of the suite. When Detective Lund asked him if he knew anything about the death they were investigating, the accused hung his head and nodded in the affirmative. He was cautioned at the police station, was cooperative and gave a statement telling what had happened. The younger man was apparently not involved in the killing and was released after giving his statement to the investigators.

The accused said in his statement, read to the jury by one of the senior police witnesses, that he had gone to the suite hoping to borrow some money and had no intention of using any force. The occupant of the suite, he said, was a long-time friend but he refused to give or lend the accused any money. An argument ensued. The argument escalated into a pushing and shoving situation and finally into a violent beating. He killed his friend and took some money from his pocket. Mr. Greenberg suggested to the jury he was acting out of character and had not intended to hurt the deceased.

In my charge to the jury I told them the various verdicts they should consider - murder, manslaughter or not guilty. The death was obviously a violent one, and was caused in the course of a robbery. That probably decided the direction the jurors would go. They only took two and a half hours to reach their verdict: Guilty of murder. Without delay I imposed the sentence prescribed by the *Criminal Code* of Canada. Without comment, I sentenced the friendly and remorseful culprit to imprisonment for life. The sheriff closed court and the jury and I were escorted from the room.

The case was an example of the stupidity of many crimes and the effect of booze on an otherwise simple and well-meaning individual. He didn't mean to kill his friend, but he did.

As mentioned earlier, the only criminal cases I sat on as a judge were with a jury. My task was to rule on the admissibility of the questions being asked by counsel, to help the jury understand the proceedings and what they should consider when deciding whether the accused was guilty of the main or some lesser offence or whether they were not guilty. To do that, and to impose an appropriate sentence if the accused was found guilty, I had to take extensive notes and make rulings as the case progressed.

The reason my involvement in criminal cases was limited in this way was due to two factors. When appointed to the Queen's Bench, there were only eight judges and they all heard criminal cases with juries. The non-jury or "judge alone" cases were heard by County Court judges. By the time the two courts amalgamated in 1984, I had been appointed the Associate Chief Justice of the Court, responsible for the administration of the newly formed Family Division. After the fall of 1983 until I took early retirement in 1993, I did no criminal work.

Although I didn't realize it at the time, my introduction to sitting as a judge in criminal cases had been gradual. The nature of my earliest cases show that Chief Justice Tritschler was testing my ability to handle simple cases before turning me loose on murder and other involved cases. The actual assignment of cases was done by the Chief's right hand man, Mr. Justice Israel (Izzy) Nitikman.

The accused in the first criminal case I sat on in Winnipeg was charged with pointing a firearm and possession of an offensive weapon. The jury found the accused not guilty on the first count and guilty on the second. I sentenced the accused to two years in the Penitentiary. His counsel appealed the case but the Court of Appeal dismissed it. The next case was one of robbery and the jury found the accused not guilty. The third was a charge of drug trafficking and I sentenced the accused to nine years. The sentence was appealed but the Court of Appeal upheld it as well.

By October I heard a fraud trial and a charge of distributing obscene material. Both cases drew probation orders and fines of $5000 and $1000 respectively. Apparently having survived the testing period, my next three cases in Winnipeg were murder, manslaughter and murder. In the first case I sentenced the accused to be imprisoned for life. In the manslaughter case, the jury acquitted and the second murder trial resulted in the jury finding the accused not guilty of murder but guilty of manslaughter. I sentenced him to seven years in jail.

Importing Drugs

The international cooperation of police forces in Asia and North America not only led to the detection and destruction of an international network of drug growers and peddlers, but also turned out to be one of the most dramatic trials I heard with a jury. It was also one of the longest.

The federal Crown was represented by Bruce McFarlane and Judith Webster. Jay Prober acted for Ashok Dass, the accused. After the jury was empanelled, Mr. McFarlane addressed the jury and began to give an outline of the Crown's case. As he was obviously going to take some time, we recessed for lunch at 12:25. When we reconvened, the empty chair in the jury box made it obvious that a juror was missing. We waited for some time but finally decided the missing juror wasn't coming.

Mr. Prober suggested we call the jury panel back and select another juror. The panel had been discharged so that was impossible. He then suggested we select a new jury and start all over again. I thought that might take months to organize because it was often difficult to find dates acceptable to both counsel. I decided we would proceed as the *Criminal Code* provided that a jury could carry on as long as it had at least ten members. As it turned out, the case lasted thirty-five days, of which twenty-one were sitting days, and the eleven jurors remained throughout.

The Crown Prosecutor told the jury the case involved an alleged conspiracy to import illegal drugs into Canada. He explained that all but one of the participants in the plan had been apprehended and would be tried in Minnesota. The other member of the group was arrested in Winnipeg and was the person on trial before them.

Conspiracy is a difficult thing to prove. It involves proving the intent of two or more people to commit an illegal act, whether or not the act is carried out. The drugs in question never did enter Canada. The task of the prosecution was to prove the plan or agreement to bring them in. A conspiracy charge, he said, may be proven, even if it is impossible to establish which member of a group actually did the importing.

The jury and I were to hear the facts the Crown said formed the foundation of the charge. Although the charge was complicated enough in itself, the fact that most of the conversations between the alleged conspirators were conducted in Urdu added another element to the trial. All the wiretapped conversations between the alleged conspirators had to be translated from Urdu into English so the jurors would know what had been said.

As each witness described their part in the investigation, we learned that the marijuana in question had been grown in the hills of Pakistan. It was moved by the buyers to a central location where the drugs were spread on carpets that were then rolled and covered with several layers of plastic. The authorities in Pakistan got wind of what was happening and assigned investigators to follow the shipment of the rugs.

After sitting in a warehouse for several weeks, they were assigned for shipment by Japan Air to Los Angeles. Asian police were on the plane and in cooperation with the FBI they followed the shipment to a warehouse at the Los Angeles airport where a named individual was to claim it. Again, the shipment sat in a warehouse for several weeks.

During that time the FBI brought in a trained dog which identified the rolls containing drugs. They had scientists open some of the rolls to confirm the type of drug they contained. They made notes of what they did and the analyses they performed, so they could give evidence in court if that became necessary. The carpets were then re-rolled and covered so they looked identical to the others.

It was two weeks before the authorized individual appeared at the shipping counter, inspected the goods and directed they be sent on a particular flight to Minneapolis. The FBI again watched the loading of the rugs, were on the plane with them, and saw them being unloaded and placed in storage in another warehouse.

By that time, the people who had participated in the shipment of the rugs, their delivery and transfer from one airport to another, were identified and their telephone calls were being monitored, recorded and translated into English. It was learned the rugs would be taken to a house in suburban Minneapolis before distribution to various locations, including Winnipeg.

The FBI, local police and Canadian authorities were contacted and advised what was happening. As soon as a group of people arrived at the Minneapolis airport and started loading the shipment into their vehicles, unmarked police cars and helicopters watched and followed until the rugs were being unloaded and carried into a house. The police then descended en masse, arrested everyone who was present and took possession of the rugs.

As soon as the arrests in Minneapolis were underway, the Winnipeg police arrested the accused and seized material that was intended to be used to hide the contraband. The case was the best example of police work and international cooperation I ever encountered.

The exhausted jury found the accused guilty of conspiracy and I sentenced him to the minimum prescribed by Canadian law, fifteen years in the Penitentiary. I later heard that when he had served his time he was deported.

The Roof Fire

Another case where I had known the lawyer for the defendant for years involved the destruction of a commercial building. Bud Irving and I were classmates in grade eleven at Kelvin and again in first year law. Bud was also a lineman with the Winnipeg Blue Bombers. He was envied by the rest of our law class because his principal, Norman Darcy, paid him $50 a month instead of the $25 the rest of us received.

As I listened to the case I was hoping Bud would win, although I also knew the other five lawyers who participated or had watching briefs. It may seem strange that a judge would admit to such a sentiment and I wouldn't have admitted it at the time, but such is the legal system that such sentiments can exist without affecting the final result.

The evidence was that the fire was inadvertently caused by the roofing company Bud represented. The loss was agreed to be $480,000. The witnesses, as with those in most civil cases I heard, had to educate me on the fine points of roof construction; in this case, how roofing tile and sealing tar are supposed to be applied.

The new roof was covered by a fibrene underlay with squares of insulation and four layers of tar paper interspersed with hot liquid asphalt. The asphalt was pumped to the roof through a pipe leading from a tar kettle on the ground. In it the asphalt was heated to 450 degrees. After the material went into the tar bucket on the roof, it was removed by saturating cotton fibre mops and dripping the asphalt over the steel decking or swabbing it over the layers of material.

Unfortunately, the mop was left suspended over the bucket when the two workmen went for lunch. During that time the roof caught fire. After listening to workmen and experts, I had no trouble concluding that the mop had self-ignited from a build up of heat within it. Even the roofing contractor said he had instructed his workers never to leave a mop on a roof over a lunch-hour.

Restrictive Covenant

I hadn't been on the court three months when I was faced with a restrictive covenant of the sort I had signed in Brandon. This one prohibited a salesman from starting his own business within a radius of 100 miles of Portage la Prairie for three years after the termination of his employment.

There were three lawyers on the case. They quoted the Maguire case I had consulted before going out on my own in Brandon. Fortunately they referred me to more recent cases as well. One was a decision written by Mr. Justice Dickson, then of the Manitoba Court of Appeal, who said "…it becomes necessary to examine the covenant under attack to see whether it is excessive in regards to area, time of operation and scope".

Another case they referred me to was a decision of Laskin J, later Chief Justice of the Supreme Court of Canada, saying employee restraint covenants may be held invalid because of their unreasonable duration or because of their unreasonable territorial ambit. "That principle….is the application of a rule of reason to a balancing of the interests of the employer and the erstwhile employee in respect of the need of the former for protection of his business and of the latter for economic mobility, in the light of a policy that discourages limitations on personal freedom, and, specifically, on freedom of economic or employment opportunity."

Believing that the 100 mile limitation was too wide, I concluded the covenant was invalid and dismissed the claim.

Rape

Juries in the 70s And 80s didn't like rape any more than they liked drug charges. In one case a senior lawyer was defending three young men who had forced a girl into their car, driven to a secluded spot and had sex. The men said they had been at a party where it appeared the girl was going to bed with several men. In their statements to the police they said their activities with the girl were consensual. The girl said they were not. She had a bruise on her head, some torn clothing and seminal fluid on her clothing.

I thought she might very well have been the loose person the accused suggested. I also thought, although these were just my personal reactions and were not stated out loud, that she probably did have intercourse with others at the party as the accused suggested. If I had been a judge sitting alone I would probably have given the accused the benefit of the doubt and found them not guilty.

My charge to the jury lasted an hour but the jury did not deliver its verdict until 10:30 the next morning. They convicted all three of abduction and rape. I sentenced them to three years for rape and six months for the abduction, the sentences to run concurrently. In spite of my personal reservations I had to accept the decision of the jury.

A Jury's Dilemma

The very next case involved the shooting and killing of a friend at a Legion party where all the witnesses who were called to testify had been drunk. It was hard to tell who had done what and the degree of responsibility of the accused. The jury must have been equally confused as it found the accused not guilty of attempted murder but guilty of wounding with intent, possession of an offensive weapon and possession of a restricted weapon. I sentenced the accused to one year on count two and ninety and thirty days on the lesser counts. Juries take their task seriously and I had to follow their lead when imposing sentence.

Love Gone Wild

One of the strangest murder cases I presided over involved a woman and her 'friend' giving the deceased, the woman's husband, sleeping pills then throwing him out a second storey window to his death. The jury convicted the wife and I sentenced her to life imprisonment. The case went all the way to the Supreme Court which found that I should not have allowed the Crown to re-examine the last witness on a point I thought had been raised in cross-examination. A new trial was ordered and it was heard several years later by Mr. Justice Kroft.

In the meantime, Katie Harper had married the friend and he was added as a defendant in the new trial. It was a lengthy trial as his counsel continually tried to sever the trials and then to have evidence against him excluded. The jury found Katie guilty of murder and her new husband, who had played a lesser role, guilty of manslaughter. Katie was sentenced to life in prison, probably in Kingston, with no chance of parole for ten years. The Court of Appeal dismissed the offenders' appeals.

Civil Juries

Civil juries were a rarity when I was on the court. The "*Queen's Bench Act*" provided that cases of defamation, malicious arrest, malicious prosecution or false imprisonment are to be tried with a jury unless the parties waive trial by jury.

All other cases are to be tried by a judge alone unless a judge orders a jury trial. I never had an application of that sort all the time I was on the court. Apparently a number of applications had been turned down in earlier days so it appeared to the bar it was not worth applying. Harry Walsh once complained to me about the lack of civil juries. I seriously replied: "You never applied to me to have a case tried by a civil jury."

I had two civil jury trials during my time on the bench. The first involved a shoplifter who was caught leaving a Woolworth store with merchandise he hadn't paid for. He put on quite a show. He was irate at being prevented from leaving and accused the company staff of false imprisonment and harassment. The evidence was clear that he and a confederate, who had pleaded guilty in Provincial Court, had picked up a tape, transferred it back and forth and finally put it in a bag containing other merchandise that had been paid for. They didn't stop at the checkout counter.

Two security guards had become suspicious and followed the men as they moved around the store. They waited patiently until the shoplifters were outside, then arrested them and took them to a private room where they accused them of theft and seized the tape. One of the culprits was making such a fuss they called the city police. When the police arrived some time later, they took statements from the employees and the accused, and arrested them again.

The jury trial was really a farce and the jury had no trouble finding the one who was on trial guilty of theft. None of his lawyer's attacks on the security guards and the police were credible as the lawyer and the client tried to bully or bluff their way to an acquittal. The lawyer cited a number of English and Canadian cases, trying to get me to instruct the jury to acquit. The hold-out accused was convicted. I fined him and required him to pay the costs of the lawyer representing Woolworth's.

The jury wasn't impressed either. I later learned that the foreman of the jury sent a letter to the Law Society complaining about the conduct of the lawyer for the thief and asked why he was allowed to practice law.

The second civil jury had to deal with a claim of defamation. The *Winnipeg Tribune* had printed an article describing the ambiance of a local restaurant and a description of the food the reporter tried. The article was accurate but not complimentary. The owner felt insulted, although his counsel admitted, before any witnesses were called, that if the writer expressed an opinion it could fall into the category of 'fair comment' as long as it was based on existing facts. An apology had been demanded but had been rejected by the newspaper.

Counsel for the plaintiff had the manager go into great detail about the variety of meals it served and the cleanliness of the place. As it turned out, neither had been criticized in the article. He said the food was fresh, but under cross examination had to admit that much of it, including the french fries, remained frozen until the meal was prepared. The article had described the fries as having "customary tastelessness." The cabbage and pie were partly prepared on site but were warmed in the microwave before being served. He said the kitchen cleaning practices were good but had to admit that the allegation in the article that there were pieces of lettuce or carrots on the floor was accurate.

The owner was upset by the general tone of the article and said that while the regular customers continued to come, there was some decline in the number of customers for a few months. In spite of that belief, the sales in the month the article appeared were higher than they were the year before. He didn't know the date the reviewer attended and couldn't say that many of the facts in the article were untrue.

The jury found that the article was fair and not defamatory. It unanimously dismissed the restaurant's claim. I ordered it to pay the newspaper costs of $2,500 and its court and other disbursements.

Counsel for the restaurant later told me that the owner told him, after the case was over, that he had only been in court twice in his life. The first was before a Judge Hamilton in the Juvenile Court and the second was a Hamilton again. He complained that he lost both times.

I enjoyed the two cases I did have. The fact that civil juries are made up of only six jurors, rather than the twelve in criminal trials, meant I had to do more explaining of the civil law and procedure, but I found the jurors interested and serious about their responsibilities.

Purveyors of Smut

This case introduced me to Ruth Krindle, a Crown Attorney and later a Queen's Bench judge. She was a tough prosecutor who seemed to be assigned to many of the most unpleasant and difficult cases. She was direct with witnesses and the jury. On the other side was Ray Flett, also an effective counsel. He represented a company that sold and distributed books and magazines from its local store and warehouse.

Two city detectives were dispatched to a store where they purchased a copy of the magazine in question for fifty cents. The next day another copy was seized from another Winnipeg store. A search warrant was obtained and further copies were seized from the warehouse. It was determined that the magazine had come from a distributor in New York.

When shown the issues that had been seized, the manager said, "this one got by me." He produced a box of magazines containing obscene material he had held back and refused to sell. He had also issued an immediate recall of the questionable issue and it was taken off the shelves. He agreed to cooperate with the police in any way he could.

Mr. Flett said the company in Winnipeg had acted responsibly, examined material when it came in and put a stop to the distribution of offensive material. He tried to persuade the jury not to convict, saying "what a horrible thing it is to be convicted as purveyors of smut." He pointed out it was not hard core pornography.

Miss Krindle agreed that the company was surprised to see the offensive material in its inventory and had been cooperative in having it removed from the stores to which it had been distributed. On the other hand, she advised the jury that the possession of such material is absolutely prohibited by law. She told them they had no choice but to convict.

The jury returned its verdict of "Guilty" within a few minutes. I accepted the various mitigating factors both lawyers had mentioned and imposed a fine of $1,000 payable by the middle of the next month.

I mention this case to indicate that, while the law has to be obeyed, there is still room in the system for understanding and leniency.

The Computer Age

In January 1973, a year after I joined the Court of Queen's Bench, I had a civil case in Winnipeg I considered to be on the cutting edge of new technology. It involved an industrial computer. There were news items about the wonders that rooms full of machinery could do in storing and using information, but I knew nothing more.

Feed-Rite Mills was interested in having its accounting done more quickly than by internal accounting and an outside computer. It wanted statements done within two days of the end of each month and wanted additional statements, records and analyses.

A commercial supplier of business machines recommended purchase of various units that would enable all the company's accounting requirements to be processed quickly and in their own premises. A contract was signed calling for a payment of close to $90,000, although the cheque for the first instalment said "subject to machine performance." It quickly tuned out that a punch card and sorter would also have to be purchased for another $7,000.

There were problems getting the equipment to operate properly from the outset. The vendor's technicians did their best to overcome problems but the system never operated as intended. Inaccurate statements were being printed and incorrect numbers found their way onto statements.

The warranty period was ninety days but the purchaser refused to make any further payments until the defects were cured. After a year and a half the machinery was still not operating properly. Among other defects, the computer would print out a "2" where a "3" should appear.

Finally, in November 1969, Feed-Rite gave the supplier a deadline to get the equipment operating properly. If they couldn't, they were asked to return the money that had been paid to date. Feed-Rite also demanded that the machinery be removed from its premises. The supplier refused to take the equipment back, even though all the additional programs had still not been installed, and it sued for the balance of the purchase price still outstanding. The purchaser alleged that the equipment was not fit for the purpose for which it was intended.

The plaintiff, the supplier of the equipment, admitted that the original contract did not cover the whole agreement. The vendor was to train company personnel in the operation of the equipment, prepare and insert seven specific accounting functions and install the equipment in good operating condition.

Its position during the trial was that one problem with getting the unit operating was that Feed-Rite failed to provide certain information. It also argued that the machinery had been accepted by the purchaser. The evidence I heard did not persuade me that those allegations were accurate. In addition, I was satisfied the supplier was never able to get the system to work. The purchaser had given it ample time.

I found as a fact that the supplier had failed to fulfil the contract because it had failed to get the machinery working properly. In technical terms, I found that the supplier was guilty of a fundamental breach of contract. I ordered the return of all monies that had been paid on account, the additional expenses the purchaser had incurred, interest and costs.

A fundamental breach of a contract is one going to the root or very foundation of a contract. I found that was the case here. The contract was never fulfilled in a number of important ways. I felt the purchaser should not be required to pay for machinery the seller couldn't get to work. In effect, the seller was unable to live up to the promises it had made.

I dismissed the plaintiff's claim and ordered it to repay the deposit it had received, interest on that amount of $7,000 and various other expenses it had incurred. The total judgment came to over $41,000.

My decision was appealed to the Court of Appeal. Mr. Justice Roy Matas, speaking for a unanimous court, wrote that court's decision dismissing the appeal and confirming my conclusion and the amount I had ordered be paid to Feed-Rite.

An interesting aside was that the lawyer who acted for Feed-Rite during the trial became my Chief Justice within six months – Archie Dewar. The lawyer for the supplier relied on most of the same cases, but tried to distinguish them, arguing they didn't apply to the circumstances of this case.

Should the Client Testify?

A jury trial I had in Winnipeg involved what seemed like very minor charges - possession of an offensive weapon and pointing a firearm. Bill Morton, a thorough and careful prosecutor acted for the Crown and an older lawyer who I didn't know represented the accused. I won't mention his name, because there were several lawyers with the same last name and I can't recall which one was on the case. My second reason for not naming him, even if I had a record of his name, will become obvious when I speak of the major mistake he or his client made.

The family was celebrating the 25th anniversary of the mother and father of the accused. Some trouble started at the couple's home, then spilled over to the hall where 100 relatives and guests were assembled. The witnesses called by the Crown described the condition of Walter, the accused, and what they saw and heard. Most were less than positive about their memories and seemed to me to be downplaying the extent of the troublemaker's intoxication and what he did. I don't know, of course, if the jury thought the same.

The first witness was a cousin of the accused who had been in the parents' house. On being told that Walter had a gun, he went out to the street to talk to him. "He told me not to come any closer."

"When I asked what the trouble was," he said, "It's not you I want, but my father." As I talked to him and moved closer he said, "Don't come any closer or I'll kill you and he pumped the gun twice."

When asked where the gun was pointing the witness said, "In the direction of me."

When asked what condition the accused was in, the cousin said, "He was upset, there's no doubt about that. At the hall, there was a scuffle between him and his father. His father grabbed him and put him down."

The witness was serving drinks at the hall and when asked the condition of the accused, he said, "he was underneath (*sic*) the influence of alcohol."

Another brother testified that he heard the accused say, "Keep my father away from me." When he found he couldn't settle Walter down and people were afraid of what might happen, he called the police.

A neighbour testified the rifle was his and that there were no bullets in it. He eventually took it away from Walter and handed it to the police when they arrived. The police took the accused to the Public Safety building where he was charged with pointing a firearm. When the Crown asked the officer what the accused said, he replied "I'm not saying anything until I see my parole officer."

It was said so quickly, defence counsel had no time to object. I'm not sure I could have excluded the remark in any event. The damage had been done, even though it wasn't necessary for the officer to repeat the whole conversation. Should I declare a mistrial because the Crown had, in effect, told the jury the accused had a criminal record? Basically, the accused had said he didn't want to give a statement. His reason was immaterial.

While I was struggling with what to do about the disclosure, events settled my concern. The Crown closed its case, then defence counsel foolishly said "I call Walter Pickering to the stand."

My reaction at that point still was that the Crown case wasn't very strong. Although the accused had pointed the rifle at his cousin I didn't think it was clear he had pointed it at his father. It also appeared the rifle had no ammunition in it.

The accused told of having had an argument with his father. He couldn't remember what the argument was about but did remember he had been told to "stay away from the house if I knew what was good for me." He went to the house anyway. "I took along the gun to protect myself from Jim. I knew there were no bullets for it." He denied having pointed the rifle at anyone at any time although he admitted pumping it on two occasions.

In cross examination by Bill Morton he admitted he was pretty close to drunk but said he knew what he was doing. He said his father was drunk and he was upset at the same time. He said, "I wasn't going to walk in and get bumped off myself." He admitted telling his cousin he would kill him. When asked why he had pumped the gun twice he said, "Just because I did."

The case against the accused then took a dramatic turn for the worst. Mr. Morton could not have questioned the accused about his record if he had not testified, but was now entitled to do so as he was in the witness stand giving evidence. Mr. Morton had him admit that in recent years he had been convicted of causing bodily harm with intent to wound, possession of an offensive weapon and arson, break enter and theft, and auto theft for which he had been sentenced to two and a half years. He was still on parole when this alleged offence took place.

Both counsel addressed the jury and I instructed them on the law and their options. The jury found Pickering guilty on count 1- possession of an offensive weapon and not guilty on count 2 - pointing a firearm.

It is almost an unwritten rule that defence counsel not call their client to testify if they have a criminal record, because that will enable the jury to hear what it is. If he doesn't take the witness stand the jury will never know. The real damage to the accused in this case was done during his cross examination by the Crown Attorney. It revealed to the jury, for the first time, they were not dealing with a very savoury character. The impression was likely that the accused had little or no respect for the law.

I sentenced the accused to two years in prison, hoping that would give him time to think about changing his aggressive way of life. The penalty would have been greater if there had been an actual assault or if the gun had been loaded. It would have been lighter if it had been a first offence.

Pukatawagan Tragedy

I had many jury trials in all the judicial districts involving Aboriginal people. The most tragic was a second degree murder charge heard by a jury in The Pas in 1979. Crown Counsel were P. J. Jensen and Brian Colli and the accused was represented by Bob Mayer and Lorne Giesbrecht. The jury of northerners was selected in forty minutes. The case was tragic for two reasons. It described the terrible living conditions often found on Indian Reserves and the actions of the accused that resulted in an unintended death.

It was -30 Celsius on the twenty-ninth of December when a large number of sports fans gathered at a house about six o'clock in the evening to watch television, play cards and drink. The house where the television was located had no electricity so several extension cords were used to plug into a socket in another home.

For some reason that was never explained during the trial, the power kept going off. One of the merrymakers in particular, kept blaming the young accused of disconnecting the extension cords. The accused was upset about being blamed and decided to scare his accuser into silence. He ran down a hill and across the frozen lake to his grandparents' home to borrow their '22 rifle. While at their house he fired the gun into the ceiling to make sure it was working. He then ran back across the lake towards the party house.

As he came toward it, a person was standing in the middle of the road. He thought it was his tormentor who had finally beaten him up in the house. He fired at the figure and killed him. As it turned out, the person he killed was his uncle who was coming to calm him down.

A number of witnesses spoke of the good nature of the accused. He was living with a woman in a nearby community and they had a small child. The jury convicted him of manslaughter "with a recommendation of mercy."

The maximum penalty I could have imposed was life imprisonment. The Crown suggested a "substantial period of incarceration," while the defence sought "Provincial Time," meaning less than two years imprisonment.

I sentenced the accused to 18 months in the Provincial Jail at Dauphin. I felt that was the only place his wife and child could visit him. My decision to impose that sentence was based on two other factors as well. The first was that the evidence had convinced me that the intent of the accused was only to scare the bully and not to kill anyone. The second reason was that I didn't think the Court of Appeal would let me get away with a lesser punishment if the Crown appealed. As it turned out there was no appeal.

The jury, I thought, in view of their recommendation, would be satisfied with the sentence. The lack of appeal seemed to indicate the Crown was satisfied as well.

When I was sitting in Dauphin over the next year or so I would inquire how the accused was doing. I was told he was doing well. He worked in the grounds around the jail, was a good worker and a model prisoner. His wife and child had visited twice and the family was looking forward to being reunited. He was released on parole before his time was up.

Human Rights

Labour cases where no witnesses are called to testify were dealt with on the regular weekly Chambers day. They might deal with the enforcement of an injunction or picketing but more often with interpretation of a collective agreement that had previously been negotiated by the labour and management bargaining committees.

These matters were always hard fought and I found the labour and management lawyers were a special breed. They were among the best lawyers at the bar but their antics in the courtroom took on a circus-like appearance. They would shout their staccato presentations and work one another into a frenzy as they exchanged barbs and insults and derided the opposing party's stance. Each hearing was a battle to the death. They would throw copies of the reported cases they relied on at the clerk, who would stamp them and pass them up to me.

Their rapid fire presentations, laced with objections and interruptions from their opponent, were hard to keep up with. There was of course no time for me to read the portions of the cases they referred to but they did provide copies. I learned from my earliest hearings with them that all I had time to do was make a few notes as they spoke and to write the name of the lawyer who relied on a certain case, on the copy. I would later have to sort out who was relying on which case. It got confusing if both lawyers relied on the same authority.

As soon as court finished for the day, before I forgot the issues, I would dictate a recital of the nature of the dispute and the position of each lawyer. I would then read the cases when I had time and write my decision. As lawyers involved in labour law were prone to appeal every decision they or their client didn't like, I had to be careful to cover all the issues and include legal authority for my opinion.

Labour cases were challenging and their presentation was always entertaining as well. I used to wonder whether the lawyers realized how difficult it was to keep up with them, or the problems I was having keeping track of their positions, but they seemed oblivious to my concerns. Theirs was a stage performance of which any hoofer would be proud. The young lawyers waiting their turn in Chambers were clearly impressed with these nimble-minded counsel and their mastery of the art of advocacy.

One case involved a dispute over whether Safeway was entitled to require certain employees to wear hair nets. Another was a dispute as to whether the employer could prevent its employees from growing beards. A Board of Arbitration referred to in the agreement would have to consider the cases on their merits and make a report. I gave a restraining order saying the company couldn't discharge the employee until that hearing took place.

One branch of labour cases falls into the category of human rights. The most unusual case I had involved a university professor, the union to which she belonged and the University of Manitoba. The professor, Imogene McIntire, had turned 65 and the collective agreement provided that all academic appointments automatically terminated on the date of retirement as defined in the University Pension Plan.

The Professor alleged that the age limitation was contrary to the *Human Rights Act* which provided that everyone has the right to equality of opportunity based upon *bona fide* qualifications. In particular it provided that an employer couldn't refuse to employ or continue to employ a person because of a number of matters including "age."

In what seemed unusual to me, the University and the Faculty Association both opposed the professor's application, and argued that the collective agreement between the University and the Faculty Association was valid and binding and should be respected.

Much of the argument presented by counsel dealt with the jurisdiction of the court to deal with the issue and most of my written decision was directed to that as well. I held that the jurisdiction to hear the case had not been ousted by the *Human Rights Act* or by the actions of the University and the Faculty Association, in their attempt to arrive at an agreement that was contrary to the Act.

I found that the provisions of the collective agreement, purporting to require her to retire at age 65 were void and of no effect. I declared that the provisions of Section 6(1) of the *Human Rights Act* applied to the position of the applicant.

The next year I heard an appeal from a board of adjudication that had been appointed under the *Human Rights Act*. The adjudicator had found that the government's discharge of an employee when he reached 65 was not contrary to its The *Human Rights Act* because of the contrary wording of earlier legislation. I allowed the appeal and found the province could not discharge him solely on the basis of his age.

That was still not the end of cases dealing with compulsory retirement. The applicant the next year was a Staff Inspector with the City of Winnipeg Police Department who had been required to retire when he turned 60. That was in accordance with a City of Winnipeg by-law.

The approach of the City, the Police Associations and the Police Commission was that the employee had been discharged because of his age but that he was properly discharged. Section 6 (6) of the *Human Rights Act* provided that its basic prohibition against firing did not apply where a limit on age was a reasonable occupational requirement. The Supreme Court of Canada had referred to the exception in an Ontario case that year, although it dismissed it for lack of evidence.

The matter came on before me because the adjudicator appointed by the Human Rights Commission had received a great deal of scientific and medical evidence dealing with aging and the mental and physical demands of the job, and held that the termination of this particular employment at sixty was justified. He said this case was an exception to the general rule I dealt with in the earlier cases. He dismissed the challenge and found the Inspector had to retire.

I upheld the adjudicator's decision and dismissed the challenge. The weight of the evidence before the adjudicator was substantial and there was no contrary evidence presented before me. The respondents had merely relied on my earlier rulings. The case showed the necessity of examining legislative provisions with care. The adjudicator in the last case was Marshall Rothstein who was appointed as a justice of the Supreme Court of Canada in 2006.

When a Tort is Not a Tort

A tort is a civil wrong, as distinct from a criminal wrong. In the Royal Bank case I handled as a lawyer in Brandon, the Supreme Court of Canada dealt with the injury sustained by Mrs. Campbell when she slipped and fell on the bank's wet floor. She was classed as an invitee, in that she *legally* went into the bank's property to cash one of its cheques. The bank had committed a tort.

A tort is part of the law of negligence. If you fall you may be able to sue the person who caused you to fall. You may then be entitled to receive compensation for your loss. Much has been made of class action suits where hundreds or thousands of people have suffered because of the negligence of a manufacturer. On the other hand, not everyone is entitled to receive compensation for the negligent act of another even if they have been affected by it.

In one negligence case I sat on, none of the facts were in dispute. An employee of the defendants was driving heavy machinery across a bridge over the Red River, hit and damaged the side of the bridge, and caused it to be closed for a considerable length of time. The plaintiff ran a tavern in East Selkirk and many of its customers who previously had a short distance to travel from Selkirk, had to drive south to the locks at St. Andrews, cross the river there and then drive north to East Selkirk. (The bridge that is now a few miles north of Selkirk did not exist at that time.) The extra distance for Selkirk residents was fifteen miles.

Business fell off and it was agreed that the tavern owners had sustained a considerable economic loss. The question was: did the defendants have to pay the tavern damages? That became part of a larger question; who is entitled to claim damages for another's negligence? Counsel quoted from English and Canadian cases which said that a person may recover for economic loss caused by another's negligence although there was no physical damage. The plaintiff argued that if the plaintiff could show damage resulting from the defendant's negligence it was entitled to succeed and to be paid for the damage or loss it suffered. On the surface that sounded reasonable.

The defendant, on the other hand, argued there is a limit on the application of that principle. Quoting from an article by C. Harvey in the 1972 *Canadian Bar Review*, he said the test should be:

> *"A person should be bound by a legal duty of care to avoid causing economic loss to another in circumstances where a reasonable man in the position of the defendant would foresee that kind of loss and would assume responsibility for it."*

There was a significance difference between the two approaches as far as the final result was concerned and it was such a distinction that made a study of the law so fascinating or, some might say, so baffling.

To reach a conclusion, I had to start by examining a decision of the House of Lords in England.

The case of *Donoghue v. Stevenson* arose from an incident which occurred in Paisley, Scotland, on the 26th of August 1928. When in the Wellmeadow Café one evening, a friend purchased and gave Mrs. Donoghue an opaque bottle of ginger beer. When she poured out a second portion, the remains of a snail appeared. She became ill and sued for 500 pounds for damages she sustained from drinking the contaminated ginger beer.

Her claim was allowed by a Court of Session in Scotland, but denied by a split decision of the justices in the Second Division. An appeal *in forma pauperis*, the plaintiff being indigent, was then taken to the English House of Lords. They agreed at the outset that the law that applied was the same in Scotland and England. In another split decision, that court reversed the previous decision and found in favour of Mrs. Donoghue.

The reason I refer to this case is that it, along with later Canadian cases, settled the procedure I followed in the case I was hearing. Lord Atkin, in giving the majority opinion said:

> *At present I content myself with pointing out that in English law there must be, and is, some general conception of relations giving rise to a duty of care, of which the particular cases found in the books are but instances. The liability for*

negligence, whether you style it such or treat it as in other systems as a species of "culpa," is no doubt based upon a general public sentiment of moral wrongdoing for which the offender must pay. But acts or omissions which any moral code would censure cannot in a practical world be treated so as to give a right to every person injured by them to demand relief. In this way rules of law arise which limit the range of complainants and the extent of their remedy. The rule that you are to love your neighbour becomes in law, you must not injure your neighbour; and the lawyer's question, Who is my neighbour? receives a restricted reply. You must take reasonable care to avoid acts or omissions which you can reasonably foresee would be likely to injure your neighbour. Who, then, in law is my neighbour? The answer seems to be – persons who are so closely and directly affected by my act that I ought reasonably to have them in contemplation as being so affected when I am directing my mind to the acts or omissions which are called in question.

The result of this reading required me to place myself in the position of the driver who caused the damage. I then had to ask myself, as if I was the driver of the machinery before I caused the accident, "If I run into the bridge and cause it to be blocked for some time, to whom will I owe compensation?"

In my answer to myself, I thought I might be responsible to the bridge authority for the damage I caused, but I couldn't think of anyone else to whom I owed compensation. I might feel I owed a duty to the public at large not to damage a public thoroughfare; but if through some unintentional though negligent act I caused the thoroughfare to be closed, I wouldn't feel I should have to pay any and every driver who had to take an alternate route.

Applying that process to the situation of the owner of the tavern, the driver would never have thought the damage he caused to the bridge would give rise to a claim by the owner of a tavern or by any motorist who suffered some economic loss by having to take a different route to his or her destination. Indebtedness to any of them would not have been reasonably foreseeable.

I dismissed the plaintiff's claim.

Trial in Absentia

Trials are full of surprises, but one of the most surprising occurred when I was sitting with a jury in Brandon. After the Crown and defence lawyers had challenged some of the prospective jurors, the selected twelve took their places in the jury box and were sworn in. The indictment was read to the accused and he pleaded not guilty to rape and to three lesser charges.

The case was adjourned until 10 o'clock the next Monday. When that time arrived, the accused wasn't present so I adjourned for half an hour. The lawyer for the accused said he was supposed to see the accused the day before, but he hadn't shown up. The Crown Attorney called the accused's common law wife to testify in the absence of the jury. She said he was scared and was talking about running away. After she returned from work on Saturday, his clothing and his car were missing. Counsel and I agreed he wasn't going to show up.

I adjourned the hearing for half an hour to give me and counsel time to consider what we should do. Section 431 of the *Criminal Code* seemed to provide the answer. In effect it said that where an accused absconds during his trial, the court may carry on in his absence. Today the relevant section is 475 (1). Both counsel agreed that the trial had begun when the accused was arraigned and entered a plea of not guilty. They both agreed the trial should continue.

Counsel for the accused then said he would like to be excused and relieved of his responsibility to represent the accused. I declined to release him. It was bad enough not to have the accused in court but I wanted his lawyer to remain to cross-examine the Crown witnesses and to present argument on his behalf after all the evidence had been heard. I explained the situation to the jury and said we would start hearing evidence the next morning.

After several police officers described the condition of the student nurse, she was called as a witness and told of going to a house party with a group and of being manipulated into a bedroom where she was grabbed by the accused who demanded intercourse and other sexual activity while holding his thumb to her throat. The doctor who examined her found there was swelling and bruising to her neck. Another person who was at the party said she was upset, choking and crying when he saw her in the house.

Another witness saw the accused and the nurse in the bedroom with their clothing partially removed. She was yelling and swearing at the accused and was almost in hysterics. Another man who had seen the victim with some of her clothes off, said she hollered, "the bastard tried to rape me" as she ran from the bedroom. She vomited twice and he took her to the police station.

The jury deliberated for four hours then returned a verdict of guilty of attempted rape and one of the lesser charges. I listened to the proposals of counsel on the sentence I should impose. The prosecutor told me the accused had five prior convictions. An earlier doctor's report to the Child Guidance Clinic said he had periods of violent outbursts caused by an unstable emotional temperament.

His counsel brought out the fact that he was divorced and had been living common law in Winnipeg for a year. Alcohol apparently increased his tendency for violence. His counsel recommended a psychiatric assessment. I thought that would be a good idea but I felt I couldn't order one due to the absence of the accused. I had been thinking of a sentence of five years, but after seeing the earlier doctor's report I sentenced him to ten years in jail on the major count and to three years concurrent on the lesser charge.

I didn't think it was any of my business to find out what happened to the offender, but I did hear he had been located in the United States. It also seems to me I heard some time later he was in jail in Manitoba.

Municipalities

Two unusual but strikingly similar cases came on before me in my later years in the Queen's Bench before the Family Division was created.

The first case was humorous because the lawyer protagonists had been fellow cabinet ministers in the Schreyer government. Howard Pawley had been the Attorney General and would later become the Premier of Manitoba. He acted for the ratepayer who challenged the procedure followed by the municipality in purporting to pass a by-law.

Sidney Green had been a member of the same party and the Minister of Labour. Assisted by C. L. Chappell, he acted for the Rural Municipality of St. Clements and took the position that the procedure it had followed in enacting a by-law to permit the construction of a recreational facility at a cost of $470,000 was correct.

The second case, four years later, involved the manner in which the Brandon City Council dealt with a contentious issue. Arnie Peltz and 'Butch' Nepon acted for a group of citizens. Arnie specialized in public interest law. My old adversary and unintentional mentor Frank Meighen Q. C., who had always been the City Solicitor, assisted by J. B. Mills, represented the city council and supported the procedure it had followed in enacting a by-law dealing with bus service.

In the St. Clements case, most requirements in the *Municipal Act* were followed. A notice of intent to consider the by-law had been published, the council heard representations from ratepayers, first reading was given, and the by-law was submitted to the Municipal Board for its consideration. As there were some objections, that Board heard representations in favour of and against the proposed by-law. It then issued an order permitting the Municipal Council to proceed with second and third readings.

Although not required to do so, the council heard further representations. After supper, the council met behind closed doors and gave second and third readings to the by-law. All counsel agreed that procedure was contrary to s. 114(1) of the *Municipal Act* and that the by-law could not stand.

The question I had to decide was whether the whole procedure would have to be repeated or whether the municipality merely had to pick up from where it went astray. The arguments of counsel were entertaining. They argued with vigour and often at the top of their voices. It may have been a reflection of how they debated in the legislature or the issue may have been very sensitive and hotly contested in the municipality.

I based my decision on section 189(1) of the *Municipal Act*. It gave the court authority to quash by-laws in certain circumstances. It also said that the court may "quash the by-law in whole or in part for want of jurisdiction on the part of the council."

Case law indicated that a court should "interfere as little as possible with the exercise of the legislative functions of municipal councils, when that exercise falls within the proper limits of their powers."

My ruling was that, if the municipality still wanted to proceed, it must start its reconsideration of the matter at the point where it erred in its procedure. I set aside the final passage of the proposed by-law and directed the municipality to give notice and hold a public meeting at which any affected person could make representations in favour or against the passage of the by-law. The municipality could then proceed in public to second and third reading of the by-law if it wished to do so.

The case was really a draw as far as the combative counsel were concerned. Mr. Pawley succeeded in stopping the by-law that had been improperly passed and Mr. Green did not have to start all over again.

The Brandon case was similar. Its City Council was also covered by the *Municipal Act*. The applicant, Dyck, sought an order quashing a resolution of the council that reduced the regularity of some bus service and discontinued some routes formerly served by the Brandon Public Transit System.

The first part of the challenge was that the reduction in service was invalid because the prior approval of the Public Utilities Board had not been sought or given. I agreed with counsel for the city, that while the board may involve itself in bus service, it had never done so and its permission did not have to be sought. I also agreed that an operator of a bus service did not have to seek permission to alter, change or vary service, even if the change resulted in discontinuing some service that had previously been provided.

The part of the challenge that warranted closer examination was the manner in which the City Council arrived at its decision to reduce service. My task was to examine the passage of the resolution to see if the City Council followed the correct procedure in the exercise of its jurisdiction. It was not to examine the merits of the reduction in bus service.

The evidence indicated that the "committee of the whole" of City Council considered a report from the director of operations and the city engineer, had a debate *in camera* and passed a motion accepting the recommendations. No member of the public was permitted to attend that meeting although the media was permitted to attend and to report what had been done.

Probably because of the publicity, a petition of 1405 people was presented to a subsequent meeting of council. The petitioners opposed the changes in service. A further meeting of the committee of the whole considered the objections. The meeting decided not to proceed with a fare increase but confirmed the rest of its earlier decisions. The public was excluded from that meeting.

The meeting of the committee of the whole did however adjourn and the regular meeting of counsel was convened five minutes later. The third matter referred to in the minutes said under "Reports":

"Committee of the Whole (Special) June 21st, 1978

(the names of the mover and seconder)

That the report be taken as read and so adopted. Carried"

Six councillors voted in favour of the motion and three against. There was no debate and many in the audience failed to appreciate the effect of the motion. The *Municipal Act* provided that every council shall hold its meetings openly, although meetings of committees may be held *in camera*. No reference was made to a "committee of the whole."

Counsel for the city then argued that the public became informed of the deliberations of the committee through the presence of the media. It turned out that the presence of the media was prohibited by another by-law. In my written decision I suggested that, when the media is permitted to attend the public had the same right. Counsel must, in any event, ensure that the required reporting was done at the regular council meetings.

Chief Justice Dewar, in an earlier decision, affirmed by the Court of Appeal, held that the reporting by a committee to council was intended to let the public know what was being done. He spoke of the abuse of council's powers and the suppression of public knowledge.

In this case I found there had been a breach of s. 127(2) of the *Municipal Act* because there was no written or oral report of the deliberations or decisions of the committee of the whole to the "open" council meeting that followed. In failing to make such a report, members of the public were deprived of information they were entitled to receive.

No explanation for the manner in which City Council dealt with the bus issue was given and I said in my written reasons that I could only conclude that, for some reason, council wished to keep the public from knowing the reasons for its decision or to keep the public from hearing the positions taken by various members of council. I pointed out that councillors were elected representatives of the public, doing public business and that the public was entitled to know what they were doing.

I declared that the resolution of Council adopting the report of the committee of the whole implementing the transit report was null and void and was quashed.

Understanding This Judge

Several years after I retired from the court, I was walking south on Kennedy Street across from the Law Courts and caught up to a senior Crown Attorney who had appeared before me on a number of jury trials. Just to make conversation I asked, "Do you think I was a little pro-defence?"

He nearly exploded. "A little?" he said. "It was like having another defence counsel on the bench."

I was a little hurt and taken aback by his reaction but I said nothing more. The remark nevertheless indicated how a judge's conduct and approach to the law can be misunderstood.

All the time I was on the bench and hearing criminal cases with a jury, I followed certain principles of my own. It would have been impossible and improper to explain myself at the time, but I can do so now.

If an argument about a procedural matter arose during a trial, or if there was a dispute about the admissibility of the evidence counsel wanted a witness to give, and I was unsure whether to let the jury hear the evidence, I invariably went along with the position of counsel for the accused. Usually my ruling had no bearing on whether the accused would be found guilty or not, but I didn't want to make a ruling that might be considered unfair by a higher court and have the jury's decision reversed on appeal.

To bolster that approach, I said to myself: "If the jury convicts the accused, I want him to stay convicted."

The result was that I gave each accused every possible break during the presentation of the evidence, so he would have no basis for complaint. There were other benefits of going along with a defence motion. In one case three people were accused of transporting drugs to and from Florida. The indictment called for the three to be tried together. Before the trial started, one of the accused made a formal application before me to be tried separately. The other accused joined in his request to have their trial severed so each would have a separate trial.

The Crown Attorney refused to sever and argued that separate trials would substantially increase the cost of trying the accused and would result in substantial delay as well.

I acceded to the defence request in spite of the Crown's objection and ordered separate trials. To the surprise of the Crown, each of the accused pleaded guilty. They just didn't want to be associated with some of the things their fellow accused had or might have done. They were afraid the jury might convict all of them for the actions of others.

The result of my ruling saved the Crown Attorney a great deal of work and uncertainty. He obtained the convictions he was looking for.

After completing a short custody trial in the Family Division, I immediately gave an oral decision rejecting the father's application to take custody of a young son away from the mother and give it to him. As the court clerk was taking me back to my office, she said the lawyer for the father was quite upset and said to her, "What do you have to do to win a case around here?"

Without hesitation, I replied: "Have a case."

Unfortunately some lawyers seemed to think that just because they had been at the bar for a number of years and have 'some standing at the bar' they should win all their cases. It didn't matter to me what they expected. They had to persuade me why I should go along with their position.

The reaction to what I was trying to do when sitting on a civil case was better expressed by Leon Mercury, a trial lawyer I got to know quite well after we had both retired. He said, "We were never able to read you."

He meant that when I was listening to a witness, he could never tell whether I believed the witnesses or not, let alone whether I was being swayed by the evidence or position they espoused.

While I took the remark as a compliment, the truth is I didn't want to make any decision on whether I believed a certain witness or not until the whole trial was over and I had heard the lawyers' closing arguments. After that I would still have to review my notes to see what different witnesses said on certain vital issues. I also had to read the cases the lawyers referred me to and often other cases referred to in those cases that would give me a clear understanding of the existing law.

As soon as possible after the close of a case I would write out or dictate the essential evidence I had heard and my initial reaction. As I reviewed my notes and the case law I would start amending my first draft. I'm sure I drove my secretary mad with all my amending but I often did a dozen drafts of my decision before I was satisfied with it.

On occasion, after nearly completing a decision, I would change my mind when my written decision didn't sound persuasive to me. On a couple of occasions I completely rewrote my decision to favour the other party. I didn't take long to render a decision in any event. My goal was to complete every decision within thirty days of the end of the trial.

There were times when I thought I knew the law that applied in certain situations. I nevertheless liked to review the law as the slightest change in the facts of a case could require looking at another aspect of the law.

Sentencing. Jurors decide whether an accused person is guilty or not guilty of the charge or charges they are being tried on. No judge or other person may ask them how or why they arrived at a certain verdict or found the accused not guilty of certain charges. If there is a conviction on one or more charges, it is entirely up to the judge to impose the sentence he or she thinks appropriate. The judge has to rely on his own interpretation of the evidence and apply what he or she thinks is an appropriate penalty.

The only thing a judge may be told following a conviction is the nature of any previous convictions the accused may have. A jury won't have that information unless the accused has taken the witness stand in his own defence and has had to disclose his record in cross examination by the Crown Prosecutor.

Prior to sentencing, counsel make their own recommendations to the judge on how long or short they think any incarceration should be. In some cases I would impose a sentence immediately. In other cases I wanted to read the cases counsel had referred to. In those and other cases I would also want to consult my own index on sentencing.

After my appointment to the bench, I regularly read the reported decisions of the *Supreme Court of Canada,* the *Manitoba Court of Appeal, Western Weekly Reports* and some *Dominion Law Reports* and made notes of interesting cases and sentences in my personal card index box. I kept a record of the sentences I had imposed, cases where other judges of our court had imposed a sentence and some of the cases where the *Supreme Court* or our own *Court of Appeal* had made an important comment on a certain crime or point of law.

My sentences were intended to be in line with others being handed out in Canada. Any variation depended on my personal analysis of the severity of the crime and the degree of harm and criminal intent.

It was unknown to me to have lawyers agree on a range of sentence and ask the judge to sentence within that range. I was always pleased to have the suggestions of lawyers but believed that determining the length of a sentence was the sole responsibility of the judge.

Damages. I followed a similar process in civil cases where, for example, I found in favour of a person who had suffered a broken leg in a fall or brain damage in a car accident. Counsel would make submissions on the damages they thought should apply. Invariably, expert witnesses had described the injuries in detail, the treatment that had been given and the prognosis for a full or partial recovery. Actuaries would sometimes testify on the creation of a structured settlement that would calculate the income that could be created on the investment of a lump sum award and relate that to the amount the injured person would likely receive on a monthly basis.

In addition to listening to the experts and to counsel, I would consult my other card index on damages that were being awarded in similar cases across Canada. Generally I tried not to wander too far from damages awarded or approved by the Manitoba Court of Appeal.

In one case I decided to head out on my own when the line of cases in vogue in Public Trustee cases hadn't changed for years. I tried to bring the level of damages up to date. In a judgment I signed on December 31, 1974, after I had been on the bench for three years, I decided I had an obligation to keep the law, and damage awards, up to date. In my view the courts were not even adjusting damages under the *Trustee Act* to keep pace with inflation.

I had two outstanding counsel on the case. The surviving spouse was represented by Don Baisley and the government insurer was represented by Peter Morse Q. C., later Justice Morse. The lady killed in the accident was 56. Some cases I read indicated the maximum award in Canada at the time was ten thousand dollars. I awarded twenty thousand.

Justices Gordon Hall and Joe O'Sullivan of the Manitoba Court of Appeal came down on me like a ton of bricks. In particular they seemed to be upset by my attack on the decision of Mr. Justice Ivan Schultz, a former member of our Court of Appeal, in his 1956 decision. In their decisions they reviewed the long line of English and Canadian cases which put Trustee cases in a special category where only nominal, rather than actual compensation for the loss of a spouse, was to be the norm.

The award in my case was reduced to six thousand five hundred dollars. So much for my foray into untested waters.

This didn't stop me completely from resisting the decision of other courts I thought to be wrong. During argument in Chambers about how I should rule in a family dispute, Frank Allen argued that I had to follow the decision of two Courts of Appeal in other provinces. I refused. To my surprise, Frank phoned me the next day and congratulated me for the position I took. It took several years but the Supreme Court of Canada finally said those appellate decisions had been wrong.

I mention these cases as some writers seem to think a trial judge may do whatever they want. Trial judges, generally, are supposed to be guided by decisions of the Court of Appeal and Courts of Appeal are to be guided by decisions of the Supreme Court of Canada. All courts have to respect and apply the laws enacted by the Government of Canada or their provincial government.

There is still of course considerable leeway for trial judges as most cases do not fit a narrow mold. Most can be distinguished from earlier decided cases by differing facts and evidence.

Guiding Principles. If there was one principle that guided me in my judging, it was the manner in which Sam Freedman, one of our law school lecturers, conducted himself when he was on the Manitoba Court of Appeal. When he wrote an opinion it was clear and precise. His analysis of the authorities was a work of art, but his certainty in his own ability and his own conclusions on matters of fact and law was clear.

Justice Sam Freedman, later Chief Justice Freedman, decided cases in his own way. It didn't matter to him whether the other members of the court agreed with him or not. In fact, he became known as the great dissenter as he was often at odds with his colleagues.

His grasp of the appropriate legal principle and his ability to articulate it became evident when, in case after case, the Supreme Court of Canada allowed appeals from Manitoba, confirming the Freedman dissenting opinion as the correct one. On occasion other judges of the Court of Appeal would support Sam's decision but it was usually his decision and his reasoning that carried the day in Ottawa.

I don't pretend to write as he did or to have the skill to analyse the law as he did. It was his belief in his own opinions, whether others agreed with him or not, that caught my attention.

The lesson I took from my observation of the Freedman approach was not to be afraid I might be wrong in a decision I was making or a judgment I was writing. I did what I thought was right.

Justice Brian Dickson was a judge of the Manitoba Court of Appeal when I was appointed to the Queen's Bench. I only had one jury trial before him in Brandon when he was on the Queen's Bench between 1963 and 1967 when he was elevated to the Manitoba Court of Appeal. In 1973, a year after I was appointed to the Q. B., he was appointed to the Supreme Court of Canada and was its Chief Justice from 1984 to 1990. I don't recall appearing before him in the Court of Appeal but would see him from time to time at judicial programs. I can't recall how it happened, but at one of them he gave me a piece of advice. He said, referring to cases that were appealed to the Supreme Court, "Make sure you have the facts right. We can take care of the rest."

The Canadian Judicial Council and the National Judicial Institute put on seminars throughout Canada where judges listen to law professors and seasoned judges discuss procedural matters of all kinds. Special sessions are provided for newly appointed judges. The Manitoba Court of Appeal and Queen's Bench also bring in local professors to discuss unusual issues in depth.

<u>Judges are pretty well on their own.</u> When I was appointed to the Queen's Bench, it had only eight members. The judges were busy hearing civil and criminal cases throughout the province. As far as I know, they never exchanged drafts or asked others what they thought of their writing. The facts of each case are usually so detailed and

interwoven it was impossible to explain them to anyone who hadn't been present in the court room. That is one of the reasons it takes some time for the Court of Appeal to render a decision on an appeal. The judges hearing an appeal have to read the transcript of all the evidence taken at trial and concentrate on the differences in the evidence that were likely given by the various witnesses.

I only sat in the Court of Appeal twice. One case was heard by a five judge bench. The sentencing appeals were heard by three judges. It was a good experience for me to see the Appeal Court in action. The larger case was of a corporate nature and all the judges quickly agreed on what should be done. I don't think I said a word. The sentencing cases were not hard to deal with but I didn't enjoy the raucous debate and differences between the other two judges. It was good to see how the appellate system worked but I came away thanking my good fortune to be in a trial court where I could make my own decisions and express my findings in the manner I thought appropriate.

The only person from whom I ever sought a reaction was my wife Lorna. As a former teacher I would occasionally ask her if a certain paragraph was clear and made sense to her. As a mathematician, I would ask her if some intricate calculations I made were adequately expressed.

The much larger court of today developed with the creation of the Family Division of the Queen's Bench in 1983 and the amalgamation of the Court of Queen's Bench and the County Courts of Manitoba in 1984.

Family Law

My last ten years on the bench were spent as the Associate Chief Justice of the Court of Queen's Bench, Family Division. I did no more civil or criminal trials. My time was spent attempting to resolve disputes between separating or divorcing couples and resolving disputes between parents and Child Welfare agencies over the custody and placement of children they were neglecting.

The creation of a separate division of the court was initiated by the provincial government and particularly by Attorney General Roland Penner, based on a study he asked Robert Carr, later Justice Carr, to conduct. It was supported by the Manitoba Law Reform Commission and its Chairman, Frank Muldoon.

Not everyone was happy with the creation of a specialized court. Many judges were sceptical and Chief Justice Dewar was not excited about the change. When my name was being considered, he said he would approve the creation of a new Division if I would administer it and take the anticipated flack. I agreed.

Madam Justice Bonnie Helper, Madam Justice Myrna Bowman and Mr. Justice Robert Carr were appointed to the court by the federal Minister of Justice and I was appointed as its Associate Chief Justice by the Prime Minister on the 13th of October, 1983. Mr. Justice Gil Goodman, who had been involved in establishing the Division while with the provincial Attorney General's department, was appointed in the spring of 1984.

Robyn Diamond, head of the family law section of the Attorney General's Department, continued actively to support the establishment and development of the Division until she was appointed and became Madam Justice Diamond on the 15th of September, 1989.

This group set out to visit and examine the procedures in use by the other federally appointed Unified Family Courts in Canada in Hamilton and Saskatoon. We also met with the specialized social workers attached to the Superior Court in Montreal. We attended various meetings in the United States to see how judges and their staff dealt with separating and divorcing couples and heard from researchers who had established long-term tracking projects to assess the well-being of children from broken homes. We heard how the administrators and the judges worked together.

I visited the courts in England to see how they processed family cases and examined the role of their Masters. Sitting in their Court of Appeal and the Old Bailey also provided an opportunity to view their civil and criminal courts in action.

I was appointed to the Board of the International Association of Family and Conciliation Courts (AFCC), made up of judges, court administrators, university professors and court administrators. It held one of its yearly conferences in Winnipeg. That meeting, and its other conferences, heard from experts about new systems that were being initiated and tested.

We tried to determine which system would provide the best services to separating parents and their children in Manitoba. We were particularly interested in systems that avoided long drawn out court proceedings.

Family Conciliation, with its professional social workers at Fort Osborne Barracks, was moved downtown where the Division would do all divorce and Child Welfare work in Winnipeg. Shirley Smith became the Director and the judges worked with her as new procedures were put in place. She brought in experts and writers from California and Colorado to talk to her staff and permitted our judges to sit in as observers. They spoke of child development problems and provided training in mediation.

The Judges and Family Conciliation settled on a way to process contested cases where child custody was in dispute. One social worker would meet with the parents and try to help them arrive at a custody and visitation agreement that would be good for the children. These would often be difficult to work out because of disagreements over the amount of financial support one parent would have to provide. If assets had to be valued we often referred that issue to a Master of the court.

If custody or visitation could not be resolved by Family Conciliation, another worker would do an independent evaluation of the situation and supply the court with a written assessment of that issue. When a judge was hearing a case each counsel could examine the worker on his or her recommendations.

A system of judicial mediation was also established. We decided that no case could be given a trial date until a judge, who would not hear the trial, was satisfied there was no chance of having the parties agree. In child welfare cases, where an agency was seeking an order of guardianship, a judge would question the parents and the social worker on the efforts made to reach an agreement. Often there had been none because the opposing sides did not trust one another.

In child welfare cases we would often have to ask the Agency worker what efforts had been made to find a member of the extended family to care for a child or children. If that had not been done we would adjourn the case and direct the social worker to inquire. Most often a relative or a friend was willing to care for a child until the parents got their lives straightened out. My own statistics showed that agreements were reached in 80 to 90% of the cases I pre-tried, thus avoiding a trial.

I have been out of that court for fourteen years and have no knowledge of how things are going. I do understand that Chief Justice Mercier and his dedicated judges are swamped with work.

The excitement I felt as a lawyer and judge, hardly applied to family law. That was difficult and unpleasant work but it had to be done. In contested cases, the ill will that probably played a part in a separation or divorce, often raised its ugly head once more. Some bread winners were reluctant to pay a substantial part of "their" hard-earned income to the former wife they had come to hate. Some abandoned the children they once professed to be so concerned about.

It was hard to convince a deserted spouse that it was in the best interests of the children to maintain a relationship with both parents, but that was what research had shown to be the case. Too often the needs of the children were forgotten or brushed aside.

Financial support guidelines were developed nationally and set suggested amounts to be paid to the dependent spouse for her or the children. Recent cases have held that these amounts should escalate or be reduced in proportion to changes in the income or assets of either parent. Many men say the system is stacked against them. It is not. A former wife may have an edge in getting custody of young children if the man has a full time job; but if the man retains a close and supportive relationship with his children, he may end up with custody or at least an arrangement where he is deeply involved in his children's lives.

If a former wife has custody and the husband has little or no contact with the children, he will likely lose the affection he might have had with them. Children sometimes refuse to have anything to do with an absent parent. This may be due to one parent poisoning their attitude but, more often, it is due to the absent parent's failing to keep in touch.

I will not discuss any of the family cases I dealt with as a judge but I did want to indicate some of the services the Court of Queen's Bench provides to parents and their children.

The AJI

My career took a sharp and unexpected detour in the spring of 1988. I was quietly reading files in my office, preparing for the morning docket, when my secretary announced that Deputy Attorney General Tanner Elton was on the phone. That was unusual as Crown Attorneys, and others in government, never phone judges. With the separation of responsibilities and the closely guarded independence of the judiciary, there is always a concern that someone might try to influence a judge in the performance of his or her duties.

Apprehensive as I was, I took the call. With no explanation of what he wanted, Tanner Elton asked if he could see me in my office right away. When ushered in five minutes later, he came quickly to the point.

The province was considering the establishment of a Commission to look into the deaths of Helen Betty Osborne in The Pas and J.J. Harper in Winnipeg. He wanted to know if I would accept an appointment to it as a Commissioner.

From media reports, I knew that a jury trial in The Pas had recently dealt with the stabbing death of an Aboriginal schoolgirl in 1971. I also heard and saw on television that Mr. Harper, the Executive Director of the Island Lake Tribal Council, had been shot and died following a struggle with a City of Winnipeg police officer.

The Chief of a local reserve and the Mayor of The Pas were both calling for an inquiry into the delay and the manner in which the Osborne case had been handled. In Winnipeg, groups and individuals were calling for an investigation in Harper's death. The calls increased when the Chief of Police announced that the policeman was not at fault and had been exonerated.

Tanner Elton said the government also wanted the Commission to examine how Aboriginal people were being served by the justice system. That certainly sparked my interest. I knew from working with Aboriginal accused and their families in western Manitoba, that many problems existed.

I said I might be interested in becoming a Commissioner, but that I would have to speak to my Chief Justice, Ben Hewak. Tanner Elton indicated that an attempt had already been made to discuss the matter with him but no response had been received. He said the government wanted to appoint the commission immediately so I said I would speak to the Chief Justice.

I met with him that day and told him of the visit and what I considered to be an invitation to participate in the inquiry. He must have been surprised and probably annoyed that I had been approached directly. If that was his reaction, I don't say it wasn't justified but I mentioned the urgency Elton had mentioned. It was only after several discussions that the Chief reluctantly authorized me to accept the government's invitation.

I don't think all my confreres were overjoyed with me accepting this appointment but I firmly believed that great injustices had been visited on Aboriginal people. I hoped that maybe, in some way, I might be able to come to grips with the problems and suggest solutions that might work. I realized it was going to be a massive undertaking but I was excited about assuming the task.

Most of the justices of the family division were supportive of me in this undertaking and I thank them for the encouragement they gave me at the time. My acceptance of the appointment to the commission meant extra work for them, but nevertheless the feeling among them, I believe, was that something must be done to alleviate the tragedy of the situations many on reserves were facing.

At that time the Division was dealing with difficult cases where Aboriginal children were being removed from their parents. Before a Child Welfare agency could place a child for adoption in Winnipeg, it had to obtain a Guardianship order from us. Most of them were reluctant to tell the court what their short or long-term plans were for the children. They felt that an Order of Guardianship gave them a *carte blanche*.

In most cases, little or no effort was being made to place Aboriginal children in an Aboriginal home, nor was there much of an effort to place the children with members of the extended family or other Aboriginal people in their home community.

A few years earlier, Judge Ed Kimelman, also a classmate, had done a study and a report on the adoption of Aboriginal children. He criticised the manner in which children had been removed from their parents by social agencies, often with the help of the RCMP. The practice came to be called "The 60s Scoop" because so many aboriginal children had been forcibly removed from their parents and adopted by white families, often in the United States.

That program had stopped but agencies still sought the authority to run the lives of children they legally removed from unsatisfactory parents. I felt the practice was unfair to the parents and to the children and I thought that was something the commission of inquiry might be able to do something about.

The deputy and I met again. I said I would accept the assignment. He asked what I would think of having a second commissioner. I must have appeared less than enthusiastic, so he added: "We're thinking of appointing Murray Sinclair as well." Without hesitation, I said that would be great, saying he had appeared before me in court several times and brought about a unique settlement in a trial involving Aboriginal parents and white foster parents. Not only did I find out that he was knowledgeable in Aboriginal history and current problems, he was also an outstanding student of the law. It turned out that we worked well together and became good friends.

Judge Sinclair and I met with the Attorney General, clarified the terms of reference, suggested some changes in wording, and were appointed to conduct the Aboriginal Justice Inquiry.

I was never told why I was asked to be one of the Commissioners, but an Aboriginal child welfare worker who appeared before me with several Aboriginal parents who were fighting to keep custody of their children, told Lorna he had recommended that I be one of the commissioners.

On reflection, I concluded that Murray, an Ojibway who had been brought up in the Selkirk area, was well known to the government. It had just recently shown its confidence in him by naming him an Associate Chief Judge of the Provincial Court without his having been a judge at all, an almost unheard of thing to do. My assumption was, he had probably been asked to be a commissioner before I was even approached, and asked if he could recommend another person.

We started by assembling a staff. Tom McMahon, a lawyer with the government, resigned his position to maintain his neutrality and became our Executive Director. Don Fenwick, a senior chartered accountant, agreed to supervise and audit our expenditures. Judge Sinclair contacted professors and other specialists and asked them to provide the historical information we required.

We met the Chief and senior members of the city police department and told them how we planned to proceed. He was nervous about us examining the conduct of his men, but agreed to participate in our hearings. The Mounties were enthusiastic. The Deputy Commissioner asked if he could have an officer sit in on our community hearings throughout the province. We said he could, as long as no presenter objected. In that event, we would ask his officer to leave.

The bar and bench were invited to a similar meeting. The judges understandably declined, and only one or two members of the bar showed up.

We engaged Perry Schulman and Randy McNicol as counsel to investigate the two cases, find and present witnesses at the formal hearings we had decided to hold in The Pas and Winnipeg, and to present the evidence they thought we should hear. To give them time to prepare for those hearings, we decided to start with public consultations on the question of how Aboriginal people were being treated in the legal system.

Half our research and office staff was intentionally Aboriginal. Judge Sinclair was a computer expert, and he had me and the rest of the staff take lessons on the operation of computers and our in-office network. Some of the staff were quite advanced and they helped me with my computer problems. I had never had a computer and its workings were a mystery to me. I still call on Maryanne Boulton to come to my home when I get stuck.

Each commissioner had a special assistant. Diane Gielis, a Métis, worked with Murray Sinclair and Phil Lancaster, who had taught Aboriginal people hoping to become lawyers in Saskatoon, worked with me.

We offered to hold a public hearing in any Aboriginal community that wanted us. We visited over forty reserve communities and held meetings in regional towns and cities as well. We visited all the provincial jails, including the jail for women in Portage la Prairie and the all-Aboriginal bush camp at Egg Lake where doors were usually left unlocked. We had a guided tour of Stony Mountain penitentiary and saw the near-empty carpentry shop with the latest equipment but little wood to turn into furniture.

We had a private meeting with fifty of its Aboriginal prisoners. They complained about their strict confinement, their lack of privacy and the removal of the furniture from their range months earlier because of the actions of a few prisoners. They objected to women guards walking by when they were taking a shower. Unfortunately, they didn't find any programs that met their needs. Many were from northern Manitoba and lost touch with their families.

In the provincial jails, the inmates sat behind bars, talked, smoked, played cards or just waited for the days or years to pass so they could be released.

We delayed starting the public hearings until the provincial election in June was over. We didn't want our hearings to be seen as political or used as a soap box by the public or politicians. After the government changed, we met with the new Attorney General and our appointments were confirmed. He asked if we would like to have a third commissioner in case of disagreements. By that time I had worked with Judge Sinclair for several months and was able to say: "Don't worry, we'll agree."

Most of our Winnipeg hearings were held at the Freight House on Ross and Isobel. It was a convenient location for many we wanted to hear from. People and organizations put their names on a list, received a time and appeared to present their views and be questioned by us. Eric Robinson operated the recording equipment and, as did Jeannie Daniels, went into communities ahead of us to invite the Chief, Councillors and others to come and speak to us.

The meetings in reserve communities were usually held in a school or recreation building, if there was one. We put no limit on how long anyone could speak and let people finish their presentation before we asked questions. All public presentations were video-taped and made available to the media. Even so, there was a contingent of media present at almost every meeting. We only heard two or three presentations in private where people were afraid to tell us about their problem in the presence of others.

In Winnipeg, we heard from individuals, lawyers in private practice, organizations that helped women and whole families who moved to the city from distant reserves and interested citizens.

We heard many complaints about white child welfare workers who didn't understand the problems Aboriginal parents were having adjusting to the city and were trying to find enough money to live on. Fights were common between frustrated parents and although police would go to a house and break up a fight, they provided no long term solutions. If an abused woman wanted to press charges the man was taken into custody and stayed there until he went to trial or the woman recanted.

Child Welfare agencies told of the problems they had dealing with apparently disinterested parents. They told of placing children up for adoption and in group foster homes. They felt their first duty was to remove children from their parents to prevent them from being abused. Ma Mawi Chi Itata, an Aboriginal service agency, told of how they tried to support Aboriginal parents and their children.

Both the older white agencies and the newer Aboriginal ones did what they could but the volume of difficult cases seemed to make it impossible for either of them to keep up. The inability of many workers to communicate with the parents, and their lack of experience in dealing with a different culture, made matters worse. In the early part of the new century, Aboriginal agencies have been given more authority and the older agencies have more Aboriginal employees. That is a step forward and in line with some of the commission's recommendations.

Many government people explained how their part of the justice system operated and how they dealt with Aboriginal people and their needs. Before we were done we heard from eight hundred individuals and one hundred and eighty organizations. Complaints were the order of the day and the suggested solutions had either been tried and failed or weren't working. It would be a challenge to provide solutions when the two worlds could not communicate and understand what their counterparts were trying to accomplish.

How the Other Half Lives

We chartered a plane and two pilots from Saskatchewan to fly us to remote communities. The ancient plane turned out to be a beat-up looking Twin Otter. If its seats were ever padded, they no longer were. We, a couple of our staff and a few reporters, sat on bare metal seats. Everyone's luggage was stowed in the tail of the plane, kept from sliding forward by heavy netting, ropes and leather straps.

The signs inside the plane were in Spanish and our staff lovingly named the plane 'The Spanish Fly' implying it had been used in the drug trade. The roar of the engines made it impossible to carry on a conversation. We were often dropped off in a remote reserve while the pilots left for a warm hanger or a place they could keep the plane plugged in.

Our most hairy and unsettling experience was when we were preparing to fly across Lake Winnipeg from Berens River to Grand Rapids for an evening meeting. The engine wouldn't start. We had to disembark and stand shivering on the snow packed runway. The pilots phoned some distant technician for instructions but whatever they were told didn't work.

Finally the pilots got the manual crank out of its resting place and, with both of them straining, tried to get one of the engines to turn over. Finally, after what seemed an eternity, one engine started to cough and finally came to life. The same process was applied to the other engine and it more quickly started to roar.

We got back into the plane before the engines could stop again, and were flown across the lake at an altitude of about five hundred feet. The sky was overcast and I assume no radar or landing device existed at the other end to help the pilots find the landing strip. Whether the pilots kept the engines running, or started them from time to time, I don't know, but they got us back to Berens River to spend the night.

Our first northern trip was to God's Lake Narrows and the flight was long but uneventful. I just hoped the pilots knew what they were doing as all I could see was frozen lakes and islands. Finally the plane started to descend but it was some time before I could see the little snow packed landing strip in the distance. When we landed, there was no building, no one to meet us, and no transportation.

Bob Lowery, a seasoned northern reporter for the *Free Press*, knew the way and led us along a path through the bush to an antique hotel or hunting Lodge. Sitting on the edge of a lake, it must have been picturesque in the summer but it looked old and weather-beaten to me.

There was a fire blazing in the massive fireplace. The women were assigned rooms on the second floor but Murray, Tom McMahon and I were shown to a one room construction trailer behind the Lodge. It contained four single beds. We were shown how to light the gas stove, but told to leave it alone until we were ready for bed.

It turned out we were in the Métis community and had to get into open aluminium motorboats to be ferried across open water to the Indian reserve. Icy spray stung my face until a northerner told me to turn my back to the wind. On reaching the other side, we boarded a school bus and rode to where the meeting was to be held.

We heard from the Chief and a counsellor but the strongest presenters were older women. The first woman complained about the way the courts operated. She said the judge, the prosecutor, the clerk, a court reporter and a legal aid defence lawyer all flew in together. They rushed through cases and never got to all the cases on the list. They would adjourn the remaining cases and tell those involved in them to come back again the next month. The judge and the others then flew out of the community together so they would be sure to get back to Thompson before dark.

Unless your case was going to get heard, she said, it was impossible to talk to the lawyer. She said the people didn't know what was going on most of the time as the judge and the lawyers were talking to one another. They couldn't understand the technical terms and certainly didn't know what they were doing.

Another woman complained that the Chief was having liquor flown in to the reserve so he could sell it to the residents at high prices. She had complained but the RCMP wouldn't search the planes and didn't stop the practice. She pointed out that, at the same time,

Mounties were stopping and checking cars on southern highways and confiscating liquor all the time.

Other women said things were so bad on the reserve that many women had to leave and take their children to Winnipeg where they struggled to get a job or to survive on welfare. They spoke of the lack of support on the reserve when they or their children were abused. One woman said their Chief always took the side of the husband. No one was being prosecuted for abusing their wives or children.

When we returned to the Lodge, after having something to eat on the reserve, we went to the ice cold trailer and, with some difficulty, got the gas stove to start. Before long we were sweltering and had to turn it off. We left it off in the morning, had a cold water shave and headed for the Lodge. The women who had occupied the upper rooms, fared no better. Their rooms turned cold when the fire downstairs went out.

The next day we flew to God's River. It had no police detachment and the court never sat there. If people had to go to court they either had to take an expensive flight to God's Lake Narrows or cross the treacherous lake in an open boat.

The main topic of discussion was what had recently happened to three girls from the community. They had recently taken a shotgun and shot out the windows in the school. The Mounties flew in, arrested them without speaking to their parents and flew them to Winnipeg, hundreds of miles to the south. They were placed in the Manitoba Youth Centre in Tuxedo which housed young people who had been sentenced and more who were on remand and waiting to have their cases heard.

Only when their daughter was finally sent to court in Thompson, were one set of parents able to see her. The Crown refused to have the girl released on bail even though the parents said they were non-drinkers who would look after her. The parents told us they were non-drinking responsible parents. They had to borrow hundreds of dollars just to get to Thompson for two hearings. In court, the Crown Attorney wouldn't let them speak to the judge. In the meantime the young girl continued to languish in the very unpleasant Youth Centre.

I was shocked to see the living conditions on the reserves. Small run-down houses were often occupied by several families. Many communities had no running water, no sewer and no recreation for the youth. Drinking and sniffing were out of control and were ruining the lives of children. Nursing stations and schools were established in some communities, but often the white nurses and white teachers were intimidated and left the communities.

We stayed overnight in the nursing station at South Indian Lake. Prior to the evening meeting we were given a tour of the community. Our guide pointed out a shack where children went to sniff gasoline. During the hearing we heard from three high school girls. All they wanted was to leave the community as soon as possible. In the morning, when getting ready to leave, we were told that a girl had died in the nursing station overnight. The nurse thought she died from an overdose of drugs.

Effective self- government on reserves is still non-existent and the powers of the elected Chief and Council are very limited. All major decisions are made by the Department of Indian affairs in Ottawa. Ottawa is supposed to provide adequate housing and they don't. Many reserves get into financial difficulties when trying to improve services and Ottawa takes over the administration of the reserve. They employ accountants to do the day to day administration and charge the cost to the reserve's account. The agriculture and agricultural equipment promised in the treaties is nowhere to be seen. Most reserve communities are slums and are in dire straights.

The stories of prejudice and abuse we heard in Winnipeg were as bad. The treatment by the police was seen as inadequate. A young Aboriginal man was running down the street as he was late meeting his girl friend. He was arrested and taken to the police station. The police thought he must be a criminal running from a crime scene.

Women found it almost impossible to get a job in a factory even though people were being brought in from Asia to do sewing. An older Aboriginal man told of driving his Cadillac. If he had a suit and tie on he was never bothered. If he wore casual clothing he was regularly stopped and asked where he got the car. These may seem like minor matters but they indicated to me the different rules and stereotyping that exists.

In our report, we urged that more Aboriginal police officers be hired. We thought they would be able to get to the bottom of complaints of spousal abuse, for example. The city police reacted positively and hired more Aboriginal officers.

At Hollow Water, on the east side of Lake Winnipeg, we saw a band program that dealt with abusers in a reconciliation program that successfully put a stop to abuse and provided the information children and women needed to stop any improper conduct in the future. That sort of program should exist in every reserve community but it doesn't. Indian Affairs, which is supposed to be responsible for Aboriginal people and their communities, refuses to establish similar programs in other communities. Years later I tried to help a reserve south of Clear Lake set up a similar program. Ottawa refused to include child welfare matters so the project failed.

It was probably after our visit to God's Lake that I went to the Army and Navy store across from the Bay and bought clothing for the other trips to come. My parka was good for fifty below zero and my big bush boots were the same. A smaller padded zipper jacket would suffice if the weather turned warm, but I was taking no chances. On one trip, I even took a sleeping bag and a ski suit. I bought some fur lined slippers as I noticed that all the Aboriginal people and Murray took off their boots when attending our meetings.

The northern residents were too polite to say anything to me but I imagine they had many laughs about the appearance of this greenhorn from the south.

On another of our early trips, I was glad to have all the heavy clothing I had bought. We had been flown by the government jet, which was a rare occurrence, to a meeting in Red Sucker Lake, where Elijah Harper was from. Our next stop was to be St. Theresa Point where the men would be accommodated in the Priests' residence and the women in the one occupied by the Nuns.

The meeting at Red Sucker dragged on so one of our staff phoned the nurses residence in St. Theresa to say we were running late and wouldn't arrive until eleven. Later we found out that the nuns phoned those who were going to pick us up in trucks and told them we wouldn't arrive until eleven. They couldn't imagine the caller meant eleven at night.

The government jet dropped the ten or so of us off at the St.

Theresa airport and disappeared into the southern sky. There was no one there to greet us and the few buildings were locked. We waited and waited for the trucks to arrive. We could hear the sound of skidoos in the distance, but none came our way. I was getting cold so donned my ski suit, then Murray and I decided to walk. We went down a snow packed road through the bush and finally came upon a Hudson Bay store with its lights on. It was the eighth of December and the staff was taking stock in preparation for the Christmas season. After several phone calls, Judge Sinclair got hold of someone who roused the drivers who then came in their half-tons and transported us across the ice to the mainland. The ice was barely frozen on the lake so heavy trucks and buses were out of the question.

Three of us stayed in the priests' house and the women stayed with the nuns'. We all had a full breakfast there in the morning before we headed off to the building where the meeting took place.

It was a well attended meeting. We heard from the local Chiefs and residents in the Island Lake area. We then had a presentation by the youth justice committee that had existed in the community for some time.

Several parents had lobbied for its creation in the hope it could deal with the growing number of young people who were engaged in gas sniffing and were skipping school. The committee was based on the customs and traditions of the tribe.

The young people who were called before it were lectured and rebuked in public for their inappropriate behaviour by elders. Soon the parents were also called to account. Eventually, young people who faced criminal charges were being referred to the committee by the police and by the courts.

The community also appointed a "magistrate." He was a local Elder. We were told that no one in the community ever challenged the right of the council to create that position, but it added to the importance of the committee and its standing in the community. My understanding is that the committee finally received some outside funding from the province or Ottawa to cover its salaries and administrative costs. As excellent as the program was, I am not aware of a similar program being established anywhere else in the province.

Justice for American Indians.

Judge Sinclair had met American Indian professors over the years and knew a lot about the American Indian tribal courts. I had never heard of them and didn't even know they existed. We decided to go to the States to examine their system in detail. We drove, with our wives, in our own cars, and agreed to meet in Reno and later in Chinle (pronounced 'Chinly') on the large Navajo reservation. Meeting dates and places were arranged by our staff.

In Reno we sat in on a training session for court clerks in the employ of different tribal courts in the south western states. They were receiving instructions on how to run a court office, keep track of and collect fines, organize trials, prepare jury lists, sit in court as the clerk and how to empanel juries. We heard that juries were widely used in the Tribal courts. The teachers were judges and lawyers attached to the tribal courts administration in California.

We learned there were also ongoing training sessions for elected and appointed tribal judges as well. There are no educational requirements for anyone wanting to become a judge but in some reservations they must have lived on the reservation for at least six months prior to election day. Former residents, who had worked off reserve for years, often decided to return home, re-establish their residence, and run for office.

Training sessions for judges are a permanent fixture in the system and are held at various locations across the country. New judges receive instructional books on civil, criminal law and procedural matters. They may also call on one of the national training offices for advice at any time.

In Canada, we use the terms 'Indian Reserve' and refer to the residents as 'Aboriginal.' In the United States, the terms are 'Reservation' and 'American Indian.'

Our staff had arranged to have me meet three Chiefs on my own. I went to the Hila River reservation between Phoenix and Tucson, a reservation at Mesa and the Hopi reservation which is surrounded by the Navajo. Most had elected judges although I was told the family and youth judges require special skills and are normally appointed. One Chief said you could be a truck driver one day and a judge the next. The only qualification for office was residence on the reservation for at least six months prior to the election.

In the Hopi reservation there were a number of men in orange coveralls working on the street in front of the court building. When I asked who they were, I was told they were prisoners. I asked if they ever ran away and the person I was talking to pointed out they wore no shoes.

The judges I spoke to said the system was operating well and served the needs of the residents on the reservations. A prosecutor said she found no problems with juries. She said the residents liked the personal involvement in the legal system juries provided, and said the jurors had no difficulty in coming to a decision.

In Chinle, on the large Navajo reservation with a population of 200,000, Judge Sinclair and I met with a judge in charge of one of the many regional courts. We were told the tribal courts have unlimited civil jurisdiction. The judge told us of a case where a jury awarded over a million dollars in damages against an outside corporation. The case went to the State Court of Appeal and the decision of the reservation court was upheld.

We also learned that an accused can have the assistance of anyone they wish to assist them in a criminal trial. A few people, although not legally trained, who had a good record of success, were often engaged by people wanting to plead not guilty.

After an hour or more of questioning, the judge brought in three peacekeepers who worked for him from time to time. One was a lady who had been a teacher. Another was an older man who was a preacher and the third was involved in family services. They all had experience in settling disputes and they had all been selected by their communities.

We were told how a recent case had been resolved and how the local court and the State run system cooperated. A young man had been charged with rape and appeared in the State court as the offence was beyond the jurisdiction of the tribal court. After looking at the case, a State attorney reduced the charge so the tribal court could deal with it.

The judge we were visiting was told the nature of the offence and, rather than going ahead with a trial, he called in the older peacemaker and asked him to see what he could do. He met with the young man who admitted his responsibility. He then met with his parents. Both the boy and his parents apologized for what had happened. The peacekeeper then went to see the girl and her parents. Apparently the offence was not too severe and they agreed to accept the apology if they received some traditional recognition of the offence.

The peacekeeper brought both families together and the guilty family agreed to give the offended one some of its cattle. The peacemaker then submitted a written report to the judge who still had the right to have the case heard in court. The judge accepted the report, ordered that it be followed, and the case was over.

Our second trip, some time later, took us to a university in Seattle Washington where we met with Professor Johnson, an expert on tribal courts and their civil and criminal codes. I was amazed to learn that, while many of the codes are similar, every court system has its own laws that have been voted on and passed by its residents.

We also learned that, at that time, there were 250 separate tribal courts in operation in the United States. Some small reservations that couldn't afford a full time judge, would hire a judge from another reservation to come to their community and hold court when necessary. We were also told that more and more of the tribal judges were legally trained.

From Seattle, we drove to the North West Inter Tribal Court system in the Puget Sound area, where we met their chief judge. We chose that system as it included small, scattered communities similar to those in Manitoba.

Judge Elbridge Coochise, a Hopi, had been hired and brought from Arizona to be the Chief Judge. An important factor was that he had no personal connection with any of the local people and was seen as independent. He visited each community once a month and dealt with whatever matters were on the docket. A lawyer, also in the employ of the system, travelled with him and acted as a friend of the court to help accused people present their case and bring out the facts in their favour. He also gave legal advice to the judge if requested.

The judge mentioned that incarceration of an offender was avoided whenever possible. If he sentenced someone to a term in jail, the local system had to rent a cell from the State. He said he had no difficulty in imposing another form of punishment that was equally effective.

As a result of the information we received during these trips, we decided to have some of the experts come to Winnipeg to tell one and all of a better way of dispensing justice in Aboriginal communities. We advertised a Tribal Court Symposium and flew in eleven experts from the United States including Professor Johnson and Judge Coochise.

Hardly anyone came. The government had a few junior people from the Attorney General's office there. A few lawyers attended and there were some representatives of the Aboriginal community. It was a disaster. This should have been a warning about what was to come when our report was delivered.

Helen Betty Osborne

Helen Betty Osborne was a bright Cree girl who was brought up in The Pas. Her mother, aware of her potential, sent her to the Guy Hill residential school near Clearwater Lake north of The Pas. For high school, she moved to The Pas Collegiate and boarded with a supportive white family. She had a number of good friends and was doing well in school.

In the early hours of November 13, 1971, after leaving her friends downtown and heading home, she was dragged off the street and into a car by four drunken white youth. She begged to be released and fought off their sexual advances as best she could. She was driven to a cottage area on Clearwater Lake where they continued to assault and molest her. She was able to stop them from having intercourse with her but they beat her. Then they put her back in the car and drove further east on the airport road and stopped near a pump house and a rock and rubble fishing pier.

It was there she was stabbed fifty-two times with a screwdriver and died. Her body was dragged into the bush. When I heard the manner in which she was killed, I assumed the killer must have been a maniac acting in a fit of rage.

The next morning, a man was fishing from the pier while his young son explored the area. The boy ran to his father and led him to the body he had come across while wandering through the bush. They drove to the airport where the father phoned the police. The father and son returned to the pump house to wait for the investigators.

At that time, The Pas had two detachments of Mounties. One policed the town and the other looked after the rural area. Both became involved in the investigation. The rural detachment went to the scene, saw the body and taped the area so it wouldn't be disturbed. Some officers searched the area while others took measurements and photographs, including the marks that might have been caused by a body being dragged from the side of the road into the bush. Others located a screwdriver at the side of the road some distance to the west.

The police let it be known that an Aboriginal girl had been murdered near the pump house and asked members of the public who might have seen anything unusual to come forward.

A taxi driver did just that. He reported that he had seen a car on the highway in the vicinity of the pump house about four in the morning. He followed it for a time and saw its license plate, but couldn't remember the numbers. At the suggestion of one of the officers, he agreed to be hypnotized to see if that would improve his memory.

The town detachment obtained photographs of the body and started rounding up and questioning a number of Helen Betty's friends. Their methods were brutal. Without warning, they showed them gruesome pictures that had apparently been taken in the morgue. They suggested to the Aboriginal girls and Helen Betty's boy friend that they were involved in or knew something about her death. We heard from the friends when our hearings began and were shocked at the lack of tact and sympathy the officers displayed. The friends had no idea their friend was even missing when the questioning began. They had no information that could help the police other than to give the approximate time she headed for home.

When the results of the hypnosis of the taxi driver were received, the numbers he recalled were sent to the provincial licensing department. They identified The Pas as the place where the licence had been issued and, on further digging, determined that the owner of the vehicle was a Mr. Colgan who was a well known and respected citizen. He was the manager of the province's liquor store.

The rural detachment wanted to have the car taken to a shop where the seats could be removed so it could be searched for anything that might show that Helen Betty had been in it. The town detachment refused.

The arrangement between the detachments apparently required that the rural detachment obtain the permission of the town detachment before they could conduct an investigation within the town. Their request was denied, or at least delayed for quite some time. When a constable in the town detachment was told of the desire to search the car, he said it wasn't necessary as he had checked the car after the death and there was no need to search it. Even the explanation of how the licence plate had been identified, failed to sway him.

The evidence we heard on the point failed to convince me that the town officer had done anything more than look in the window of the car and it wasn't clear whether he had done that before or after the death had occurred. It seemed to me to be obstructionist to prevent the rural detachment from investigating.

It was impossible to tell why the town constable acted in the way he did. Was it because a leading citizen was the owner of the car, or was it because of some jealousy or antagonism between the two branches of the RCMP? Whatever the reason, the refusal to have the car thoroughly examined as soon as possible was an early set back to an investigation that had been making some progress.

This was probably the worst example of the lack of cooperation between the two detachments. It is impossible to say whether other attempts to get the younger Colgan to talk to the police would have borne fruit in the early days of the investigation, but as time passed the four suspects kept one another away from the police. They were assisted by Darcy Bancroft, who said he was acting for all four. He had died before our inquiry began and I can only leave it to legal debate whether he should have been so aggressive in keeping the suspects away from the police or whether he should have told at least some of them to get their own lawyer.

That is what eventually happened. When it looked as though at least some of the suspects were going to be charged and the case was going to trial, Colgan went to see Don McIvor, another local lawyer, who was able to get him immunity from prosecution in return for his evidence, such as it was. In the meantime, according to what we heard, Colgan had become a physical and emotional wreck. He drank, his marriage broke up and he was emotionally upset when he gave testimony before us, sixteen years after the death. It is not that I have any sympathy for him, but if he had seen a lawyer of his own choosing earlier on, he would have been spared a great deal of grief.

The fourth suspect had been a passenger in the car. Norman Manger was also being protected by Darcy Bancroft. After being spoken to by an officer who had been brought in from distant duties,

Manger agreed to take a lie detector test in Regina. Two undercover officers were keeping an eye on him in a beer parlour when a couple of men spirited him out a side door and took him to Bancroft's office. Bancroft refused to have him take the test and the police were never able to find out whether, as Manger said, he was too drunk to see or remember anything, or whether, if he did remember what happened, he could have been a Crown witness.

I hesitate to refer to the part Darcy Bancroft seemed to have played in the case, because I always thought he was a good lawyer, but I do so in the hope that law professors and experts in legal ethics will find something in my recital that will assist other lawyers faced with a similar situation.

The decision of the Crown to sign an immunity agreement and refrain from prosecuting Colgan is not open to criticism. Colgan was a timid person and would not likely, in my opinion, have been a direct participant in the killing itself. Without his testimony, it is quite possible that no one would have been convicted of the murder.

That leads me to a matter that concerned me. It too is a matter of tactics. The two men who were eventually charged with murder, were not charged with the included offences of abduction and sexual assault. I felt that all the suspects participated in dragging the girl into the car and assaulting her. I thought all the suspects could have been charged with assault and abduction.

My guess is that the Crown didn't want the jury to have a choice for fear it would opt for the less serious charges and find the accused not guilty of murder. Nor do I fault the trial judge for taking his lead from the Crown. It was their case to present and try to prove. The jury was not at fault either. The evidence was unclear on whether, or the extent to which, Houghton had participated in the killing. He clearly lied to us about his reason for avoiding the police, but the evidence we heard wouldn't have been strong enough to convict him of murder.

Another issue we considered, was the belief on the part of many Aboriginal people, that "everyone in The Pas knew what had happened and who the killers were."

We found that was not the case. The killing was certainly discussed by everyone in town but the community at large was shocked by it.

There were a few exceptions. One storekeeper pretended to have an inside track and enjoyed the attention that gave him when talking over coffee, but he knew nothing the police did not know. He might have assumed that his employee, the younger Colgan, was involved in some way, but that was all.

A number of friends of the suspects knew more, partly because Johnston, who was later convicted of the murder, did a lot of bragging. He admitted, at one party, that he had stabbed her, without saying who *her* was. He also said it felt great to kill someone. He didn't mention any specific killing but the implication was clear as he threatened to kill anyone who spoke to the police.

Johnston was known to be a violent person. His threats were taken seriously and caused his listeners to keep quiet. When the cold file was re-opened by Constable Urbanowski in 1984, and he advertised and asked people with information to come forward, two people who had heard Johnston's bragging finally told the police what they had heard.

Johnston apparently had a number of local friends, including some bikers, who must have known of his involvement in the killing. It was some of them, I assume, who got Manger out of the beer parlour and delivered him to Bancroft's office.

When Colgan testified before us, although I don't think he told us everything he knew, he gave us an outline of what had happened. I assume he told us what he had told the jury during the recent trial of Johnston and Houghton.

He said the four suspects had been drinking and were driving around The Pas in his father's car. It was late at night. Houghton was driving when they saw a native girl walking down a deserted street by herself. They pulled alongside as she kept walking and tried to persuade her to get in and go for a ride with them. She refused and kept walking.

The car stopped and two of the occupants got out, grabbed her and pulled her into the back seat. Helen Betty struggled and resisted their advances. She was apparently giving them so much trouble, they decided to drive to a cottage area at Clearwater Lake, some twenty miles north of The Pas on the road to the airport where the Houghtons once had a cottage. Their intentions were clear. They wanted to have intercourse with her and they were infuriated by her resistance.

She was making so much noise resisting them, they decided to drive to a more isolated spot. They drove to the pump house where Johnston dragged her out of the car while the others stayed inside. Sounds of banging on the side and back of the car lasted for some time. At one point Colgan saw Johnston reach into the car and take a screwdriver that had been lying on the floor. The banging sounds continued.

After awhile, Colgan asked Houghton to go and see what was happening. He got out of the car and Colgan said he couldn't see and didn't know what was happening, but the banging stopped. The theory of the police was that, whether Houghton did anything to the girl or not, he helped Johnston drag her body into the bush. The officers who examined the scene the next day and others who examined the photographs, couldn't say whether the drag marks were made by one person or two.

During our hearings, we heard that Johnston hated Aboriginal people and we heard examples of his cruelty. My assumption is that he was furious that Helen Betty, this Aboriginal woman, would reject his sexual advances and refuse to do what he wanted. I believe he killed her in a fit of rage. There was no evidence to cause me to believe that any of the other suspects participated in the killing itself. The extent of their involvement in the earlier abduction and assaults, is of course, another matter.

A major objection I did have to the trial of Johnston and Houghton, was that there were no Aboriginal people on the jury. They were intentionally excluded by one or more counsel, using their peremptory challenges. That was not unusual, nor was it legally wrong, but it is not right either. The Jury Act of Manitoba gives all citizens, with a few exceptions, the right to serve on a jury. It is an insult to remove jurors merely because they appear to be Aboriginal. My own experience is that they are exceedingly honest and fair minded. Possibly because of their own experience as a people, they have a strong belief that justice be done.

It is standard procedure for a lawyer, depending which side of a case they are on, to exclude Aboriginal jurors where the victim or the accused is Aboriginal. The AJI report suggested the *Criminal Code* be amended to do away with peremptory challenges. That hasn't happened and I still urge it be done. There should only be challenges for cause and the judge should be the only person to decide, after counsel questions a prospective juror, whether they have the required independence to serve on the jury.

Our report recommended the change. I have continued to recommend it in other writings, and within the last few years I wrote the federal Minister of Justice in the Martin government recommending the amendment of the *Criminal Code*. The response from the Minister merely said that the department wasn't considering any such amendment. It should still be done.

Our hearings in The Pas were recorded and the television and newspaper coverage was extensive. If nothing else came from our examination of the case, it gave the public a picture of what had happened and the efforts that were made to bring the perpetrators to justice.

J.J. Harper

J. J. Harper was from northern Manitoba, but he and his wife lived in Winnipeg where he was the executive director of the Island Lake tribal council. He was a leader in the Aboriginal community and was well known and popular in Winnipeg and throughout the province. Members of his large extended family were active in Aboriginal affairs as well. It is little wonder that his death, in an encounter with a Winnipeg police officer, caused an outpouring of antagonism by Aboriginal people.

Harper had spent the evening before his death with friends at a hotel near his home. He was quietly walking home by himself on the ninth of March, 1988, when he was approached by a city police officer who grabbed his arm and turned him around. The officer started to question him about what he was doing and where he was going. Harper, in effect, told the officer it was none of his business and started to walk away. He was stopped again and a scuffle ensued.

Constable Cross, when he finally gave evidence before us, said his gun had been in its holster at all times that evening, that it must have come out during the struggle, went off and killed Mr. Harper. At one point in his testimony, Cross said he had hold of the barrel of the gun while Harper was pulling on the butt.

We heard from the police officer who usually took fingerprints. In this case, he said the gun was not 'fingerprinted.' In fact, he said he was instructed not to examine the gun for prints. He couldn't remember who gave him those instructions. Unfortunately, I say with some suspicion, all the police officers who testified before us, suffered from a similar loss of memory, forgetting who told them what to do or refrain from doing.

In all the jury trials I presided over, I never heard of a weapon that was involved in a death that was not subjected to the closest scrutiny. If the weapon had been properly examined, that would have established whose fingerprints were on the gun and where they were. It would have confirmed what Cross told us, or shown that his evidence was false. We didn't have the benefit of knowing.

As with the Osborne case, we were faced with having to examine the conduct of a substantial number of police officers in our attempt to find out what happened.

As a limited provincial inquiry, we concluded that we had no authority to attribute any criminal or civil liability to anyone. That responsibility could only be exercised by a judge or jury in a civil or criminal trial. We did make some findings of impropriety but had to stop short of saying who we thought was responsible for the death.

We did find, and Cst. Cross in his testimony agreed, that he had no *probable cause* to believe that Harper was committing, or had committed any criminal offence. He agreed with our counsel that he had no right to grab hold of him. Harper was entitled to refuse to talk to the officer and was entitled to continue walking home. During our public hearings, we heard from many Aboriginal people who said they had been stopped and questioned by police officers for no reason at all. What happened that morning fitted the pattern.

A substantial number of police were in the area because, not long before Harper was seen on the sidewalk, a car and a case of beer had been stolen in the same area. The police had a description of the car and officers in three patrol cars descended on the area looking for it and its occupants. When they caught sight of the stolen car, they chased it through the neighbourhood until it turned into a lane and stopped. The juvenile passenger was quickly apprehended but the driver ran up the lane, in and out between houses, and disappeared.

The police spread out and finally found Pruden, the driver of the stolen car, hiding behind some houses on the other side of the park Harper was soon to pass. As soon as they apprehended him, the arresting officers advised the other officers, by radio, that he was in custody. At that time, we learned from other evidence, Cross and his partner were still in their patrol car. That raised several questions. Why did Cst. Cross keep looking for the fugitive? Why did he stop Harper at all? We never received a satisfactory explanation. His feeble excuse was that Harper matched the description of the thief. The only similarity was that both were Aboriginal.

Although there was no other evidence that could tell us whether

Cross was telling the truth or not, my suspicion was aroused by the manner in which the other officers conducted themselves. I say '*my* suspicion' as I think it inappropriate to assume what Justice Sinclair was thinking, or to presume to speak for him.

I accepted the evidence of the police on what they did when trying to find the driver of the stolen car and their arrest of the culprit, but I had to reject what they had to say about their weapons. Each made a point of saying they never had their gun drawn. To their and our surprise, an independent and reliable witness came forward. He had been watching television coverage of our hearings at home and was surprised to hear the police say they never had their guns drawn when looking for the car thief.

The witness told us he was driving through the area and was stopped at a stop sign, when he clearly saw a police officer leaning over a fence with a gun in his hand. He was thoroughly cross examined but wouldn't agree that he was mistaken. He had even phoned the police station, given his name, what he had seen, and that he would talk to them if they wished. We didn't know who took the call but I was satisfied the witness was telling the truth.

We also heard from some young people who had driven past the park. They said they had seen police on the street and around the houses with their guns in their hands. Counsel for the police tried to discredit them during cross examination, but I believed what they said. They had no axe to grind and merely said what they had seen.

Another suspicious piece of evidence that remained unchallenged, was Pruden's statement that after he had been arrested and was sitting in a police car, he heard a senior officer telling Cross what to say.

The most startling revelation during our hearings was when a constable testified that a senior officer objected to what he had written in his report. As a result he had to change and completely re-write his entire report. He had also lost his memory and couldn't tell us the name of the officer who gave him that direction.

It was obvious that the witnesses were not telling us the truth, inspired no doubt, by their loyalty to one another and to the police department. That is another ethical matter for others to consider.

Also disturbing, was the manner in which Cross prepared his official statement. Instead of giving it to one or two officers in his own words, he prepared his statement with the assistance of some unidentified senior officers.

Unfortunately, the whole matter got off to a very bad start. Instead of saying that the death of Harper would be carefully examined, the Chief of Police said there had been an internal board of inquiry that had reported to him. He publicly exonerated Cross, saying he had conducted himself properly and was not responsible for the death. The desire to protect the good reputation of the force apparently trumped the obvious need for openness and a full and careful examination of why and how the death occurred.

The death of J. J. Harper was a tragedy, but it was not the only one. A senior police officer who was scheduled to give evidence to the inquiry, took his own life the morning he was to appear before us. The amiable Chief of Police, Herb Stephen, who tried to protect his men, had to resign. Constable Cross was never able to work again and died some years later. The manner in which the investigation of Harper's death was derailed, left a black mark on the performance of the police department.

There were other matters that concerned me as well. Police officers took the position that their note books were their own private property. They kept them at home. We heard that was not the practice in Toronto. There, the books are the property of the police force and have to be left at the police station when they are not in use. We recommended the same procedure be adopted in Winnipeg. Not only would that protect the books from getting lost, they would be readily available if a case had to be reviewed years after the original trial.

With more and more cases being reviewed because of DNA evidence, the note books should be safely kept. If a police officer dies, or moves away following retirement, I wonder what happens to his or her note books.

Mainly because of the complaints we heard at our community meetings which spoke of the need of police officers to respond to complaints of spousal abuse at Aboriginal homes, we recommended that the police force recruit and engage more Aboriginal officers. We also suggested that social workers and police officers work more closely together to settle marital disputes and to work on long term solutions.

Another reason we made the suggestion was that we thought greater numbers of Aboriginal officers would help other officers better understand Aboriginal people and their problems and how to deal effectively with them. The Winnipeg force responded positively to the suggestion and added more Aboriginal officers.

We also raised a long-standing concern of mine. When presiding with a jury, I found that alleged offenders often challenged the authenticity of the statement the police said they had voluntarily provided. When a police officer is called as a witness by the Crown and is asked to tell of a statement they received from an accused, a voir dire is usually held in the absence of the jury to see if the statement was voluntary and can be shown or read to the jury. If counsel for the accused has shown the statement to his client and the client says the statement is not correct or was given under duress, he will cross examine the officer and challenge the admissibility of the statement. The onus is on the Crown to prove that the statement accurately represents what the accused said and that it was voluntarily given.

The judge is faced with a difficult decision. How does he resolve the issue? He may allow the statement to be read to the jury or he may reject it. In that event the jury will never hear it and the case for the Crown may collapse. If the statement is allowed, the jury may later find itself in the same position as the judge. They will have to decide whether to accept what the statement says or to reject it if they are concerned about its contents or the manner in which it was obtained.

The difficulty can easily be removed with the use of modern technology. All statements should be video taped or at least tape recorded. Any suspicion the judge or jury might have about whether the statement is true and voluntarily given should be removed.

The unwillingness of the police to do that only reinforces my concern. I know that other judges have urged that statements taken in the privacy of a police station be properly recorded. If necessary, the *Criminal Code* should be amended to require taping. That should make the police feel better about their efforts as well, rather than having to have their actions criticized by a criminal and questioned during a trial.

Of late, a number of old convictions have been set aside and people have been released from prison. In many cases, large cash settlements have been paid by government for the wrongful conviction that occurred because of an overzealous, incomplete or one-sided investigation or prosecution.

The public doesn't like to see the work of police officers challenged but it doesn't want innocent people sent to jail either. The taping of statements and interviews would, in my opinion, be of considerable advantage to the police and a necessary protection for innocent suspects. If the police continue to oppose the change, I have to ask what they have to hide.

The Result of the AJI

The province is responsible for the establishment of the courts and the administration of justice. In our two volume report we told it what we had found and we made hundreds of recommendations. Nothing happened.

At first I thought the failure to act was because it was an NDP government which established the commission and a Conservative government was in place when we delivered our report; but then, years later, the NDP again formed the government. It too failed to act on our major recommendation.

When he was the Minister of Justice in the Filmon government, Vic Toews said "there will never be a separate Aboriginal court in this province." When the NDP returned to power, our former associate Eric Robinson, became a Minister in the government and he too announced that the government was not going to create a separate Aboriginal justice system.

Unfortunately, most commissions that have been appointed in Canada meet the same fate. The national commission on Aboriginal matters that was established shortly after ours concluded, spent years and a massive amount of money examining many of the same issues. I see no sign of action in response to their report either.

In some reading I have recently done on Royal Commissions and Commissions of Inquiry, writers have suggested that their main purpose is often to take the heat off government when a difficult issue arises. That is probably the answer to the lack of action on our recommendations.

Years ago I heard it said that judges who become commissioners of public inquiries get burned out and have a difficult time returning to the bench. That may apply to me although I cannot be precise. I retired from the court in 1993, less than two years after our report was released and three and a half years before I had to retire. Whatever the reason for government inaction, it is a shame that the hopes and expectations of Aboriginal people were dashed once again.

I have kept busy with a variety of matters. People ask if I miss being on the court. Somewhat to my own surprise, I say what I miss the most are jury trials.

Summing Up

At the end of any trial, lawyers are expected to 'sum up' their case and indicate what they think the judge or jury should decide. I seek neither approbation nor condemnation for the decisions I made as a lawyer or as a judge. I made them because I believed they had to be made, according to both law and justice.

I have merely touched on the variety of the work I did as a lawyer and a judge to give readers some idea of the inside workings of one legal and judicial mind. My love of the law began when our law school teachers breathed life into the apparently impenetrable intransigence of the law and showed how trained practitioners of the art could help people caught in its web.

The cases I have related are intended to provide a sampling of the work I did. They are also intended to show the foibles and frailties of human nature laid bare in the courtroom and in the decisions of judges and juries. They talk about real people caught in a system they didn't understand. It was up to serious lawyers, judges and juries to discover what happened, and to design a solution that would put an end to a dispute.

No judge and no jury is perfect, but in my experience both take their duties seriously and do the best they can. They often have to try to unravel a complicated, often contradictory, set of facts and opinions. There are, fortunately, courts of appeal and the Supreme Court of Canada to examine the record, analyse the conduct of the trial judge and the verdict of the jury. The system is intended to avoid the possibility of error but we know that advances in DNA examination, for example, have revealed holes in the system. Hopefully, further changes will eliminate problems that have come to light.

The law deals with ordinary people and ordinary feelings, some more acceptable than others. It is a study of human nature, sometimes of its unexpected and humorous side and at other times its deviations that bring people into conflict with the accepted norm.

What we were never told in law school, was the challenge a practitioner of the art would feel when trying to defend an undefendable blaggard or the pleasure felt in helping a needy person find justice when they had abandoned all hope.

After I retired from the bench I attended a two week course on mediation at Harvard Law School. The subject was when and how mediation can be used to resolve disputes outside the court system. In retirement, I was fortunately able to resolve two disputes that involved a million dollars without the cases having to go to court at all.

I only mention that because methods for resolving disputes are starting to change. The existing ways of processing criminal and civil cases almost overwhelm the courts. My hope is that Canada will examine some of the advances being made in other countries and bring its outmoded requirements and procedures up to date.

As someone who is now outside the legal system, I still follow its workings with interest and I like to think I can see some of its glaring problems. One is the unbearable delay between an arrest and bringing a criminal case to trial, often with the suspect, who may or may not be guilty, languishing in custody.

In this day and age, with disclosure requirements, the preliminary inquiry is totally unnecessary. It adds months and sometimes years to getting a case to trial. It costs an immense amount of money and ties up Crown and defence counsel who should be processing other cases and eliminating the unseemly backlog. I see no reason why it should not be eliminated.

A great deal of time and money is wasted if a jury in a criminal trial is unable to reach a unanimous verdict. We don't know why some juries are unable to bring in a unanimous verdict. Is it because one holdout is so stubborn they will not agree with the others? Is it because of an honest disagreement, or because one juror has taken a dislike to the judge, the accused or one of the lawyers? We don't know. In any event I suggest that Canada move to the English system and permit a jury to bring in a verdict after two hours or more of deliberation if at least ten are in agreement.

Possibly mediation should be applied to criminal cases as well. As I indicated, there were no disclosure requirements when I practiced law and I like to think accused people got a fair trial. If the Crown can't bring a trial on within a reasonable time, the accused should be released.

This is a situation, like others I have mentioned, where the federal and provincial departments of justice should examine what is happening in other countries, in this case England, to see how it avoids interminable re-trials and unacceptable delays. Canada's record is so bad that the Charter of Rights and Freedoms' guarantee of a trial within a reasonable time, has become a meaningless and unenforceable farce.

Our courts should now accept the assistance mediation can offer and does offer in other countries. As I mentioned, I was involved in judicial mediation when going to trial seemed to do more harm than good, but times have changed. Judges can't keep up with the volume of work and trained mediators often have little to do.

In certain courts in the United States, a civil suit cannot proceed until an outside, often non-legally trained mediator, has tried to bring the parties to an agreement. Only when a mediator signs a certificate saying he or she could not settle the case, can it proceed to court. My understanding is that a similar system exists in Ottawa and used to exist in Toronto.

Years ago in California, senior lawyers who were not involved in the case, were mediating other lawyers' civil cases. I don't know if the practice continues, but Canadian lawyers should examine those and other alternatives. I am no longer a fan of trial judges trying to mediate or settle cases after they have been in the court system for years. I say this with respect to family and all civil cases.

With the use of outside mediators, the courts could save themselves a great deal of time by refusing to accept the filing of a civil claim until the parties present a document, signed by a recognized mediator, certifying that mediation has been tried but was unsuccessful. This would provide work for the legal profession, keep the courts clear of mediation, and provide the time the courts need to hear cases on a timely basis.

The courts, in my view, owe the litigating public the most modern and effective means of resolving civil and criminal cases.

Above all else, I make one more plea that provincial governments begin the establishment of Aboriginal courts, manned by Aboriginal judges and other personnel, whether legally trained or not, so that each community, with the help of its elders, can deal with first time offenders in a traditional way. Examine the American system and start applying it in Canada!

Lessons Learned

With that I draw my odyssey to a close. Whitby Kerr, an elderly gentleman and the head of the largest law firm in Brandon was retiring not long after I arrived in town. His firm hosted a reception in his honour at the Prince Eddy and a number of dignitaries spoke of his years of service to the community or to them personally. As Frank Meighen brought the proceedings to a close, after speaking about his years working with Mr. Kerr, he called on him to say something.

Mr. Kerr said he had enjoyed being part of the Brandon community and his years of practice with his partners. He then told the sizeable gathering that he had always tried to keep his clients out of trouble and out of court. He said his advice was always **"stay out of court."** This only repeats what Aristotle and others have urged for more than two thousand years, but how many listen?

The more I have thought about the remark over the years, the more sense it makes when we know there are alternatives. Criminals have no choice, unless they decide to change their ways. Separating spouses can work out a financial settlement if they put the interests of their children first. Civil suits can be settled between the parties with a little give and take.

Rather than winning everything and destroying the opposition, or losing everything and be destroyed, a compromise settlement can save years of strain and uncertainty and the expenditure of huge sums of money.

I recognize that people don't change and that out-of-court settlements may be a fanciful suggestion, so I conclude by saying:

> If people want to fight, the courts provide the best arena there could be. The contestants will have their say. Their lawyers will assume the role of gladiators.

A judge will be their Referee.